OXFORD MONOGRAPHS ON MUSIC

NORTH GERMAN CHURCH MUSIC IN THE AGE OF BUXTEHUDE

North German Church Music in the Age of Buxtehude

GEOFFREY WEBBER

CLARENDON PRESS · OXFORD

Oxford University Press, Great Clarendon Street, Oxford OX2 6DP
Oxford New York
Athens Auckland Bangkok Bogota Bombay
Buenos Aires Calcutta Cape Town Dar es Salaam
Delhi Florence Hong Kong Istanbul Karachi
Kuala Lumpur Madras Madrid Melbourne
Mexico City Nairobi Paris Singapore
Taipei Tokyo Toronto Warsaw
and associated companies in
Berlin Ibadan

Oxford is a trade mark of Oxford University Press

Published in the United States by
Oxford University Press Inc., New York

© Geoffrey Webber 1996

British Library Cataloguing in Publication Data
Data available

Library of Congress Cataloging in Publication Data
Webber, Geoffrey.
North German church music in the age of Buxtehude /
Geoffrey Webber.
p.   cm.—(Oxford monographs on music)
Includes bibliographical references (p.   ) and index.
1. Church music—Germany, Northern—17th century.   2. Church
music—Germany, Northern—18th century.   3. Music and society.
4. Buxtehude, Dietrich, 1637–1707.   I. Title.   II. Series.
ML2929.W43   1995   782.2'2'094309032—dc20   95-35104
ISBN 0-19-816212-X

3 5 7 9 10 8 6 4 2

Printed in Great Britain
on acid-free paper by
The Ipswich Book Company, Suffolk

To my mother,
in memory of my father

ACKNOWLEDGEMENTS

◊

It is with pleasure that I offer my thanks to all those institutions and individuals that have facilitated my research and helped with the writing of this book. In particular, I must thank the following libraries and their staff: the Staatsbibliothek zu Berlin (both the former Deutsche Staatsbibliothek in Unter den Linden and the Staatsbibliothek Preußischer Kulturbesitz in Potsdamer Straße); the Staats- und Universitätsbibliothek, Hamburg; the Niedersächsische Landesbibliothek, Hannover; the British Library, London; the Ratsbücherei, Lüneburg; the Bibliothèque Nationale, Paris; the Universitetsbiblioteket, Uppsala; the Herzog August Bibliothek, Wolfenbüttel; the Biblioteka Uniwersytecka, Wrocław. I am also grateful to Peter Ward Jones and the Bodleian Library, Oxford, for acquiring microfilms of the Düben collection, and to Jürgen Kindermann and the Deutsches Musikgeschichtliches Archiv, Kassel, for supplying microfilms of numerous other sources. For financial support, my thanks are due to the British Academy, the British Council, New College, Oxford, and Gonville and Caius College, Cambridge.

I am particularly grateful to Andrew V. Jones, Basil Smallman, and Susan Wollenberg for their valuable comments on a first draft of this book, and to John Sturdy and Peter Bradley for their assistance with the German and Latin translations respectively. My thanks are also due to many others who have helped me along the way in diverse manners, particularly Paul Trepte, who first convinced me that any music before Bach was worthy of attention, to Edward Higginbottom, for securing my devotion to Baroque music, to my two research supervisors at Oxford, John Caldwell and James Dalton, to Albrecht Weber and the Evangelische Gemeinde in Oxford, who allowed me to live for a time in the world of Lutheranism without even stepping outside my own organ loft, and above all to my wife Tessa, for her ceaseless encouragement and scholarly advice.

G.A.W.

Gonville and Caius College, Cambridge
August 1994

CONTENTS

◊

NOTE ON MUSICAL EXAMPLES
AND ABBREVIATIONS

◊

C-clefs have been replaced by modern clefs throughout, and the original barring has been made regular. The figured bass given is that provided in the sources, though minor alterations have been made (such as the use of a natural sign rather than sharp sign in places where flat notes have been raised). Editorial corrections have been carried out without being noted. Details of the instrumentation of the basso continuo lines are not indicated.

ABBREVIATIONS

S	Soprano (Canto)
A	Alto
T	Tenor
B	Bass
vn	violin
va	viola
vdg	viola da gamba
vno	violono (at 8-foot pitch)
ct	cornett
cl	clarino (or trombetta)
tbn	trombone
fl	flauto dolce (recorder)
ob	oboe
fag	fagotto (the German *Fagot*)
bn	bassoon (the French *basson*)
bc	basso continuo

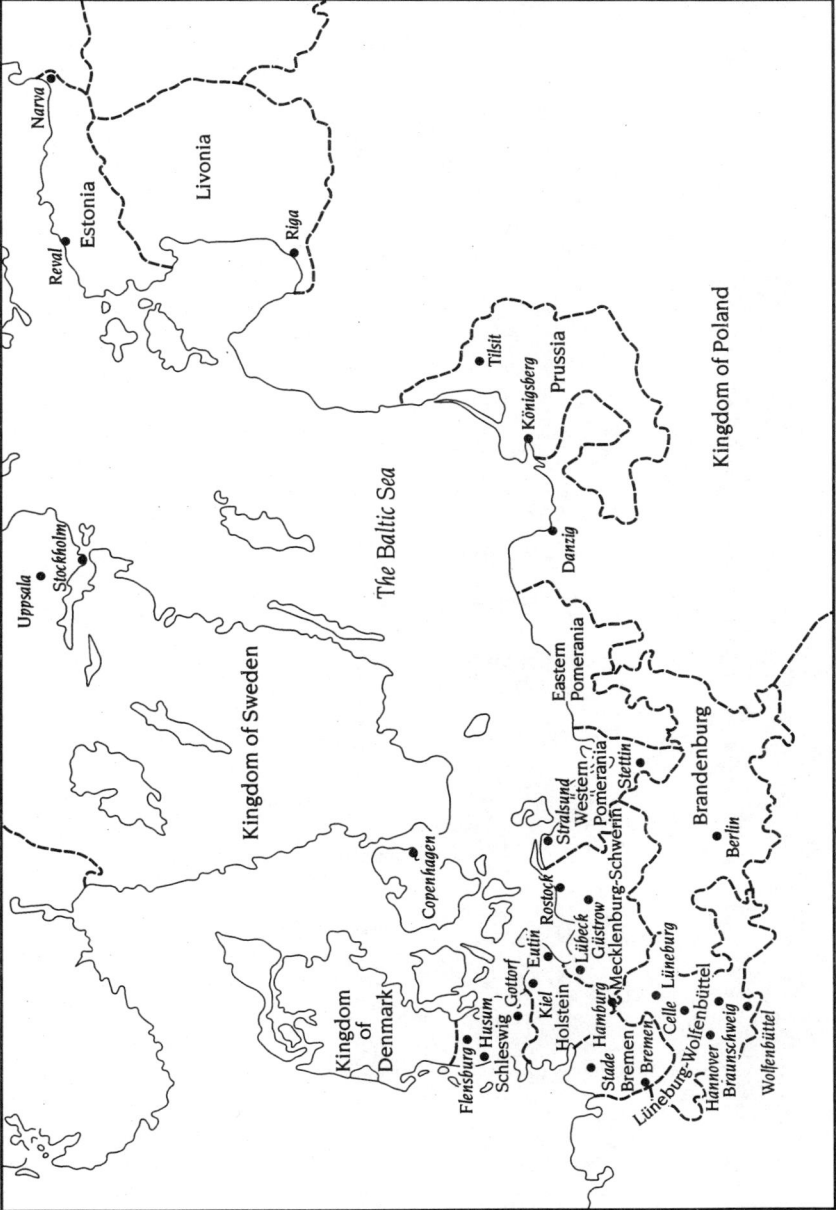

The North German and Baltic region in the second half of the seventeenth century

INTRODUCTION

◊

DIETERICH BUXTEHUDE has stood pre-eminent in the study and
performance of German music of the mid-Baroque period ever since
the awakening of interest in his music in the mid-nineteenth century. The early figures in the Buxtehude revival, among them
Johannes Brahms and Philipp Spitta, focused their attention principally on Buxtehude's organ music, and it is still this part of
Buxtehude's *œuvre* that receives greatest attention today. However,
recent scholarship has provided a more rounded view of the composer's musical activities, and Buxtehude is now also well established
as the most outstanding figure in the history of German church
music between Schütz and Bach. Much of the interest in Buxtehude
has come about through the search for a historical context for understanding the music of J. S. Bach, but the context in which
Buxtehude himself lived and worked has received comparatively little attention. Only a handful of Buxtehude's contemporaries have
been studied, notably Nicolaus Bruhns, Matthias Weckmann, and
Franz Tunder, mainly because they, like Buxtehude, were composers
of organ music. Many others have languished in relative obscurity, so
that names such as Balthasar Erben, Georg Österreich, Kaspar
Förster, and Georg Schürmann remain almost totally unknown,
although much of their church music is of a quality to match that of
Buxtehude. Moreover, it is only by studying the entire surviving
corpus of late seventeenth-century North German church music that
Buxtehude's own contribution can be properly understood and
assessed.

The aim of this book is to examine the surviving repertoire of
North German church music composed during Buxtehude's lifetime
(*c.*1637–1707), excluding occasional works for weddings or funerals

and settings of the Passion narrative, and to give due consideration to the context in which the music was composed and performed. The geographical area covered is that of the northern part of the German Protestant territories stretching as far east as Estonia, together with the neighbouring Baltic kingdoms, as shown in the map on p. xi. The career of one of Buxtehude's North German contemporaries, Johann Valentin Meder, covered almost this entire area, from Bremen through Danzig (now Gdańsk in Poland) to Reval (now Tallinn in Estonia)—all German-speaking Lutheran towns at this time. Although politically quite distinct from the German territories, the kingdoms of Denmark and Sweden are included in this study, since both adopted German Lutheranism, and their royal families maintained strong connections with the German nobility. Moreover, the musical retinues of the Danish and Swedish courts were dominated by German musicians. Heinrich Schütz's period as *Kapellmeister* of the Danish court is well known, and the leading musical dynasty in Sweden for most of the seventeenth century, the Düben family, was of German origin. The southernmost area under consideration here is defined by the borders of the territories of Brandenburg and Braunschweig (Brunswick)-Lüneburg, and thus includes the towns and courts of Wolfenbüttel and Berlin.

In general, the seventeenth century was not a period in which the arts flourished in the German-speaking lands, due in part to the destructive and demoralizing effects of the Thirty Years War (1618–48), which laid waste many German towns and severely reduced the population in certain areas.[1] However, a general decline of German cultural life is discernible during both the sixteenth and seventeenth centuries; the disparate nature of the German political map meant that there was no single concentration of noble and civic wealth that could attract and foster the arts in the way that occurred in Paris or London. Nevertheless, church music prospered, supported by tenets of Lutheranism. Although much of the kind of artistic expression of religious fervour that took place within Roman Catholicism in the form of painting, sculpture, and architecture was avoided by the Lutherans, music formed a notable exception. Luther

---

[1] For further reading on the historical background of the period see R. Vierhaus, *Deutschland im Zeitalter des Absolutismus (1648–1763)* (Göttingen, 1978), translated as *Germany in the Age of Absolutism* (Cambridge, 1988); D. Kirby, *Northern Europe in the Early Modern Period: The Baltic World 1492–1772* (London and New York, 1990); and T. Munck, *Seventeenth Century Europe: State, Conflict and the Social Order in Europe 1598–1700* (London, 1990).

himself spoke repeatedly of the value of music in church worship, and stressed in particular the importance of singing, so clearly advocated in the Book of Psalms. But whereas the Calvinists held that this manner of worshipping God should remain in the domain of the congregation, Lutherans argued strenuously that more elaborate forms of singing, including instrumental accompaniment, also had their place in regular church worship. Thus the more prosperous Lutheran towns and courts supported, as far as finances permitted, a regular company of professional singers and instrumentalists to adorn the church or chapel worship, and allowed for the training of boy choristers, many of whom later joined the ranks of the professional musicians. However, not all Lutherans were equally keen about the use of elaborate music in church, and some held more to the Calvinist point of view; thus the cultivation of church music was not evenly spread throughout North German Lutheranism. Moreover, some ruling families in the region were Calvinist, including the most powerful North German noble dynasty in the second half of the century, the Brandenburg Hohenzollerns, which accounts for the fact that none of the surviving repertoire of late seventeenth-century North German church music can be associated with the patronage of this family. Furthermore, although the main towns of Brandenburg-Prussia, Berlin in the west and Königsberg in the east, were predominantly Lutheran, the influence of their Calvinist rulers seems to have restricted their musical development.

The vast proportion of extant North German church music from Buxtehude's lifetime can be found in two manuscript collections—the Düben collection, now in Uppsala, Sweden, and the Bokemeyer collection, now in Berlin. By good fortune, these two extensive collections are chronologically complementary. Gustav Düben compiled the bulk of his collection for use in Stockholm in the 1660s, 1670s, and 1680s, whilst the compiler of the early part of the Bokemeyer collection, Georg Österreich, assembled his music for use at the Gottorf court during the 1690s and at the Wolfenbüttel court after 1702. In addition to the manuscript repertoire, roughly a dozen printed collections of church music were issued during Buxtehude's lifetime, mostly containing works for small forces. A summary of the surviving North German church music of the period in both manuscript and printed form is given in Appendix I.

Without the efforts of Düben and Österreich our knowledge of the church music of Buxtehude's time would be meagre indeed.

Unfortunately, our knowledge of the lives and careers of these two men is rather thin, as is our understanding of how the collections came to be assembled, though extensive investigation into such matters has been carried out by several scholars, notably Friedhelm Krummacher, Bruno Grusnick, and Harald Kümmerling.[2] Gustav Düben succeeded his father Andreas (a pupil of Sweelinck) as *Kapellmeister* at the royal court and organist of the German church in Stockholm in 1663. The link between the royal castle and nearby German church was strong since German members of the royal family attended services in the church, and musicians from the court were frequently engaged to sing at the services there. The bulk of the Düben collection seems to have been assembled for use at the court, though some music from the German church which survives now in the Royal Library in Stockholm has clear connections with the collection in Uppsala. The manuscripts of the Düben collection contain some 1,300 sacred works, nearly all by German and Italian composers, of which approximately 430 compositions are by North German composers. Two composers are particularly prominent in the collection, each represented by around 100 works, namely Dieterich Buxtehude and Augustin Pfleger. The next most prominent composers are Christian Geist (a member of the Swedish *Hofkapelle*) with fifty-seven works, Kaspar Förster with thirty-five, and Christoph Bernhard with twenty-four. The manner in which Düben acquired his collection has been the subject of much debate. He had certainly travelled widely in Europe before assuming the post in 1663, but much of the music he collected was composed after this time. It is clear that he received individual works and groups of pieces over some length of time, and that he maintained good connections with certain places and people (most obviously Buxtehude). A group of manuscripts written in the same hand, for example, contains works exclusively by composers active in Danzig, suggesting that he had a single source for acquiring these works. One of the most significant features of the make-up of the collection is that the

---

[2] Both collections are investigated in F. Krummacher, *Die Überlieferung der Choralbearbeitungen in der frühen evangelischen Kantate* (Berlin, 1965). On the Düben collection see B. Grusnick, 'Die Dübensammlung: Ein Versuch ihrer chronologischen Ordnung', *Svensk tidskrift för musikforskning*, 46 (1964), 27–82, and 48 (1966), 63–186, and for details and a full list of contents of the Bokemeyer collection see H. Kümmerling, *Katalog der Sammlung Bokemeyer* (Kassel, 1970). There is no published catalogue of the Düben collection, but a typed catalogue by F. Lindberg exists in the Carolina Rediviva at Uppsala, where the collection is housed, together with a more accurate card index compiled by J. Rudén.

manuscripts comprise both individual vocal and instrumental parts and scores written in tablature. Some works survive in either parts or tablature, but many are present in both forms, and the existence of parts gives considerable information concerning performance practice. Viewed in a wider context, the Düben collection represents the musical branch of that large influx of foreign culture that took place during Sweden's most illustrious period of history, the so-called Age of Greatness. The process was well under way in the early part of the century during the reign of Gustavus Adolphus, whose army collected many cultural artefacts during its exploits in the German lands during the Thirty Years War. Music received a particular boost from Queen Christina, well known for her subsequent patronage of Corelli and others in Rome following her abdication, who engaged a group of Italian musicians at her Swedish court during the last years of her reign (1652–4). Düben worked under his father during these years, and the earliest pieces which survive in the collection display clear links with the Italian musicians.

The Bokemeyer collection is rather less uniform in origin than the Düben collection. Over 1,800 sacred and secular works survive, which can be divided into three chronological sections. The earliest part consists of the sacred music assembled by Georg Österreich at the Gottorf court in the last decade of the seventeenth century. He left Gottorf in 1702 and moved to the Wolfenbüttel court, taking his collection with him. He continued to collect music at Wolfenbüttel, now focusing his attention on secular rather than sacred music, and at some point passed the collection on to his pupil Heinrich Bokemeyer, who then added further scores and printed material. The Gottorf court underwent considerable changes in fortune during the course of the seventeenth century, and the funds for music were increased or cut back along with other elements in the court budget, according to the particular predilections of the ruler at the time. When Friedrich IV assumed power in 1694 his first action was to dismiss many of the musicians. Österreich left briefly at this time but appears to have been tempted back by Duke Friedrich following an assurance of greater support for music at the court. Despite these less than ideal circumstances, he appears to have collected some 1,700 sacred works during his time at Gottorf, although only about half of them have survived in the collection to the present day.[3] The

---

[3] See Kümmerling, *Katalog der Sammlung Bokemeyer*, 10.

total quantity of extant North German church music in the collection dating from before Buxtehude's death in 1707 amounts to approximately 330 works. Many of the works collected during the Gottorf period are by composers who were active at the Gottorf court, among them Johann Philipp Förtsch (82 works), Johann Theile (21), and Österreich himself (46), and others are by composers who worked nearby, for example Nicolaus Bruhns in Husum (13 compositions) and Johann Friedrich Meister in Flensburg (14). Österreich thus seems to have had fewer outside contacts than Düben, though he managed to obtain small numbers of works by most of the best-known North German composers of the time. A similar picture emerges with the sacred music collected during the early Wolfenbüttel years, with much of the music being related to composers either employed by or strongly associated with the court, such as Georg Schürmann. By contrast with the Düben collection, the Bokemeyer collection contains only scores, written in staff-notation. There are more difficulties concerning composer attributions than in the Düben collection, together with a larger proportion of works that survive only anonymously. However, Österreich shared Düben's passion for Italian music; both collections are important and under-explored sources of Italian as well as German church music.

One of the adverse effects of the tendency of some commentators to view the church music of Buxtehude and his contemporaries as a kind of proto-Bach repertoire is apparent in the area of terminology. Just as Buxtehude's organ works entitled 'Praeludium' are still frequently given the misleading description 'Prelude and Fugue', the term 'cantata' pervades modern literature on seventeenth-century German church music, even though it was never used to describe church music by contemporary musicians in the seventeenth century, and it has only partial relevance in such a context after 1700. The most important German theorist of the early eighteenth century, the Hamburg musician Johann Mattheson, explained that the description 'cantata' properly refers to a secular genre for solo voice and accompaniment which, by the turn of the eighteenth century, comprised an alternation of recitatives and arias.[4] It is in the context of the new recitative and aria pattern that the term can most correctly be employed, since it was precisely this model of the Italian cantata

---

[4] See J. Mattheson, *Der vollkommene Capellmeister* (Hamburg, 1739; facs. repr. 1987), 215.

that inspired the Hamburg pastor Erdmann Neumeister to use the word in relation to the sacred texts organized according to the same pattern that he published from 1700 onwards. However, as Mattheson also pointed out, the addition of other types of musical movements such as fugues and choruses in individual sacred works meant that the term cantata was not suitable in this sphere, and it is notable that Bach did not use it for any of his church music. During the seventeenth and early eighteenth centuries, most sacred works were referred to simply by their incipits, but the term 'motet' was sometimes employed, or, when it was felt necessary to distinguish the modern style of the work from the older polyphonic style, the more full description 'concertato motet', or just 'concerto'. The Italian version 'motetto concertato' was often used, as was the German 'Konzert'.

The late seventeenth-century North German composers who are best known today are those whose lives and careers had connections with either Schütz or Buxtehude, or who were active as organists as well as composers. They include such figures as the organists Matthias Weckmann, a chorister under Schütz at the Dresden court, and Franz Tunder, Buxtehude's predecessor at the Marienkirche in Lübeck. Collected editions were produced in the late nineteenth century of the church music by these composers, making their music known to all students of the repertoire ever since. Buxtehude's dominance in the modern perception of the period, together with Bach's youthful experiences at both Lübeck and Lüneburg, have helped focus attention on the western part of the North German region, resulting in a comparative neglect of the eastern area. Yet composers who worked in the eastern part of the region were among the most famous and admired composers at the time. These include Kaspar Förster and Johann Valentin Meder, who both received lengthy and complimentary entries in Mattheson's biographical dictionary *Grundlage einer Ehren-Pforte* (Hamburg, 1740), in which Buxtehude, by contrast, has no individual entry. Many of these largely forgotten composers worked in the free city of Danzig, a centre whose musical resources and accomplishments rivalled those of Hamburg.

Modern scholarship has not only tended to focus on one particular geographical area but has also been inclined to concentrate on music associated with the chorale or with the surviving Passion repertoire, both of central importance to the study of Bach's church

music.[5] The chorale in particular gives a distinctive German flavour
to the repertoire, and since it is a prominent feature of Bach's church
music, it is perhaps not surprising that studies of pre-Bach German
church music have been intent on tracking down earlier chorale settings. The large repertoire of works without chorales, such as Psalm
settings and solo motets, have therefore tended to be pushed into the
background.

A preoccupation with the German nature of the repertoire has
likewise resulted in a comparative lack of appreciation of the extent
of Italian influence upon it. The importance of Italian music in the
first half of the century has long been appreciated, especially in connection with Schütz's celebrated study trips in Italy. But the effects
of Italian church music later in the century have received less attention, partly because the Italian repertoire itself remains an under-
explored area, with little of the liturgical church music between the
periods of Carissimi and Vivaldi being familiar today. This study
draws upon the substantial quantity of Italian church music which
survives in the Düben and Bokemeyer collections, as well as other
North German sources, and seeks to show in detail the way in which
Italian church music maintained its influence on North German
church music throughout the age of Buxtehude.

[5] Concerning the study of chorale-based music see F. Krummacher, *Die Choralbearbeitung in der protestantischen Figuralmusik zwischen Praetorius und Bach* (Kassel, 1977), and
for settings of the Passion narrative see B. Smallman, *The Background of Passion Music: J. S.
Bach and his Predecessors* (2nd edn., New York, 1970).

I

Music in Religious Thought and Education

◊

THROUGHOUT the history of Lutheranism the writings of Martin Luther himself have provided powerful ammunition for pastors and others seeking to defend the work of church musicians. Luther declared that the study of music was second only in importance to the study of theology, and he underlined the value of music both as a fitting way of rendering praise to God and as a vehicle to convey the word of God to the listener. But despite Luther's sanction, the role of music in Lutheran worship developed during the seventeenth century into a source of considerable argument between conservatives and reformers. In order to understand this controversy it is necessary to consider music as part of the wider religious debate that existed in the Lutheran church during this period.

ORTHODOX LUTHERANISM AND THE REFORMERS

The early decades of the Protestant Reformation in the sixteenth century were marked by considerable confusion over matters of doctrine. The leading Protestant pastors and scholars, free from one form of church doctrine and hierarchy, now had to establish another. After much debate, the leaders of the Lutheran church assembled the Formula of Concord in 1577, a document which aimed to clarify the precise nature of Lutheranism. In 1580 this was superseded by the Book of Concord, which contained both the Formula of 1577 and several documents dating from the early years of the Reformation, including Luther's highly influential Catechisms of 1529. These documents may be seen to mark the beginning of the era known as the period of Lutheran Orthodoxy. However, although providing a much-needed point of reference for Lutheran thought and practice,

they did not put an end to religious debate within the Lutheran
Church.

The chief theological division that existed within the Lutheran
community during the seventeenth century concerned the nature of
personal religion. At the outset of the Reformation, strong emphasis
was placed on the belief in justification by faith alone (*sola fide*). But,
after the rapid initial spread of Protestantism through the German-
speaking lands, many religious leaders began to develop the idea that
whilst faith was indeed sufficient for salvation, it should also bear
fruit in matters of personal religious practice. The religious writers
who attacked Lutheran Orthodoxy claimed that the church hierarchy had come to place too much emphasis on the tenets of the Book
of Concord and not enough on personal religion. Many writers
protested that Lutheran Orthodoxy did not, for example, place any
emphasis on individual lay people reading the Bible. In defence,
Orthodox pastors argued that the combination of the teachings of
the Lutheran Book of Concord, the Gospel readings, and the weekly
sermon heard in church provided a complete religious education for
the laity. Moreover, they thought that it was positively dangerous for
the average lay person to delve into the Bible without guidance from
the clergy; unchecked, this would lead to heresy and further religious
conflict.

The reformers felt that the accepted church teachings in the Book
of Concord were not in themselves sufficient to inspire personal religion. Rather, they saw the teachings as a basis on which true religion
could be developed. In addition, the reformers complained that
much Orthodox preaching dwelt on complex theological points and
in so doing obscured the essence of the Christian Gospel. As one
leading reformer, Jacob Spener, put it:

When men's minds are stuffed with such a theology which, while it pre-
serves the foundation of faith from the Scriptures, builds on it with so much
wood, hay and stubble of human inquisitiveness that the gold can no longer
be seen, it becomes exceedingly difficult to grasp and find pleasure in the
real simplicity of Christ and his teaching.[1]

The spiritual reform movement within the Lutheran Church during the seventeenth century has often been called Pietism, after the
title and influence of Spener's *Pia desideria* (Pious desires), published

[1] Jacob Spener, *Pia Desideria* (Frankfurt am Main, 1675), transl. and ed. T. G. Tappert
(Philadelphia, 1964), 56.

in 1675.[2] However, the essence of Pietist thought had taken root in Lutheranism long before this date. Many writers before Spener had expounded the principle of practical piety, with its emphasis on good works as a sign of the believing soul. The most widely read Pietist tract published in Germany during the seventeenth century was *Vom wahren Christentum* (True Christianity) by Johann Arndt, which was published in four books between 1605 and 1609. Arndt spent the last decade of his life working in the town of Celle, and his theology of practical piety found many followers, both pastors and scholars, throughout North Germany. The University of Rostock took a leading role in the promotion of piety, and three of the best-known Pietist scholars of the first half of the seventeenth century, Joachim Lütkemann, Heinrich Müller, and Christian Scriver, were all educated there. Berlin was another important centre of practical piety, and it was the organist of the Nicolaikirche there, Johann Crüger, who edited the famous hymn-book whose title allied itself so clearly with the new ideals: *Praxis pietatis melica* (Berlin, 1647).

Spener's debt to Arndt is evident in the fact that his *Pia desideria* was first published as a foreword to a new edition of Arndt's *Postille* of 1615. At the time of publication of the *Pia desideria*, Spener was a pastor in Frankfurt am Main, but he subsequently moved to the Dresden court in 1686 and then to Berlin, becoming pastor of the Nicolaikirche in 1691. He had close links with many of the leading North German Pietists; he counted amongst his friends and correspondents, for example, the influential Professor of Theology at the University of Kiel, Christian Korholt, and his acquaintances in Hamburg included Johann Winckler at the Michaeliskirche and Spener's brother-in-law Johann Horb at the Nicolaikirche. The impact of Spener's *Pia desideria* resulted from its recommendation that groups of Christians should meet together for discussion and Bible study outside Church. To the Orthodox Lutheran clergy this was tantamount to encouraging subversion. In Hamburg, controversy surrounding Spener's advocacy of Pietist meetings frequently engendered open conflict within the clergy. In 1689 the Orthodox Lutherans brought about a ban on meetings, and then attempted to bring the Pietist clergy to heel by requiring them to sign a document denouncing all non-Orthodox practices. The Pietists refused to sign,

---

[2] For further reading on the subject of Pietism see F. E. Stoeffler, *The Rise of Evangelical Pietism* (Studies in the History of Religions, 9; Leiden, 1965).

but were allowed to stay in their posts through the intervention of the secular authorities, who did not regard the document as valid.

Spener's tract emphasized the importance not only of Pietist meetings but also of private devotional reading. His recommended list of books included, in addition to the writings of Arndt, the mystical literature of Thomas à Kempis and Johann Tauler. The appeal of mysticism to the seventeenth-century reformers lay in its central theme of union, the *unio mystica*, whereby the individual believer sought to become as one with God or with Christ, and thus achieve a new life. The advocates of mysticism thus maintained that direct experience of the divine nature was within the grasp of every Christian soul. One of the most prominent Lutheran mystics of the late sixteenth and early seventeenth centuries was the famous hymn-writer Philip Nicolai, who became pastor of the Catherinenkirche in Hamburg in 1601. Two years earlier his famous chorale 'Wie schön leuchtet der Morgenstern' was published in Frankfurt am Main; Nicolai's mystical leanings are clearly evident in the title given to the chorale: 'Ein Geistlich Braut-Lied der gläubigen Seelen / von Jesu Christo irem himmlischen Bräut[i]gam' (A sacred bridal song of the believing soul concerning Jesus Christ her heavenly bridegroom).[3]

The champions of Orthodox Lutheranism were as suspicious of the study of mysticism as they were of the practical reforms of the Pietists. Again, the pure Lutheran teaching of the Book of Concord was, in their view, being undermined. Such fears on the part of the Orthodox clergy were exacerbated by the associations between the ideals of the reformers and the teaching of other Christian denominations. Although the leading reformers, including Arndt and Spener, considered themselves to be unswerving Lutherans, many Pietists were denounced as crypto-Calvinists, and the mystics as crypto-Catholics. The vast majority of North German towns and territories remained firmly Lutheran during the seventeenth century, but the threat of conversion either to Calvinism or back to Roman Catholicism was ever present. Confessional conflict erupted now and again in the towns, and some individual Lutheran rulers were converted either to the Calvinist cause (as in the case of the elector of Brandenburg Johann Sigismund in 1613) or to Catholicism (as in the case of Johann Friedrich of Braunschweig in 1651). The threat of Calvinism was felt all the more strongly after the Peace of Westphalia

[3] P. Nicolai, *Freuden-Spiegel des ewigen Lebens* (Frankfurt am Main, 1599), 409.

in 1648, since the treaty gave official recognition to the Calvinist territories in Germany for the first time.

CHURCH MUSIC AS PART OF THE RELIGIOUS DEBATE

The role of music in Lutheran worship played a major part in the
vigorous debate between Orthodox Lutherans and the reformers that
persisted throughout the seventeenth century.[4] Some tracts, including Spener's *Pia desideria*, made no specific reference to music, but
others were concerned exclusively with the problem of church
music. These writings are quite different from the better-known
musical polemics of the period, such as the Monteverdi–Artusi controversy or the Scacchi–Siefert dispute, since they deal not with a
specifically musical problem, but with the suitability and function of
music in a particular context, the church. Within the conservative
wing of Lutheranism, elaborate church music was accepted not only
for its power to convey a particular text but also simply as an offer-
ing to God. By contrast, the reformers favoured the cultivation of the
spiritual song for use both in church and at home, and argued that
other forms of church music should be simple and serious in style,
and easily understood by the congregation. The new Italian styles
that spread into Germany during the early decades of the seventeenth
century were associated by the Pietists exclusively with the secular
world. If the Pietists allowed the performance of any artistically
worthwhile music in church, it had to be in the older, polyphonic
style, which to them bore an air of gravity that was wholly lacking
in the newer styles. The seeds of this controversy can be observed as
early as the Hamburg *Melodeyen Gesangbuch* of 1604, the introduction
of which emphasizes the importance of a serious style of music as
against more frivolous styles of vocal and instrumental music used at
times in church:

Wo nicht feine ernsthaffte *Motteten* und hertzrürende bewegliche Psalmen
und Gesenge / sondern leichtfertiglich einher hüpffende Stücke und
Lieder auff Chor und Orgeln gesungen / und mit frembden Welschen
Buhlensprüngen und Ticktacken / oder wunderlichen Fugen / als wans
zum Tanz gienge / gespielet werden / da kan nicht allein keine andacht
folgen / sondern muß auch noch wol damit ein eckel für der lieblichen und

---

[4] The principal study of this topic is C. Bunners, *Kirchenmusik und Seelenmusik: Studien
zu Frömmigkeit und Musik im Luthertum des 17. Jahrhunderts* (Berlin and Göttingen, 1966).

herrlichen *Musica* in die anwesenden hertzen hinein geschoben und gepfropffet werden.[5]

(Wherever instead of fine, serious motets and moving psalms and songs that touch the heart, pieces and songs that come frolicking in with a skip are sung by choir with organ, and played with foreign, Italian lascivious leaps and tick-tacks, or strange fugues, as if one were going to the dance, then not only can no devotion ensue, but a distaste for lovely and magnificent music must thereby be inserted and grafted on to the hearts of those present.)

The debate continued and intensified during the course of the seventeenth century as the new Italian styles became synonymous with the lighter style of music so disliked by some of the clergy. The three most significant publications to expound the Pietist view which appeared in the second half of the century were Theophil Großgebauer's *Wächterstimme aus dem verwüsteten Zion* (A watchman's voice from devastated Sion) (Rostock, 1661), Christian Gerber's *Unerkandte Sünden der Welt* (Unacknowledged sins of the world) (Dresden, 1690), and J. Muscovius's *Bestraffter Mißbrauch der Kirchen-Music* (The abuse of church music punished) (Lauban, 1694). Großgebauer was a product of the notably Pietist theology faculty at Rostock. His *Wächterstimme*, which was published only months before his death in 1661, concerns itself with many different aspects of church life at the time, but the subject of music draws from him some of his most passionate criticism. He complained that most church musicians were unspiritual people, and that their music, inspired by Popish practices, was at once frivolous and incomprehensible:

Und gleich wie die Welt nun nicht ernsthafftig ist / sondern leichtsinnig / und die alte stille Devotion verlohren hat: Also sind uns Gesänge auß Welschland in Teutschland zugeschickt / worinnen die Biblische Texte zerrissen / und durch der Gurgel geschwinde Läuffte in kleine Stücke zerhacket werden . . . Da gehets dann an ein ehrgeiziges Zusammenschreyen / welcher den Vögeln am besten und gleichsten singen kann. Bald ist's Latein / bald ist's Teutsch / die wenigsten können die Worte verstehen: und wenns verstanden wird / so hafftets doch nicht . . .[6]

(And in the same way that the world today is not serious but frivolous, and has lost the old quiet devotion, songs are sent us to Germany from Italy in

---

[5] *Melodeyen Gesangbuch* (Hamburg, 1604), 8.

[6] T. Großgebauer, *Drey geistreiche Schrifften* (which includes a reprint of the *Wächterstimme*) (Rostock, 1667), 209.

which the biblical texts are torn apart and chopped into little pieces through rapid runs of the throat . . . This results in an ambitious shouting together, to discover who can sing as well as and most like the birds. Now it's in Latin, now in German; only very few can understand the words: and when it is understood nothing sticks . . .)

Großgebauer objected most strongly to elaborate music performed during the communion, when the congregation should be encouraged to contemplate the suffering and death of Christ. Both Gerber and Muscovius took inspiration from Großgebauer's *Wächterstimme* and quoted him at length in their own publications. Like many Pietists, Muscovius likened the concerto style to the shrieking of animals. Following closely the language of Großgebauer, he tirades against the use of this style by choirboys:

Dergleichen auch / wann in einer grossen Kirche etwan ein paar Knaben auffgestellet werden / die auffs allerkünstlichste mit einander *concerti*ren / der Nachtigal am ähnlichsten und subtilesten nachschlagen / daß ein andächtiger Zuhörer ein solches durcheinander geworffenes welches Capaunen Gelächter geschwind nach- und durcheinander *coloraturi*ren / *tremuli*ren / und drüllern / eher gar vor ein Katzen- oder Hüner-Geschrey / als vor eine der Kirchen erbauliche *gravi*tätische Music halten und urtheilen muß / daß solche Music viel besser in einem Frauenzimmer-Gemach bey einem Ehren-Gelag / mehr zur Menschlichen Lust / als in der Kirche zur Erbauung verrichtet würde . . .[7]

(In the same way also when in a large church a few boys are placed, who concert with each other in the most artful way possible, imitating the nightingale most closely and subtly, so that a devout listener might hold and adjudge such confused laughter of castrati, in their ornamenting, quavering, and trilling rapidly one after the other and together, as more like the cry of cats and hens than edifying and solemn church music; and that such music would much better be performed in a women's chamber, at a feast, more for human pleasure, than in the church with a view to spiritual edification . . .)

However, the outpourings of the reformers provoked virulent counter-attacks from both church musicians and Orthodox pastors. Großgebauer's publication was answered by Heinrich Mithobius, a Lutheran pastor at Otterndorf (near Hamburg). In his *Psalmodia Christiana* of 1665, Mithobius argued that music must be seen as a gift from God:

---

[7] J. Muscovius, *Bestraffter Mißbrauch der Kirchen-Music* (Lauban, 1694), 38.

Indem er [Gott] zu dieser unserer Zeit viel treffliche Meister mit seinem
Geist erfüllet / so die herrlichsten Musicalischen Kunst-Stücke comoniret,
und darin ihren hohen Verstand und Kunst in der Music bewähret . . .[8]

(Meanwhile at this time of ours he [God] fills many excellent composers
with his spirit, who have composed the most magnificent musical art-
pieces, and proved therein their high understanding and art in music . . .)

Moreover, he claimed that contemporary Italian composers were
highly skilled at expressing the text in their music, and advocated that
their music should be performed and imitated by Lutheran composers:

Also sind auch die schönen und andächtig gesetzte Italiänische /
schriftmäßige Stücke / nicht zuverwerffen / denn wir mögen ihnen eben
so wol das Gute ablernen / und die Gaben / so ihnen GOtt für andern /
verliehen / uns auch zu Nutz machen / wo wir nur GOttes reine Wort /
neben der Kunst / Lieblichkeit und Andacht darinnen finden.[9]

(Thus the beautiful and devotionally composed Italian, scriptural pieces are
also not to be rejected, for we may equally well learn from them what is
good, and make use for ourselves too of the gifts that God has given to
them for others, if only we find in them God's pure word beside art,
beauty, and devotion.)

Gerber's *Unerkandte Sünden der Welt* received a particularly thorough critique from the cantor of Tilsit (near Königsberg), Georg
Motz, in his publication *Die vertheidigte Kirchen-Music* (Church music
defended) of 1703. Motz sets out to demolish Gerber's arguments
one by one, quoting his statements and then providing 'proof' of
their error. For example, Gerber had attacked not just the musical
abilities but the moral standing of many of the singers engaged in
some Lutheran churches and chapels, singling out the Italians for his
fiercest remarks:

Man findet unter ihnen abgöttische Baals Diener / Päbstische Marien
Knechte / unzüchtige Italiäner / und Capaunen / welches Lutherus . . . ein
unseelig Volck nennet. Denn / sagt er ob sie wol untüchtig sind zur Ehe /
so sind sie doch böser Lust nicht loß / und werden Frauensichtiger dann
vorhin / und gantz Weibisch und gehet ihnen nach dem Sprichwort: Wer
nicht singen kan will immer singen.[10]

(One finds amongst them idolatrous worshippers of Baal, popish servants
of Mary, immoral Italians, and castrati, whom Luther called . . . an ill-fated

[8] H. Mithobius, *Psalmodia Christiana* (Jena, 1665), 217.   [9] Ibid. 305.
[10] Quoted in G. Motz, *Die vertheidigte Kirchen-Music* (n. p., 1703), 17–18.

people. For he says that although they are incapable of marriage they are nevertheless not free from evil desire, and become more like women in appearance than before and completely effeminate, and it is with them as in the proverb: He who cannot sing always wants to sing.)

Motz replied by pointing out that the morals of the individual singers have nothing to do with the value and suitability of the music sung by them:

Das Singen der *Italiaener* in unsern Kirchen / weil ihnen nichts böses zu singen verstattet wird / ist gut und bleibet gut / wann gleich die *Italiaener* und *Castrati* böß und gottloß sind.[11]

(The singing of the Italians in our churches, since they are not allowed to sing anything evil, is good and remains good, even when the Italians and castrati are themselves evil and godless.)

Gerber had also complained about the moral standing of the German church musicians, whose principal vice appears to have been drink. Motz retorted that the normal Sunday congregation also contained 'godless' people, adding the rhyme:

> Keine Gemein
> Ist gantz rein[12]
>
> (No congregation is wholly pure)

Motz, like Mithobius, stressed the divine origin of music, emphasizing that artful compositions were inspired by the 'Heil. Geist' (the Holy Spirit) and not the 'Weltgeist' (worldly spirit). He also tackled the frequent complaint on the part of all the reformers concerning the incomprehensibility of the new concerto style of church music, and enlisted the help of the famous Orthodox theologian Dietericus. Concerning those occasions when the whole text cannot be understood by the congregation, Motz writes as follows:

so ist es eben nicht nöthig sagt *D. Dietericus* in seiner Orgel-Predigt daß man allezeit wisse oder verstehe / was gesungen und *musici*ret werde; was man auff der Orgel schlage; und was man auf andern *Instrument*en spiele; sondern es ist gnug / daß man das *genus* weiß / was gesungen / gespielet / und georgelt wird / nemlich geistliche liebliche Lieder / Psalmen und Lobgesänge / so zu GOttes Lob und Ehre *componi*ret / und gemachet worden sind.[13]

(thus it is just not necessary, says Dr Dietericus in his Organ Sermon, that one always knows or understands what is being sung and played; what is

---

[11] Ibid.   [12] Ibid. 34.   [13] Ibid. 72.

being played on the organ; and what on other instruments; but it is enough that one knows the *genus* of what is being sung, played, or performed on the organ, that is to say, sacred, beautiful hymns, Psalms and songs of praise that have been composed and created to the praise and glory of God.)

Of particular importance here is Motz's thesis that it is enough for the listener merely to know the *genus* of what is being performed. If one accepts this, then all further reasoning about the audibility or comprehensibility of the text is rendered irrelevant. But perhaps the most remarkable passage in his book is that in which he discusses the relative merits of congregational music, 'Choral-Gesang', and music performed separately by the church musicians, 'Figural-Gesang'. Motz does not deny the value of congregational singing, but he identifies some of the problems of this form of worship so beloved by the reformers. Carefully using the language of the reformers, he points out that the congregation usually sings out of habit and 'ohne Andacht' (without devotion), and that many important texts have been altered considerably in order to fit with a particular metrical pattern and rhyming scheme. He argues that because in 'Figural-Gesang' the text can be set sensitively and without alteration, God is worshipped more completely and reasonably in this way than with 'Choral-Liedern' (congregational hymns).

Although many Orthodox Lutherans and Pietists held diametrically opposed views concerning the use of music in church, it would be misleading to suggest that there was no middle ground between the opposing factions, and that all Lutherans held views conforming to one extreme or the other. Even Motz and Gerber expressed moderate views on some matters. Gerber strongly favoured purely congregational singing, but he also tolerated music sung by a separate group of musicians if it satisfied a number of conditions:

Wenn auch mit feinen mäßigen und *mode*sten Instrumenten ein feiner Text der Schrifft / oder sonst ein geistreiches Lied abgesungen würde ohne Einmischung gekünstelter Phantaseyen / daß es die Gemeine deutlich verstehen könte / wäre es auch wohl zu leyden . . .[14]

(If also a fine scriptural text or otherwise spiritual hymn were sung with good, restrained, and modest instruments without the inclusion of artificial elaborations, so that the congregation could understand it clearly, this would be something to tolerate . . .)

---

[14] Quoted in G. Motz, *Die vertheidigte Kirchen-Music*, 229.

Motz drew the line at the performance of purely instrumental music in church, if it had no connection with a sung text. In his view, instrumental music had to be connected in some way to a sacred text. He thus supported the use of instrumental music if it appeared as part of a vocal work, as an introductory Sinfonia, for example, but did not accept the performance of a purely instrumental piece (though there is evidence to show that such music was indeed performed in some churches and chapels). Gerber's advocacy of a moderate style of music clearly had many supporters, as is shown by the immense popularity in the North German region of the music of the central German composer Andreas Hammerschmidt. His music eschews virtuosity, and delivers the text (usually in German) in a clear and direct manner, thus meeting Gerber's requirements. However, the large majority of North German church music of the time was of a more ambitious nature—more than acceptable to Motz but abhorrent to Gerber.

The Preface to the *Hannoverisch Voll-Ständiges Gesangbuch* of 1657 offers an interesting compromise between the Orthodox and Pietist extremes. In order to placate both the Orthodox love of elaborate music and the Pietist concern for spiritual edification, it recommends the reading of Pietist texts by Habermann, Arndt, and Gerhardt during the playing of the organ and the performance of 'Figural-Music'. However, at the same time it warns against the use of too much music of this sort:

Es wäre wol zu wünschen / daß beym sontäglichen und festtägigem Gottes-Dienst an manchem Orte nicht so viel orgelns und unverständlichen musicirens oder lateinischen singens geschehe . . .[15]

(It would be desirable if at the services on Sundays and feast-days at many places there did not occur so much organ-playing and incomprehensible performing or singing in Latin.)

Although it is easy to underline the negative effects of the Pietists on the fortunes of church music in the seventeenth century, it should be remembered that the Pietists promoted directly one specific, if limited, form of music, the spiritual song. Songbooks formed a large part of seventeenth-century German music publishing, and there can be little doubt that the enthusiasm of the Pietists for this genre accounts for the level of their popularity. Some publications contained exclusively new songs, but others contained new songs

[15] *Hannoverisch Voll-Ständiges Gesangbuch* (Lüneburg, 1657), p. v^v.

alongside the traditional chorale repertoire. The Pietist tone can clearly be observed in the introduction to the second edition of the influential *Geistliche Seelen-Musik* (Rostock, 1659, 2nd edn. 1668) of Heinrich Müller, a contemporary of Großgebauer in Rostock and pastor of the Marienkirche. He opens by stating that song ('der Gesang') is beyond all doubt established as one of the most important items in both private and public worship. Later he stresses the importance of the book for private devotion, and comments that much church worship is frequently adversely affected by an over-familiarity with the customary liturgy. Müller's desire to provide new material of an appropriately Pietist nature for his congregation led him to include several new songs in the publication, and for the music he turned to his own organist at the Marienkirche, Nikolaus Hasse. Similar collaborations of pastor and musician at other major North German towns brought forth many other such volumes, such as those by Johann Rist and cantor Thomas Selle at Hamburg. More important for the development of North German church music as a whole was the fact that many composers used the newly composed Pietist songs as ingredients in larger works, either to satisfy their own interests or possibly to placate pastors and congregations. Buxtehude, in particular, made much use of the new Pietist song repertoire.

A further positive effect of the spiritual reform movement on church music was brought about by the study of mysticism, an activity encouraged by many of the leading Pietists. Theological mysticism traversed the confessional barrier between Lutheranism and Catholicism, for medieval mystical texts were as vital to the heart of the Lutheran reformers as they were to the Catholic Counter-Reformation. In addition, many books of mystical literature by Italian authors were translated into German by Protestant writers, and the works of German Catholic mystics were also widely read in Lutheran circles. It should also be noted that although many Lutherans wrote fierce anti-Catholic polemics, others showed considerable tolerance towards Catholicism, choosing instead Calvinism as the main object of their invective. A large number of seventeenth-century Italian motets were settings of mystical texts, and because of the interest in mysticism encouraged by the Pietists, such works found a welcome place in many Lutheran churches and chapels.

Religious attitudes towards music in Lutheran worship during Buxtehude's era thus covered a wide spectrum of opinion, not unlike that found in the Anglican church. Even within a single town, the pastors of the principal churches sometimes held very different views, ranging from strict Orthodoxy to Calvinistic tendencies, and so may have had very different expectations from their church musicians. But although the anti-church-music lobby was extremely vocal and well connected, the evidence of the surviving seventeenth-century church music suggests that Orthodoxy held sway in many of the largest and most prosperous Lutheran churches and chapels.

MUSIC IN THE LATIN SCHOOLS

Music was a vital ingredient in the educational philosophy of the Lutheran Latin schools. The chief town cantor was often expected to teach music along with other subjects in the Latin school, giving general instruction to the whole school and more specialized instruction to the half dozen or so boys chosen to sing in the church choir. Some idea of the manner in which music was taught can be gleaned from the surviving books of music instruction, including Daniel Friderici's *Musica Figuralis* (Rostock, 1618), Christian Frick's *Music-Büchlein* (Lüneburg, 1631), Otto Gibelius's *Seminarium Modulatoriae vocalis* (Celle, 1645) and *Kurtzer, jedoch gründlicher Bericht von den Vocibus musicalibus* (Bremen, 1659), Conrad Matthaei's *Bericht von den Modis Musicis* (Königsberg, 1652), H. Metzelius's *Compendium Musices tam Choralis quam Figuralis* (Hamburg, 1660), Johann Crüger's *Der rechte Weg zur Singekunst* (Berlin, 1660), and Martin Fuhrmann's *Musicalischer-Trichter* (Frankfurt an der Spree, 1706).[16]

Music was taught in the Latin schools as the science and skill of singing, whose function was the worship of God. Friderici's book opens with the simple question and answer: 'Was ist die Musica? Eine Wissenschaft zu singen' (What is Music? A science of singing). Frick's book 'von dem ohrsprunge, gebrauche und erhaltung Christlicher Music' (on the origin, use, and maintenance of Christian music) explains the theological basis of music, tracing its origin and development from biblical times onwards. The remaining books

---

[16] None of these treatises is as yet available in English translation. For a more complete bibliography of books of musical instruction and a detailed investigation into their contents, see J. Butt, *Music Education and the Art of Performance in the German Baroque* (Cambridge, 1994). On Crüger's theoretical writings, see E. Fischer-Krückeberg, 'Johann Crüger als Musiktheoretiker', *Zeitschrift für Musikwissenschaft*, 12 (1929), 609–29.

listed above deal more directly with musical matters: some, most notably those by Friderici and Crüger, dwell principally on singing exercises and technique; others, in particular Fuhrmann's *Musicalischer-Trichter*, provide a more general guide to music. Friderici's book on singing is particularly thorough, and appears to have been widely used during the course of the century, reaching its fourth edition by 1649. The title-page of the fourth edition explains that the book was originally written for the instruction of schoolboys in Rostock, where he was cantor of the Marienkirche. The book concerns itself not only with the notation of music but also with a number of practical matters concerned with singing in church. The boys are cautioned about several matters: they should not fiddle with their hands, beat time with their feet, hold their hands in front of their mouths, rush the tempo, and so on. The last part of the book is devoted to an explanation of the modes, a matter also taken up by the Braunschweig musician Matthaei in his *Bericht von den Modis Musicis* (Commentary on the musical modes). It is interesting to note that a demand for a treatise on the modes obviously continued to exist after 1650, despite the fact that their use was becoming increasingly less significant in the music of the time. However, it should be remembered that a large amount of sixteenth- and early seventeenth-century music was sung regularly at this time, and that plainsong was still used in services. Both Friderici and Matthaei take their readers through each mode in methodical fashion. Matthaei gives the following information for every mode: the range, final, and principal chord, the possibility of transpositions, the use of that mode for a specific mood (quoting from several authors), the Psalm tone, Canticle tone, Introit and Response tones, and examples of chorales and motets written in that mode. However, signs of a changing attitude can be found in Crüger's manual, published in 1660. Crüger explains the notation of music just as Friderici had done, but rather than taking the reader through all the modes in turn, he concentrates on the solmization of major and minor hexachords. With Fuhrmann's volume of 1706 the development is complete: he ridicules the study of the old church modes, and asserts that of the old modes only two remain, the Ionian and the Dorian (i.e. the major and minor), which can be transposed to other pitches.

In the conclusion of his *Musica Figuralis*, Friderici refers briefly to the new Italian styles of embellishment, mentioning the *accentus*, *tremulo*, *gruppo*, *tirato*, and *trillo*, but he does not explain them, saying that they are too difficult for young boys. In *Der rechte Weg zur Singekunst* (The correct way to the art of singing), Crüger also notes that such things are not appropriate for schoolboys, pointing out that this style of Italianate singing belongs rather to 'Königliche und Fürstliche wolbestalte Capellen' (well-staffed royal and princely chapels). However, he does go on to explain and give examples of the principal Italian embellishments, stating that schoolboys should at least be able to employ the *accentus*, a family of simple ornaments, and 'etliche der leichtesten *Passaggien*' (several of the easiest *Passaggi*) (see Ch. 9). He also gives explanations of several Italian musical terms, noting that they are now customary in *Concerten*. Both Friderici and Crüger conclude their books with a large number of vocal exercises. Crüger's volume concludes with seventy-five practical exercises for young singers, arranged into four groups. The first three groups contain monodies and two-part canons and exercises to be sung with solmization, and the final group comprises eleven short motets (ten in Latin and one in German) by various unnamed authors for two discantists and continuo. Friderici's book contains canons for from two to four voices; Ex. 1.1 gives a flavour of the style and nature of the exercises.[17]

If it were possible to eavesdrop on a typical music lesson at one of the principal Latin schools during the second half of the seventeenth century, one would expect to hear the cantor explaining that singing was the principal form of music, whose function was the praise of God. He would also be instructing the boys in musical notation and the origin and function of the church modes, and leading them in musical exercises such as those found in the practical manuals of Friderici and Crüger. A more progressively minded cantor might also be instructing his more musical boys in the decline of the church modes and the use of some of the more simple Italian embellishments.

Another subject that may have been tackled by some teachers was that of the relationship between music and rhetoric.[18] Since the underlying educational philosophy of the Latin schools was the

---

[17] The exercise shown in Ex. 1.1 is no. III in Friderici's *Musica Figuralis*: '*Fuga* mit zweyen Stimmen ohne Text. *In unisono*, nach einem halben *Tactu*' (the publication has no page numbers).

[18] For further reading on the relationship between music and rhetoric in German music theory, see G. Buelow, 'National Predilections in Seventeenth-Century Music Theory, a Symposium: Germany', *Journal of Music Theory*, 16 (1972), 36–49, and B. Vickers, 'Figures of Rhetoric/Figures of Music?', *Rhetorica*, 2/1 (1984), 1–41.

Ex. 1.1. Vocal exercise from Friderici, *Musica Figuralis*

humanist tradition of grammar, logic, and rhetoric, a study of the relationship between rhetoric and music fitted comfortably within the
normal curriculum. Moreover, the first North German author to
tackle the subject, Johann Burmeister, was a schoolteacher, working at
the principal town school in Rostock.[19] However, the extent to which
rhetoric was in practice part of the general pattern of musical instruction is not clear. Although some books of musical instruction make no
mention of the subject, others, such as Burmeister's *Musica Poetica*,
place great importance on the relationship, and even if it was not frequently included in class-room teaching, it was certainly held in high
regard at the more advanced level of musical composition and performance. In terms of the overall structure of a composition and the
desire to communicate it effectively to the listener, the principles of
rhetoric could be transferred to music without difficulty. The same
rules that governed the writing and delivery of a speech applied

[19] J. Burmeister, *Musica Poetica* (Rostock, 1606, facs. repr. ed. M. Ruhnke, Kassel, 1955).
For an English translation, see B. V. Rivera, *Musical Poetics* (New Haven, 1993).

equally well to the composition and performance of a musical composition. A musical composition must be born out of inspiration
(*inventio*) which is then carefully set down (*dispositio*) and elaborated
(*elaboratio*). The work must then finally be well performed to an audi-
ence (*enunciatio*). At a more detailed musical level, the duty of both
composer and performer was to employ specific rhetorical devices to
enhance the processes of *elaboratio* and *enunciatio* respectively. Several
German writers presented their own interpretations of the relationship
between music and rhetoric at such a level, using both Latin and
Greek terminology. Chief amongst these were Burmeister's *Music
Poetica* (Rostock, 1606), Johannes Nucius' *Musices poeticae* (Neisse,
1613), Christoph Bernhard's manuscript treatises 'Von der Singe-Kunst
oder Manier' and 'Tractatus compositionis augmentatus', Athanasius
Kircher's *Musurgia Universalis* (Rome, 1650), and Johann Walther's
manuscript treatise 'Praecepta der musicalischen Composition'
(1708).[20] Although no set terminology was ever established, and defi-
nitions often varied, most writers referred to such devices as *Figuren*.

The German Jesuit Athanasius Kircher identified two categories of
Figuren in his highly influential Latin treatise *Musurgia Universalis*:
figurae principales and *figurae minus principales* (corresponding to the *figurae fundamentales* and *figurae superficiales* described by Bernhard and
Walther).[21] The first type included the more fundamental ways of
enlivening music, including passing notes and suspensions, whilst the
second referred to devices more obviously related to the latest compositional styles and singing techniques. This second category
included many different ways of varying a melodic line, either creating particular forms of dissonance or simply by adding diminutions
(*passaggi*) or ornaments. Bernhard's explanation of figures includes,
for example, entries such as the *heterolepsis*, a common technique in
recitative style where the voice leaps to a note that is dissonant with
the bass but makes sense as part of an imaginary second voice, and
passaggio, comprising numerous diminution patterns.[22]

[20] Bernhard's treatises are reproduced in J. M. Müller-Blattau, *Die Kompositionslehre
Heinrich Schützens in der Fassung seines Schülers Christoph Bernhard* (Kassel, 1926; repr. 1963).
For translations, see W. Hilse, 'The Treatises of Christoph Bernhard', *Music Forum*, 3 (1973),
1–196. For Walther's treatise, see J. Walter, *Praecepta der musicalischen Composition*, ed. P.
Benary (Leipzig, 1955). The other treatises listed are not currently available in modern edi-
tions, but for a study of Kircher's treatise, see U. Scharlau, *Athanasius Kircher (1601–1680) als
Musikschriftsteller* (Marburg, 1969).

[21] A. Kircher, *Musurgia Universalis*, 1 (Rome, 1650), 366.

[22] See Hilse, 'The Treatises of Christoph Bernhard', 96 and 118.

It is clear that the principal function of *Figuren* was to assist both the composer and performer in moving the emotions of the listener. Some treatises described the use of *Figuren* as part of the compositional process itself, whilst others highlighted the role of the singer in adding them to a composition. The relationship between composer and performer was certainly a highly complex one during the seventeenth century, although the gradual trend appears to have been that as more composers became familiar with the new Italian styles during the course of the century, particular figures became an increasingly essential part of the composition of a piece, being too important to be left to the performer.[23] A further grey area concerns the extent to which composers employed the figures laid down by Bernhard and others as building bricks, as it were, for their own compositions. Were the figures learnt and then consciously applied as part of the compositional process, or did composers simply employ the figures from their knowledge of Italian music without necessarily being aware of their categorization by the theorists? In all likelihood both processes took place, depending on the circumstances of individual composers. What cannot be ignored, however, is the obvious importance of the relationship between music and rhetoric in the minds of several theorists and composers. Moreover, Bernhard was no obscure theorist, but a first-rate composer who was well known to many of the most significant composers of the time.

The concept of music as rhetoric was an almost exclusively German one. One might even interpret the process of codifying the contemporary Italian style in a manner close to the educational philosophy of the Latin schools as an attempt to rationalize the improvisational inspirations of the Italians, in order to make the Italian style more fit for German consumption. Certainly the discussion of music as rhetoric helped to spread knowledge of the latest Italian singing techniques around the German territories, particularly to individuals who were not able to discover them first-hand in Italy or at one of the German courts.

---

[23] For further examination of these issues, see ch. 5 of Butt, *Music Education and the Art of Performance*, 121–65.

2

Music in the Lutheran Liturgy

◊

ALTHOUGH the Reformation was brought about through disagreement over matters of religious doctrine, the new freedom that resulted from the separation from Rome affected all aspects of church life, including the liturgy. In England, the church, now under the authority of the sovereign, soon developed its own liturgy, which was adopted throughout the kingdom. However, in the German Lutheran territories the complex political situation militated against the adoption of a single new form. Each town or territory settled upon its own liturgy, printed in a *Kirchen-Ordnung*, which was employed exclusively in that place or region. Many of the early and mid-sixteenth-century *Kirchen-Ordnungen* held force through to the eighteenth century, but some were reprinted in revised editions to incorporate minor changes in liturgical practice.[1] Such alterations were often concerned with language. Martin Luther produced two models for liturgical practice, one in Latin, the *Formula Missae* of 1523, and the other in German, the *Deutsche Messe* of 1526, and most subsequent *Kirchen-Ordnungen* were macaronic in nature, with Latin retaining its importance for the central parts of the liturgy such as the Ordinary of the Mass. The general trend during the course of the sixteenth and seventeenth centuries was towards an increasing use of German, but a compromise was sometimes reached by the singing of individual sections of the liturgy twice, once in Latin and then again in German.

---

[1] For further reading on the *Kirchen-Ordnungen*, see R. von Liliencron, *Liturgisch-musikalische Geschichte der evangelischen Gottesdienste von 1523 bis 1700* (Schleswig, 1893), and for further discussion of the place of music in the liturgy see W. Blanckenburg, 'Der mehrstimmige Gesang und die konzertierende Musik im evangelischen Gottesdienst', *Leiturgia*, 4/5 (1961), 661–719.

GOTTESDIENST

The two principal Lutheran services were the Sunday morning *Gottesdienst*, which usually began at around 7.00 a.m., and the afternoon service of Vespers, held on Saturdays and Sundays at about 2.00 p.m. The basic outline of the *Gottesdienst* was that of the Catholic Mass, although changes were made, particularly to the Proper of the Mass. The five sections of the Ordinary of the Mass—the Kyrie, Gloria, Credo, Sanctus, and Agnus Dei—all remained in the Lutheran liturgy, but the Agnus Dei was often listed among several optional items that could be sung during the communion, rather than as an essential item in the order of service. Of the sections of the Mass Proper, only the Introit remained a permanent fixture in the Lutheran liturgy. The other parts of the Proper remained in use in some places, but there was a general trend towards replacing Propers with German hymns. The main theological difference between the Catholic Mass and the Lutheran *Gottesdienst* was the shift in emphasis from the sacramental part of the service, the communion, to the liturgy of the word, which in the Lutheran tradition contained the sermon. This meant that the first half of the service, containing the Kyrie, Gloria, and Credo, gained primary significance within the service as a whole, and for this reason many Lutheran composers wrote settings of the Ordinary in which the latter parts were omitted—the so-called Lutheran *Missa brevis*. This often contained only the first two sections of the Ordinary, the Kyrie and Gloria, since the Credo was often sung by the congregation, due to its doctrinal importance. The liturgy of the sacrament, containing the Sanctus and Agnus Dei, did remain part of the Lutheran *Gottesdienst*, but many people did not see it as an essential part of the service. The Lüneburg *Kirchen-Ordnung* of 1643 instructs the preacher to remind the congregation that they should remain in the church for communion; this suggests that quite a few members of the congregation may have felt inclined to extricate themselves after the sermon.[2] Table 1 gives an example of the order of the Lutheran *Gottesdienst*, taken from the territory of Mecklenburg's revised *Kirchen-Ordnung* of 1650.[3] The characteristic mix of Latin and German may be observed, as well as the

---

[2] 'Auch sol der Prediger zu Zeiten die Leute vermahnen / dass sie in der Kirchen bey der Communion bleiben'. *Kirchen-Ordnung des Durchleuchtigen . . . Herrn Friederichen, Hertzogen zu Braunschweig und Lüneburg* (Lüneburg, 1643), 183.

[3] *Revidirte Kirchenordnung . . . Im Hertzogthumb Mecklenburg* (Lüneburg, 1650), 151–7.

TABLE 1. *The* Gottesdienst *(Mecklenburg, 1650)*

The Ordinary sections are indicated by 'O' and the Proper sections by 'P'.

	Item	Instructions
P	INTROIT of the Sunday or feast-day	Sung by the choir
O	KYRIE	Sung by the choir
O	GLORIA IN EXCELSIS	Intoned by the priest and sung by the choir, either in Latin or German
	RESPONSE	Sung, either in Latin or German
	COLLECT	Read in German by the priest
	EPISTLE	Read by the priest, facing the people
(P)	SEQUENCE, or HYMN *de tempore*	Sung by all
	GOSPEL	Read by the priest, facing the people
O	CREDO	Intoned by the priest and sung by the choir in Latin to the prescribed melody
O	CREDO repeated	Sung by all in German
	SERMON	
	PSALM or HYMN	Sung by all
	PREFACE	Sung by the priest in either Latin or German
O	SANCTUS	Sung in either Latin or German
	THE LORD'S PRAYER	Sung by the priest
	COMMUNION	During which hymns should be sung:
		'Jesus Christus unser Heiland'
		'Gott sey gelobet'
O		Agnus Dei
(O)		Esaia dem Propheten (the German Sanctus)
		Also, if there are many communicants:
		'Ich danke dem Herrn'
		Other German hymns
		The Litany
		'O Lamb Gottes unschüldig'
		At the conclusion:
(O)		Christe du Lamb Gottes (the German Agnus Dei)
	COLLECT	Read by the priest
	BLESSING	
	CONCLUDING HYMN	'Erhalt uns Herr bey deinem Wort'
		'Verleihe uns Friede gnediglich'
		'Ehre sey dem Vater und dem Sohn'

common practice of singing the Credo first in Latin, by the choir alone, and then in German by the congregation. The Mecklenburg book contains the full melody and text of some of the Latin parts of the service, such as the Credo, and refers the reader to the hymn-book for the German versions of these items.

VESPERS

The Lutheran service of Vespers retained, like the *Gottesdienst*, the basic outline of its Catholic antecedent. Its traditional language remained Latin, but German was employed increasingly as an alternative during the seventeenth century. The order of Sunday Vespers set out in the Lüneburg *Kirchen-Ordnung* of 1643 is given in Table 2.[4] This order illustrates well the flexible approach frequently adopted with regard to the singing of Psalms at the Lutheran Vespers. In the early decades of the Reformation the choice was simply a matter of how many of the traditional Vespers Psalms should be sung in Latin at a particular service. The Prussian *Kirchen-Ordnung* of 1525 states that one, two, or three Psalms should be sung in Latin, depending on their length ('darnach sie lang oder kurz sein'), without antiphons.[5] But by the seventeenth century the choice was extended to the singing of Psalms either in Latin or in German. The traditional Vespers Psalms of the Roman rite remained the most commonly used Psalms for Vespers in the Lutheran church. In addition to the evidence of the *Kirchen-Ordnungen*, such as that given in Table 2, it may be observed that most of the extant complete settings of Psalms by Lutheran composers are settings of the traditional Vespers Psalms. Antiphons were generally dispensed with, but these, together with other remnants of the Roman rite, remained in sporadic use. The order for Saturday Vespers in the same Lüneburg order of 1643 calls for an antiphon to be sung with the Psalms, and for the responsory (or hymn *de tempore*) to be sung after the lesson.

---

[4] *Kirchen-Ordnung . . . Braunschweig und Lüneburg*, 184–5.
[5] E. Sehling, *Die evangelischen Kirchenordnungen des XVI. Jahrhunderts*, iv (Leipzig, 1911), 31.

TABLE 2. *Vespers (Lüneburg, 1643)*

Item	Instructions
PSALMS	One or two Latin or German Psalms, such as *Dixit Dominus*, *Confitebor*, *Beatus vir*, *Laudate pueri Dominum*, and at times *In exitu Israel*, and indeed excellent German Psalms, sung by the schoolboys
LESSON	Read by a boy in German, such as the Ten Commandments, Creed, or Lord's Prayer
HYMN	*de tempore*, sung either in Latin or German
SERMON	Based on the morning's Epistle or *de festo*
MAGNIFICAT	Sung in either German or Latin
COLLECT	
BENEDICAMUS DOMINO	

LITURGICAL AND NON-LITURGICAL MUSIC

The church music provided by the cantor and his musicians took the form of either settings of the strictly liturgical texts, or of texts with some or no clear liturgical origin. The Mecklenburg *Gottesdienst* given in Table 1 makes specific mention of the choir in connection with four parts of the liturgy: the Introit, Kyrie, the Latin Gloria, and the Latin Credo. However, since the choir is directed to sing the Latin Credo to the traditional plainsong melody given in the book, the only strictly liturgical items which could be sung by the choir to settings by various composers were the Introit, Kyrie, and Gloria. This is also the pattern found in other *Kirchen-Ordnungen*. At Vespers, the primary liturgical music consisted of the Psalm or Psalms and the Magnificat. Music with a strict liturgical function, often in Latin, formed a substantial proportion of the North German church music of Buxtehude's time. For example, a printed catalogue of the music of Johann Theile, published in 1708, is entitled 'Opus Musicalis Compositionis . . . Super Textus Ecclesiasticos diversos' and contains twenty-three settings of the Mass (which, to judge from his extant settings in the Berlin Staatsbibliothek, were probably of the *Missa brevis* variety), eight settings of the Magnificat, one each of the Nunc dimittis, *Deus in adjutorium* (the Preces at Vespers) and *Veni sancte spiritus* (often prescribed to be sung as an Introit), and several settings of the Psalms, mostly those appropriate for Vespers. An inventory of lost music composed by Augustin Pfleger at Güstrow, dated 1664, contains much liturgical music in Latin. The first eighteen items comprise settings of the Benedictus, Et in terra (Gloria in excelsis), *Veni sancte spiritus*, Te Deum laudamus, *Dixit Dominus, Beatus vir, Laudate Dominum*, Nunc dimittis, and *Laudate pueri*.[6] Settings of the Vespers Psalms in Latin by German composers are found in all the major collections and inventories of the period, together with settings of many other liturgical texts. A Lüneburg inventory, for example, lists Vespers Psalms in Latin by Kaspar Förster, Johann Gerstenbüttel, Johann Philip Krieger, Nicolaus Strungk, and others, as well as settings of the Magnificat and the Mass, including some settings of the Sanctus alone.[7] The Bokemeyer collection contains some extant examples of independent settings of the Sanctus by Michael Österreich, one of which follows on from a setting of the *Sursum corda*, confirming that these works were indeed designed for their correct liturgical use. They may have been intended to complement settings of the *Missa brevis* by other authors on occasions when more music was required.

With respect to the use of non-liturgical church music in Lutheran worship, it should be remembered that the *Kirchen-Ordnungen* were designed to give the basic outline of the liturgy, and that one would not expect them to contain full information concerning the music that might be employed in the services. For this type of information it is necessary to consult other sources such as headings on the title-pages of manuscript scores and parts, and surviving orders of service for specific occasions. These indicate that music was at times employed in the service at places not specified in the various *Kirchen-Ordnungen*. A publication of the complete texts sung at the Marienkirche in Lübeck over Christmas and New Year 1682 shows that, besides the normal liturgical music, a non-liturgical work was performed each day during the communion to either German or

[6] A. Nausch, *Augustin Pfleger: Leben und Werke* (Kassel, 1954), 100.

[7] M. Seiffert, 'Die Chorbibliothek der St. Michaelis-Schule in Lüneburg', *Sammelbände der Internationalen Musik-Gesellschaft*, 9 (1908), 593–621.

Latin texts.[8] The published order of service for the consecration of the new Michaeliskirche in Lüneburg in 1700 indicates that pieces were performed after the Gospel, after the sermon, and at the conclusion of the service.[9] Such specific information is quite rare, but it would seem that non-liturgical church music was performed at times in at least four places in the *Gottesdienst*, roughly corresponding to the places formerly occupied by the Proper of the Mass: after the Epistle, after the Gospel, after the sermon, and during the communion. Settings of Gospel texts were probably sung after the Gospel or after the sermon, which would have been based on the Gospel reading. The Mecklenburg *Kirchen-Ordnung* of 1650 states that 'Wenn die Predigt geendet / sol man einen Deutschen Psalm singen / vom Feste / oder der sich sonst auff das Evangelium schicket' (When the sermon is ended a German Psalm of the feast or concerned with the Gospel reading should be sung), and it seems likely that more elaborate compositions connected with the Gospel were also performed at this position in the service.[10] Compositions based on more overtly devotional texts, such as those in the mystical tradition, were sometimes employed during the communion. A number of such works copied in the Düben collection, for example, bear the heading 'sub communione', such as the Buxtehude motets *Lauda Sion salvatorem* (BuxWV 68), *O wie selig* (BuxWV 90), and *O clemens, o mitis* (BuxWV 82), and Johann Sebastiani's aria *Jesu, Jesu du mein Licht* (copied from his publication *Parnaß Blumen* of 1672). However, no fixed rules appear to have governed the use of different types of texts during the *Gottesdienst* at this time. For example, although works based on mystical texts were frequently sung during the communion, they were not restricted to this point in the service. The most obviously mystical text listed in the Lübeck book of texts from 1682, the *Jesu dulcis memoria*, was sung not during the communion but before the Sermon. Although evidence concerning the use of specific pieces during the *Gottesdienst* is rare from the North German region at this time, a wealth of such detail survives in the court diaries at Dresden, with which many of the most prominent North German composers held strong connections.[11] The *Ordnung* established in the reign of

---

[8] *Natalitia Sacra* (Lübeck, 1682), reproduced in M. Geck, *Die Vokalmusik Dietrich Buxtehudes und der frühe Pietismus* (Kassel, 1965), 230–7.

[9] H. Walter, *Musikgeschichte der Stadt Lüneburg: Vom Ende des 16. bis zum Anfang des 18. Jahrhunderts* (Tutzing, 1967), 114.

[10] *Revidirte Kirchenordnung . . . Im Hertzogthumb Mecklenburg*, 155.

[11] See E. Schmidt, *Der Gottesdienst am kurfürstlichen Hofe zu Dresden* (Göttingen, 1961).

Duke Johann Georg II made provision for the performance of church music after the Gospel and after the Sermon, and the court diaries indicate that great care was taken over the choice of works with texts appropriate to the day or season, taken either from the Proper of the Mass in the Catholic Rite or from the biblical readings of the day. However, works based on more general texts were also sometimes employed, including many on mystical themes. That additional non-liturgical church music was occasionally performed at Vespers on Sundays and major feast days is also demonstrated by the Lübeck book of texts of 1682, but the Lübeck publication does not indicate the precise place in the service at which the non-liturgical works were sung. Evidence from the Dresden court diaries suggests that the principal places for additional music were after the Psalm or Psalms, and after the Magnificat. Thus in the same way that the additional music in the *Gottesdienst* replaced parts of the Proper of the Mass, the non-liturgical music sung at Vespers was employed in place of the old Latin chants, in this case the Psalm and Magnificat antiphons.

Although it is convenient to draw a distinction between works composed to liturgical and non-liturgical texts, it would be false to suggest that individual pieces were only performed at the times suggested by the nature of their texts. Even in the more uniform liturgy of the Roman Catholic Church the distinction between liturgical and non-liturgical music was becoming increasingly blurred during this period.[12] Thus liturgical texts were used not only at their appointed time, but also at other times when the text was appropriate. In the Düben collection, the motet *O vos populi* by Carissimi, for example, is headed 'Tempore Paschatos vel ad libitum Sub Communione', indicating use either at Easter or, if desired, during communion. Similarly, the first motet in Buxtehude's cycle *Membra Jesu nostri* (BuxWV 75), 'Ecce super montes', is headed 'Pasch. aut per ogni tempo', indicating use at Easter or at any time. Texts gained a popularity in their own right, and those expressing general sentiments such as joy and grief could be used at several different times during the year. Settings of brief Psalm texts were particularly useful in this regard, and such works account for a large proportion of non-liturgical texts set by both North German and Italian composers at this time. In some cases a text was deemed to be suitable for any time

[12] See ch. 3 of J. Roche, *North Italian Church Music in the Age of Monteverdi* (Oxford, 1984), 32–47.

of the year. Buxtehude's setting of the popular text of St Bernard of Clairvaux *Jesu dulcis memoria* (BuxWV 56), for example, is headed simply 'per ogni tempo'.

In addition to supplying music for the usual round of *Gottesdienst* and Vespers, composers also provided music for weddings and funerals, depending on the social importance of the person or persons involved. Many fine works written for funeral services survive from this period, varying from simple strophic arias to large-scale works with texts drawn from different sources specifically for the occasion. The frailty of earthly life was in any case a popular Lutheran theme, and so works composed for funerals based on this theme may well have been used at other times. Amongst the more extended examples of funeral music are Christian Ritter's *Miserere Christe mei*, composed for a funeral in 1681, and Georg Österreich's 'Actus funebris' *Plötzlich müßen die Leute sterben*, which dates from 1702. Settings of the Nunc dimittis, either in Latin or German, may also have been used at funeral services, as is suggested by Buxtehude's *Mit Fried und Freud ich fahr dahin* (BuxWV 76), composed for the funeral of a Lübeck superintendent in 1671 and performed again at the funeral of Buxtehude's father in 1674.[13] They may also have been used for the service of Compline. A small number of settings of the principal liturgical items in the services of Matins and Compline can be found in the repertoire, suggesting that these services may on occasion have been sung with full musical forces. As well as the Nunc dimittis, settings of the Te Deum may be found, including a published setting by the Danzig composer Crato Bütner (1662), as well as complete Compline Psalms with Gloria Patri, such as the *Cum invocarem* by Johann Theile.

MUSICA CHORALIS AND MUSICA FIGURALIS

The church music composed by Buxtehude and his contemporaries formed only one part of the overall musical make-up of Lutheran worship at this time, and some consideration will now be given to the other forms of sacred vocal music that were employed in the services. The basic distinction that was described by several authors of the time was between *Musica choralis* (singing in unison) and *Musica*

---

[13] See K. Snyder, *Dieterich Buxtehude: Organist in Lübeck* (New York, 1987), 214.

figuralis (singing in parts). Martin Fuhrmann's *Musicalischer-Trichter*, published in 1706, defines *Musica choralis* as singing 'nach gleichen *Noten* ohne *Tact* (bißweilen Octaven-Weise / ohne *Alt, Tenor* und *Bass*)' (according to the same notes, without metre (at times in octaves, without alto, tenor, and bass)).[14] The sound of a full church singing in unison (or octaves) without accompaniment either by the organ or other instruments is rarely heard today, but was greatly prized in Lutheran worship of this period.[15] Pastor Frick of Bardowick, near Lüneburg, wrote in his *Music-Büchlein* of 1631:

O wenn eine gantz Kirche und Gemeine mit dem Chor fein einhellig mit singet / und mit einstimmet / das stehet trefflich schöne / und singet und klinget in den Himmel hinein.[16]

(When a whole church and congregation sings together and joins in with the choir it is extremely beautiful, and the sound of the singing reaches right to heaven.)

Some of the *musica choralis* regularly sung in Lutheran worship was sung by the choir or choirboys alone. Many *Kirchen-Ordnungen* refer specifically to the singing of the schoolboys, particularly at services other than the main Sunday morning *Gottesdienst*, such as the Saturday Vespers, and some sources indicate the use of the choirboys alone in alternation with the congregation. Frick's *Music-Büchlein*, for example, recommends that for the singing of the three-verse *Nim von uns lieber Herre Gott*, the whole church should sing the first and third verses and the boys alone should sing the second verse.[17] *Musica choralis* formed the musical core of Lutheran worship. *Musica figuralis* was employed only as a substitute for texts that would normally have been sung *choraliter*, or as an addition to the *Musica choralis*, depending on the occasion and the availability of skilled musicians.

The *Musica choralis* of Lutheran worship comprised the traditional Latin plainsong melodies for the *Gottesdienst* and the tones for the Psalms and Canticles at Vespers, together with the German versions of some of these liturgical items, and chorales. The music was available to the choir and congregation either in the *Kirchen-Ordnungen*, which often contained the traditional Latin melodies, or in hymn-books. Most main towns or territories, besides producing their own

---

[14] M. Fuhrmann, *Musicalischer-Trichter* (Frankfurt an der Spree, 1706), 34.

[15] This manner of congregational singing can, however, still be heard today in Orthodox Jewish synagogues.

[16] C. Frick, *Music-Büchlein* (Lüneburg, 1631; facs. repr., Leipzig, 1976), 126.

[17] Ibid. 154–5.

Kirchen-Ordnung, also provided their own general *Gesangbuch* (hymn-book) for use both at church and in the home. In addition, separate volumes were also printed which were devoted to collections of particular texts, such as the Psalms. As an example of a typical seventeenth-century Lutheran hymn-book, some details follow of the *Hannoverisch Voll-Ständiges Gesangbuch* of 1657. The frontispiece shows the whole church engaged in song under the direction of the cantor, whose hand is raised. The preface extolls the virtues of sacred song, pointing out that a text is easily learnt and remembered if written with clear rhyme and an exact metre, and especially if it is provided with a fitting melody. The *Gesangbuch* proper opens with a selection of German metrical versions of several central liturgical texts which could be used in the absence of *Figuralmusik*. The first four items are all versions of the Magnificat; then follow two versions of the Canticle of Zechariah, one of the Te Deum, and two of the Gloria in excelsis Deo. The next group contains seventeen metrical versions of Psalm texts, and the remainder of the book contains hymns grouped according to the main Lutheran themes, such as the Lutheran Catechism. Several recently composed melodies may be found in the book, though in all cases an alternative traditional melody is suggested.

Many hymn-books contain lengthy indexes indicating the suitability of individual hymns for specific liturgical use. Heinrich Müller's *Geistliche Seelen-Musik* (Rostock, 1668), for example, contains a liturgical index covering all Sundays and feast-days of the year, indicating which hymns could be used in association with both the Gospel and Epistle readings. The continued popularity of Psalm-singing in the Lutheran tradition can be seen not only from the Psalm sections of most hymn-books, but also from the considerable number of separate publications of metrical Psalms in German that appeared during this period. The most widely used German metrical version of the complete Psalter was that by the celebrated Dresden court poet Martin Opitz, which was published in many of the main Lutheran centres, including the North German towns of Lüneburg and Danzig. The preface to Opitz's *Die Psalmen Davids* (Lüneburg, 1641) acknowledges the debt owed to the French Calvinist tradition of metrical Psalm-singing, and the book itself provides each Psalm with its own melody (written in a C_3 clef with solmization also provided), though some melodies are repeated during the course of the Psalter. Following the Psalms, the book also contains metrical versions by Opitz of the Sunday and feast-day Epistles 'Auff die Weise der Französischen Psalmen in Lieder gefasset' (arranged as songs in the manner of French Psalms). Although no melodies are given in this section, a melody from the Psalm section is prescribed for each Epistle. Many of the hymn-books that appeared during the explosion of publishing that followed the end of the Thirty Years War contained, like the *Hannoverisch Voll-Ständiges Gesangbuch*, new melodies alongside traditional ones. The style of the new melodies was influenced by the contemporary Italian strophic aria and was thus quite different from the older Lutheran melodies. The foreword to the *Kirchen- und Hauß-Buch* (Dresden, 1694), for which Christoph Bernhard edited the music, makes a clear distinction between the new '*Arien-Manier*' and the '*Kirchen-Stylo*', revealing more than a hint of preference for the older style.[18] The new style, however, had many advocates, particularly when used in conjunction with texts concerned with mystical or generally Pietist themes. It is clear from the title-pages and forewords to many of the hymn-books that the publications were intended for use in the home as well as in church, and it seems likely that the more elaborate aria-style melodies were aimed more at the former than the latter. Domestic use is suggested in particular by the mention of accompaniment by instruments such as the regal, lute, or gamba. However, melodies such as that shown in Ex. 2.1, composed by the Rostock organist Nikolaus Hasse and included in Heinrich Müller's *Geistliche Seelen-Musik*, were probably not too difficult for congregational use.

The traditional manner of Lutheran hymn-singing was, like plainsong, unaccompanied, but this norm was expanded and enriched by the use of instruments in a variety of ways. The organ was used, not so much as an accompanying instrument, but as a solo instrument to introduce a hymn with a prelude, to perform solo verses, and to provide interludes between verses and even between lines of a hymn or liturgical item such as the Magnificat. The use of the organ as an accompaniment to the actual singing of the congregation was a practice that seems to have developed only gradually during the course of the seventeenth century; the task of leading the congregation in their singing was the responsibility of the cantor, not the organist.

---

[18] 'Die neuen Melodien aber hat der Editor bis auf etliche wenige / die sich selbst melden werden / nicht in heut üblicher *Arien-Manier*, sondern / mit gutem Wohlbedacht / in rechtem Kirchen-*Stylo* zu setzen /', *Kirchen- und Hauß-Buch* (Dresden, 1694).

Ex. 2.1. Hasse, from Müller, *Geistliche Seelen-Musik* (1659)

Sol- len Herr die ei - fers ruh- ten   Auff mich schla- gen tag und nacht:
Sol- len gleich den was - ser - fluh- ten   Mei - ne thrä- nen sein ge - acht?

Mei- ne thrä- nen wel- che flies- sen   Gleich wie was - ser - strö- me gies- sen

Eng- sten hertz ge - müt und sinn   Daß ich nicht weyß_____ wo ich bin.

The cantor was responsible for the instruments used in church other than the organ, and there is much evidence to suggest that these instruments were used to reinforce the congregational singing just as much as the organ. It is noticeable in the frontispiece of the *Hannoverisch Voll-Ständiges Gesangbuch* of 1657, for example, that the use of both the organ and many other instruments can be seen. Instruments may have been used just to reinforce the melody line or to provide harmony. Fuhrmann refers explicitly to the use of a 16-foot pitch string instrument for hymn accompaniment:

Violone Grosso, eine *Octav-Bass*-Geige / darauff das 16füßige Contra-C. Eine solche grosse Geige solte billich in allen Kirchen vorhanden seyn / und nicht nur beym *Musici*ren / sondern auch unter den *Choral*-Liedern immer mitgestrichen werden . . .[19]

[19] Furhmann, *Musicalischer-Trichter*, 93.

(*Violone Grosso*, a bass-octave violin, on which [is found] the 16-foot Contra-C. One such large violin ought properly to be available in all churches, and be played not only for composed musical pieces but also always during the chorale-hymns . . .)

Although many hymn-books published during the course of the seventeenth century contained just melodies, some offered either melody and bass line (sometimes figured), and others simple four-part harmonizations of the melodies. The former was most often used in books that favoured hymns in the modern Italian aria style, since such compositions were conceived from the start as a melody and bass line. But older melodies that were originally conceived monodically were also increasingly provided with bass lines and figures during the course of the seventeenth century. Bernhard's music for the Dresden *Kirchen- und Hauß-Buch* of 1694, a general hymn-book for church and domestic use, contains a setting of the Magnificat in German which combines the traditional plainsong tone with a figured-bass accompaniment, as shown in Ex. 2.2.[20]

Ex. 2.2. Bernhard, from *Kirchen- und Hauß-Buch* (1694)

Four-part harmonizations with the melody in the top voice became increasingly the norm following publications such as the Hamburg *Melodeyen Gesangbuch* of 1604. But like figured bass, this form of simple elaboration of a traditional melody also extended beyond the strict chorale repertoire. The Bokemeyer collection contains a rare example of harmonized plainsong—a four-part rendition of the *Sursum corda*, probably by Michael Österreich, shown in Ex. 2.3.

Sixteenth- and early seventeenth-century polyphonic music remained an important musical ingredient in Lutheran worship

---

[20] *Kirchen- und Hauß-Buch*, 4.

Ex. 2.3. Österreich, Responses before the Sanctus

Dominus vobiscum:

Sursum corda:

Gratias agamus Deo nostro:

throughout the seventeenth century and beyond. Indeed, such music was often preferred to the more modern style of church music, and many libraries contained the large anthologies of church music published during the early years of the seventeenth century, in particular those by Erhard Bodenschatz and Abraham Schadaeus. The older style was often perceived as more conducive to devotion in the hearts and minds of the listeners, and was favoured by many who held Pietist leanings. In a document written in the 1670s by the rector of the school attached to the German Church in Stockholm, the author characterizes the motets composed in the new style as 'zwar sehr künstlich, aber wenig erbaulich' (indeed very artful, but scarcely edifying), and expresses his preference for 'die alte geist[r]eiche Moteten' (the old spiritual motets), written for full choir.[21] The library of the German Church at the time contained all four volumes of the series *Promptuarium musicum* edited by Schadaeus and Vincentius in the period 1611–17, and it seems likely that this was the type of music favoured by the school rector.[22] Such volumes were the bread and butter of the cantor's art throughout the seventeenth century, providing a wide selection of motets by Italian and German composers. The motets were carefully selected to provide a range of pieces for the whole of the liturgical calendar, and the musical style was only of moderate difficulty. The appeal of this music, as well as that of the similarly unvirtuosic music by the popular central German composers, was considerable, and it was against the background of this type of music that music in the modern style was composed and performed.

[21] E. Kjellberg, 'Kungliga musiker i Sverige under stormaktstiden. Studier kring deras organisation, verksamheter och status ca 1620–ca 1720' (Ph.D. thesis, Uppsala, 1979), 229.
[22] RISM 1611[1], 1612[3], 1613[2], 1617[1].

3

The Influence of Italian Music

◊

WHILE the importance of Italian music in the development of German music in general during the seventeenth century is widely recognized, its specific influence on late seventeenth-century German church music has received little direct attention.[1] Modern scholars of German music have tended to focus their attention on the chorale; yet the large majority of sacred works composed by North German composers during Buxtehude's lifetime had no connection with the chorale and were composed in direct imitation of Italian works. In this chapter I examine the background to the Italian features found in North German church music of the period, and explore the channels through which the Italian style was transmitted to the North German region.

THE BACKGROUND OF ITALIAN INFLUENCE

The influence of Italian music in the German-speaking lands was part of a much wider domination of Italian culture at this time. In literature, for example, German writers had for some time followed the Italian lead in genres such as the Latin lyric and madrigalian verse. Italy was the chief foreign destination for the German nobility, and, on returning home, many individuals sought to emulate Italian taste, whether in art, architecture, literature, or music, as far as their finances would permit. The city of Rome was the main goal of German visitors, both Catholic and Protestant, and many would have visited in particular the German College, where Giacomo

[1] The principal exception is the work of the Danish scholar Søren Sørensen. See in particular his article 'Monteverdi–Förster–Buxtehude: Entwurf zu einer entwicklungsgeschichtlichen Untersuchung', *Dansk Aarbog for Musikforskning*, 3 (1963), 87–100.

Carissimi was the *maestro di cappella* from 1629 until his death in 1674.[2] The high musical reputation of the German College was well established even before the arrival of Carissimi. In the early 1620s the German traveller H. Neumayr was overwhelmed by the musical experience of attending Vespers at S. Apollinare, the church of the German College, and recorded that so many people came to hear the fine singing that it was hardly possible to get inside the church.[3] Some German noblemen maintained permanent residences in Italy. Duke Christian Ludwig of Hannover, for example, had a palace in Venice, where he financed operas, ballets, and other festivities, thereby placing considerable strain on the court finances in Hannover. The Italian language was fashionable at the courts, and several German musicians employed there became fluent in the language. But the taste for things Italian permeated the towns as well. Buxtehude composed two Italian wedding arias for important town figures in Lübeck, both of which were published (BuxWV 117 and 121). The taste for Italian culture reached as far north as Stockholm and Uppsala. During the reign of Queen Christina in particular, Italian culture was imported at a dramatic rate. She engaged the services of a Leiden professor, Nicolas Heinsius, to collect books for her library from Italy. Heinsius wrote to the Queen that 'The Italians began to complain that ships were laden with the spoils of their libraries, and that all their best aids to learning were carried away from them to the remotest north.'[4] Many new buildings were erected in Sweden in the mid-seventeenth century according to Italian design—notably the Oxenstierna and Wrangel palaces—and both members of the chief Swedish architectural dynasty of the period, Nicodemus Tessin the Elder and the Younger, had studied in Italy.

Surviving German literature concerning music written in Buxtehude's lifetime is unequivocal as to the supreme position held by Italian music at this time. The Königsberg composer Heinrich Albert wrote in 1645 that Italy was 'die Mutter der edlen Music' (the mother of noble music), and the German Jesuit theorist Athanasius Kircher proclaimed in his monumental and widely read treatise

[2] See T. D. Culley, *Jesuits and Music*, i. *A Study of the Musicians connected with the German College in Rome during the 17th Century and of their Activities in Northern Europe* (Rome, 1970).

[3] Neumayr's account may be found in F. Noack, *Das Deutschtum in Rom* (Berlin and Leipzig, 1927), 72.

[4] F. Gribble, *The Court of Christina of Sweden, and the Later Adventures of the Queen in Exile* (London, 1913), 92.

Musurgia Universalis (Rome, 1650) that 'Itali in musica principatum tenent' (the Italians hold the principal place in music).[5] Fuhrmann exhibits an element of frustration with the domination of Italian music in his *Musicalischer-Trichter* of 1706. He writes that 'Jedermann spricht: Die Italiänische *Nation* hat des *Monopolium Musices* unter allen Völckern auff der Welt'[6] (Everyone says: The Italian nation holds a musical monopoly amongst all peoples of the world), and himself admits that 'Die Italiäner . . . sind ausser Streit die berühmtesten Künstler in der Music auff der Welt'[7] (The Italians are without question the most famous musicians in the world). But not content with this situation, he attempts a sociological examination of its causes, touching on all levels of society.

All German theorists of the late sixteenth and seventeenth centuries drew extensive amounts of material from the work of their Italian contemporaries and predecessors. The three extant musical treatises by Bernhard, which form the single most important contribution to seventeenth-century music theory by a North German composer, are all completely immersed in the spirit of Italian music theory. The division of musical styles in his 'Tractatus compositionis augmentatus' feeds on the 1649 treatise *Breve discorso sopra la musica moderna* by the Italian *Kapellmeister* at Warsaw, Marco Scacchi.[8] In chapter 43 Bernhard gives a list of composers whose music he considered worthy to be emulated. Under the category 'stylus luxurians communis', which encompasses sacred vocal music in the new style, he provides the following list, placing Monteverdi firmly at the head:

Monteverde, welcher denselben *Stylum* wohl erfunden und hochgebracht /: andern, so vor ihm etwas dergleichen versuchet, ihr Lob unbenommen: / Sein Nachfolger *Rovetta*, der *Cavalli*, der *Bertali*, *Stefano Fabri*, *Francesco Porta*, *Turini*, *Rigatti*, *Cassati*, *Carissimi*, *Vincenzo Albrici*, *Marco Scacchi*, *Bontempi*, *Peranda* etc. und unter denen *Deutschen*, Herr Schütze, *Caspar Kerl*, Herr Förster und einige andere.[9]

(Monteverdi, who indeed founded and elevated this style (without detracting from the praise of others who had attempted something similar before

---

[5] Albert's comment may be found in the introduction to the sixth volume of his *Arien* (Königsberg, 1645), and Kircher's statement occurs in *Musurgia Universalis*, i. 543.

[6] *Musicalischer-Trichter*, 5.   [7] Ibid. 17.

[8] See C. V. Palisca, 'Marco Scacchi's Defense of Modern Music (1649)', in *Words and Music: The Scholar's View . . . in Honor of A. Tillman Merritt* (Cambridge, Mass., 1972), 189–235; repr. in id., *Studies in the History of Italian Music and Music Theory* (Oxford, 1994), 88–145.

[9] J. Müller-Blattau, *Die Kompositionslehre Heinrich Schützens*, 90.

him), his successor Rovetta, Cavalli, Bertali, Stefano Fabri, Francesco Porta, Turini, Rigatti, Cassati, Carissimi, Vincenzo Albrici, Marco Scacchi, Bontempi, Peranda, etc., and among the Germans, Schütz, Caspar Kerl, Förster, and a few others.)

It is particularly noteworthy that the only three German composers that Bernhard mentions had all, like himself, travelled and studied in Italy. Bernhard's knowledge of Italian music is perhaps displayed most vividly in his treatise 'Von der Singe-Kunst oder Manier'. Here the art of singing is divided into three geographical categories: 'cantar alla romana', 'cantar alla napolitana', and 'cantar alla lombarda'. The first category, applicable to instrumentalists as well as singers, refers to the addition of simple ornaments, the second refers to the careful interpretation of the text, and the third to the use of *passaggi* (diminutions). Bernhard also advises that Latin should be sung with Italianate rather than German pronunciation. It is clear that the Italian manner of singing was considered the finest form of the art, not just at the courts but also amongst aspiring singers elsewhere, as is demonstrated by the following remark made by the Frenchman Charles Ogier in 1635 concerning the singing abilities of Konstantia Czirenberg, the daughter of one of the chief town councillors in Danzig: 'In der Musik ist sie ein wahres Wunder, sie hat eine ganz vortreffliche Stimme und singt in italienischer Manier, die in Polen und Deutschland die allein gebräuchliche ist'[10] (In music she is a true marvel; she has a quite superb voice, and sings in the Italian manner, which is the only customary one in Poland and Germany).

Some writers, whilst acknowledging the overall supremacy of Italian music, distinguished different national musical characteristics between Germans and Italians, thus anticipating the more extended and well-known comments of eighteenth-century writers such as Johann Quantz.[11] The composer Tobias Eniccelius, cantor at Tönning, writing in the introduction to his collection of Epistle-arias *Melismata epistolica* (Kiel, 1667), echoes the observation of Kircher in his *Musurgia Universalis* that many Germans do not like the Italian style on first hearing it, since it is unusual and contrary to their nature. He goes on to identify differences between the German, French, and Italian musical characteristics, observing that the

---

[10] H. Rauschning, *Geschichte der Musik und Musikpflege in Danzig* (Danzig, 1931), 173.

[11] See, in particular, ch. 18 of J. J. Quantz, *Versuch einer Anweisung die Flöte traversiere zu spielen* (Berlin, 1752), transl. as *On Playing the Flute*, ed. E. R. Reilly (London, 1966), 295–342.

Germans particularly love 'die vielstimmige gravitätische / wie auch die gebrochene in Fugen Künstlich versetzte Arth' (the multi-voiced, serious style, as well as the artfully written fugal style), and that the chief characteristic of the Italians is their desire not just to entertain the listener but also to move strongly 'das Gemüth und dessen Affection' (the soul and its affection).[12] Eniccelius thus reminds us that although many of the finest German composers were fully trained and familiar with the Italian style, the idiom was not necessarily instantly or easily absorbed by many ordinary Germans. Moreover, he underlines the German affinity for sober counterpoint, thus identifying one of the ways in which German music retained some individuality during this period.

CONTACT BETWEEN GERMAN AND ITALIAN MUSICIANS

The manner in which Italian music spread to the North German region can be divided into two categories: first, through personal contact between German and Italian musicians, and second, through the dissemination of printed and manuscript copies of Italian church music. Personal contact between German and Italian musicians was gained both by German musicians travelling to Italy, and by Italian musicians seeking employment in the North. The most famous of all German musicians of the seventeenth century to visit Italy was the central German composer Heinrich Schütz, and many North German musicians would have heard of Schütz's travels either through direct contact with him at Dresden, Copenhagen, or elsewhere, or by reading the accounts of his Italian visits in the introductions to some of his publications. When German musicians were granted leave from court employment to travel to Italy, they were often expected to engage the services of Italian musicians on behalf of their employer. Mattheson records two trips made to Italy from the Dresden court by Bernhard. The first lasted a year and took place specifically on the command of the ruling Elector, who instructed him to bring back singers for the Dresden *Capelle*. Whilst in Rome, according to Mattheson, Bernhard set about imitating the musical style of the Italians, in particular Carissimi:

---

[12] Quoted in H. Schilling, *T. Eniccelius, Fr. Meister, N. Hanff: Ein Beitrag zur Geschichte der evangelischen Frühkantate in Schleswig-Holstein* (Kiel, 1935), 14.

In Rom besuchte er zum ersten den berühmten Carissimi, hernach auch alle andere Künstler; bermeckte ihre Art zu setzen, auf das genaueste; und verfertigte, nach solcher, zwo Missen mit zehn Stimmen rein und mit eben so vielen Instrumenten zur Gesellschafft: darüber sich die Welschen verwunderten.[13]

(In Rome he first visited the famous Carissimi, and afterwards also all other artists; he observed how to compose in their manner, to the very last detail, and composed, in this way, two masses for ten voices alone and with as many instruments for accompaniment: the Italians marvelled at his achievement.)

With regard to Bernhard's second visit to Italy, during which he also recruited Italian singers for Dresden, Mattheson writes as follows:

Diese Reise währte drey viertel Jahr, und setzte den Bernhard in allen seinen Wissenschafften und Künsten nur desto fester; absonderlich im damahligen Geschmack, und in der Urtheils-Krafft.[14]

(This trip lasted three-quarters of a year, and Bernhard's composing skills became all the stronger in all scientific and artistic aspects, especially concerning the taste of that time, and in matters of discernment.)

The composer Kaspar Förster the younger (1616–73) spent more time in Italy during the course of his career than any other major North German composer of the period. As a young man he worked under Carissimi at the German College in Rome for three years, and later in life he visited Italy at least twice, staying in both Venice and Rome. Mattheson gives details of the trips in his *Ehren-Pforte*, noting that Förster's skill, like that of Bernhard, even inspired jealousy in many Italian musicians. During one of his visits, Förster recruited Italian singers for the royal court of Copenhagen. A number of other North German composers are reported as having visited Italy, usually at the expense of a court employer, among them Nicolaus Strungk in 1685, Johann Förtsch in 1681, and Georg Schürmann in 1701. Some town councils also granted leave for foreign travel. Balthasar Erben, born in Danzig ten years after Förster, was given a travel grant by the Danzig town council in 1653. His travels took him all over Europe during the space of five years, and eventually to Rome in 1657.[15]

Numerous Italian musicians found work in the North German

---

[13] J. Mattheson, *Grundlage einer Ehren-Pforte* (Hamburg, 1740), ed. M. Schneider (Berlin, 1910, repr. 1969), 18.

[14] Ibid.   [15] Rauschning, *Geschichte der Musik und Musikpflege in Danzig*, 229.

and Scandinavian courts during the seventeenth century. They were employed principally for operatic work, but many also became involved in the music of the court chapels. One of the earliest examples of the employment of Italian singers at a North German court occurred at Berlin in 1616, when the tenor Bernardo Pasquino Grassi and castrato Giovanni Gualberto (a pupil of Caccini who had sung the title-role in Monteverdi's *Orfeo* in 1607) were employed as soloists, probably for the celebrations of the marriage of Georg Wilhelm.[16] But, by the second half of the century, nearly all the major North German and Scandinavian courts employed Italian musicians from time to time, as finances permitted, including those at Wolfenbüttel, Gottorf, Hannover, Stockholm, and Copenhagen. Italians were sometimes even appointed *Kapellmeister*, presiding over both German and Italian musicians, as in the case of Agostino Fontana at the court of Copenhagen between 1647 and 1650. Two of the largest complements of Italian musicians were those maintained at Stockholm during the last few years of Queen Christina's reign, and at Hannover during the rule of the Catholic Duke Johann Friedrich. Between 1652 and her abdication in 1654, Queen Christina employed a total of twenty-two Italian musicians at the royal court in Stockholm. They came principally from Rome and included the composer Vincenzo Albrici, who subsequently became one of the leading musicians at the Dresden court.[17] Manuscripts of secular music associated with those Italian musicians survive in Stockholm and elsewhere, and there is evidence to suggest that they also brought sacred music with them from Rome.[18] By contrast, the Italians employed at the Hannover court during the reign of Duke Johann Friedrich, 1665–79, came mainly from Venice. About seven or eight Italian singers were maintained at the court throughout his rule, including the composers Antonio Sartorio and Vincenzo de Grandis. The latter was assistant *maestro di cappella* at San Marco in Venice before moving to Hannover in 1675.

Although many Italian musicians found employment at North German courts during the seventeenth century, few found work at

[16] See C. Sachs, *Musik und Oper am kurbrandenburgischen Hof* (Berlin, 1910, repr. Hildesheim, 1977), 48–9.

[17] For a study of Albrici's church music, see C.-A. Moberg, 'Vincenzo Albrici und das Kirchenkonzert', in *Natalicia musicologica Knud Jeppesen* (Copenhagen, 1962), 199–216.

[18] See G. Webber, 'Italian Music at the Court of Queen Christina: Christ Church, Oxford, Mus. MS 377 and the Visit of Vincenzo Albrici's Italian Ensemble, 1652–54', *Svensk tidskrift för musikforskning*, 75/2 (1993), 47–53.

the churches in the region. This was due to both financial and sociological factors. The courts deliberately cultivated a cosmopolitan social environment, and many could afford the large salaries required to engage the best Italian musicians. However, some evidence survives to show that Italian singers were at times engaged by the principal North German town churches for special occasions. At the Marienkirche in Danzig, for example, a payment was made in 1679 to some unnamed Italian musicians.[19] Similarly, Italian musicians were engaged at the Marienkirche in Lübeck during Buxtehude's tenure as organist—an Italian castrato in 1672, the singer 'Longlio' in 1687, and another unnamed Italian in 1693.[20] These singers were probably hired from nearby North German courts just for the occasion. Italian instrumentalists were sometimes given occasional employment in town churches. The highly orthodox environment at Danzig even allowed the performance of solo violin music by the Italian Carlo Farina during the services, though this seems to have caused difficulties with the *Kapellmeister*.[21]

There was, therefore, frequent direct contact between Italian and North German musicians, but indirect contact, via central German musicians, also played its part in spreading the knowledge of Italian music in the North German region. The most famous central German intermediary between Italy and Germany during the seventeenth century was Schütz, but later central German composers who studied in Italy and then had close connections with the North German region included Johann Rosenmüller and Johann Philipp Krieger. Rosenmüller began his career in Leipzig but was forced to leave after being imprisoned on charges of indecent behaviour with his choirboys. He eventually settled in Venice, where he worked as a trombonist at San Marco, but subsequently became one of the very few German musicians to hold a prominent post there, being appointed composer at the Ospedale della Pietà in 1678. However, Rosenmüller maintained close connections with his homeland, and spent his last two years back in Germany at the court of Wolfenbüttel. His compositions show a complete sympathy with the Italian style, and were well known in the North German region:

---

[19] Rauschning, *Geschichte der Musik und Musikpflege in Danzig*, 241.

[20] W. Stahl, *Franz Tunder und Dietrich Buxtehude* (Leipzig, 1926), 50.

[21] F. Kessler, Introduction to *Danziger Instrumentalmusik des 17. und 18. Jahrhunderts* (Stuttgart, 1979), p. xii.

some ninety-six are listed in the Lüneburg inventory,[22] and a total of 126 compositions by him survive in the Bokemeyer collection. Johann Philipp Krieger, who probably developed a taste for Italian music during his time spent studying composition with Förster in Copenhagen, himself studied in Italy between 1673 and 1675, where his teachers included many famous Italian musicians as well as Rosenmüller. Krieger then worked for most of his life at Weissenfels, but his Italianate music travelled further north, and survives in both the Düben and Bokemeyer collections. Rosenmüller appears to have returned to Wolfenbüttel from Venice with Italian compositions as well as his own music. The Psalm setting *Laudate pueri Dominum* by Antonio Dalla Tavola bears the inscription by Österreich 'Diese Partitur hat . . . Johan Rosenmüller in Italien mit eigner Hand geschrieben' (Johann Rosenmüller wrote this score in Italy with his own hand).

ITALIAN CHURCH MUSIC IN NORTH GERMAN SOURCES

In the Introduction to the *Secunda Pars* of his *Symphoniae sacrae* (Dresden, 1647), Schütz makes two significant observations regarding the state of music in Germany around the middle of the seventeenth century: that the profession of music had suffered greatly during the Thirty Years War (1618–48), and that modern Italian music remained largely unknown or misunderstood by the majority of German musicians at the time. During the first half of the century, Italian music written in the *prima prattica* was widely known and performed in North Germany, but Italian music written in the *seconda prattica* was, as Schütz asserts, much less familiar. The new style was known in the larger courts of central Germany and Poland, but reached the courts and towns of the North German region only sporadically before the middle of the century, due at least in part to the Thirty Years War. The spread of the new style came about mainly through music written for dramatic productions, including opera. As an artistic reflection of status, opera was unrivalled; full-scale Italian operas were staged for important occasions at several major central German centres during the first half of the century. Amongst the earliest known instances of this are Schütz's lost opera *Dafne*, performed

---

[22] See Seiffert, 'Die Chorbibliothek der St. Michaelis-Schule in Lüneburg'.

at Torgau in 1627, and the anonymous opera *Galatea*, staged at Warsaw in 1628. The earliest known appearances of the new style in the northern region came about almost exclusively through connections with the courts of Dresden and Warsaw, where the most influential *Kapellmeister* were Schütz and the Italian Marco Scacchi respectively. The first reported use of the monodic style in Denmark is said to have occurred at the celebrations for the marriage of Prince Christian in 1634—an event for which Schütz was specifically engaged as director of music.[23] The first recorded operatic production in a North German town occurred in 1646 at Danzig, where celebrations were held in honour of the marriage of the Polish King Władysław IV with Maria Luigia of the Italian Gonzaga family. Two operas were performed at a specially built wooden opera-house holding over 3,000 people (paid for by the city of Danzig), and the music was by Scacchi and Angelo Brunerio, one of Scacchi's singers at the Polish court.[24] The first appearances of church music composed in the new style also seem to have come about through links with Dresden and Warsaw. The two and a half years that the Wolfenbüttel composer Michael Praetorius spent at Dresden (between 1613 and 1616), for example, made a deep impression both on his writings and music. Similarly, the Italianate features of Johann Vierdanck's *Geistliche Concerten* (Greifswald, 1641 and 1643) and Heinrich Albert's eight volumes of *Arien* (Königsberg, 1638–50) can be traced back to the training which both composers received under Schütz at Dresden.

But it was only around the middle of the century, after the end of the Thirty Years War, that the new Italian style gradually changed from an isolated phenomenon to the dominant force in the musical life of the North German region. This process was given a considerable impetus by the new availability of contemporary Italian music in printed form, made possible largely through the efforts of one man, Ambrosius Profe of Breslau (now Wrocław). During the 1640s Profe published six anthologies which contained almost exclusively Italian music, which may be summarized as follows (each composer is represented by a single work unless otherwise indicated).[25]

---

[23] A. Hammerich, *Dansk Musikhistorie indtil ca. 1700* (Copenhagen, 1921), 166.

[24] R. Brockpähler, *Handbuch zur Geschichte der Barockoper in Deutschland* (Emsdetten, 1964), 121–2.

[25] For a fuller list of contents of the volumes, see RISM, B/I/1.

Erster Theil geistlicher Concerten . . . ausz den berühmbsten italiänischen und andern Autoribus . . . (Leipzig, 1641) (RISM 1641²):

    I. Donati, P. Francesco, A. Grandi (10), T. Merula, C. Monteverdi, G. Rovetta (5), F. Sances, O. Tarditi (2), O. Vecchi

Ander Theil geistlicher Concerten . . . aus den berühmbsten italiänischen und andern Autoribus . . . (Leipzig, 1641) (RISM 1641³):

    G. B. Aloisi, G. Arrigoni (4), G. Casati, G. B. Chinelli, I. Donati, N. Fontei, A. Grandi, T. Merula, C. Monteverdi, G. Priuli, G. Rovetta (4), G. Sabbatini, F. Sances (2), O. Tarditi

Dritter Theil geistlicher Concerten . . . aus den berühmbsten italiänischen und andern Autoribus . . . (Leipzig, 1642) (RISM 1642⁴):

    G. B. Chinelli (2), P. Cornetti, N. Fontei, A. Grandi, R. Honorio, T. Merula (3), M. Minozzi, C. Monteverdi (5), A. Pesenti, G. Rovetta (4), G. Sabbatini, G. Scarani, O. Tarditi (2)

Vierdter und letzter Theil geistlicher Concerten aus den berühmbsten italiänischen und andern Authoribus . . . (Leipzig, 1646) (RISM 1646⁴):

    A. Cremonese, G. B. Aloisi (2), S. Bernardi, G. Casati, M. Cazzati (3), P. Cornetti, I. Donati, A. Grandi (3), R. Honorio (2), F. Marini (2), T. Merula, G. Priuli, A. Rigatti (3), G. Rovetta (10), G. Sabbatini (3), M. Scacchi (3), Sessa d'Aranda, O. Tarditi, F. Turini (4)

Cunis solennib. Jesuli recens nati sacra Genethliaca . . . (Breslau, 1646) (RISM 1646³):

    G. B. Aloisi, A. Cremonese (2), G. Casati (3), M. Cazzati, A. Grandi (2), G. Priuli (4), G. Rovetta, G. Sabbatini, M. Scacchi, F. Turini (2)

Corollarium geistlicher collectaneorum, berühmter authorum . . . (Leipzig, 1649) (RISM 1649⁶):

    G. Arrigoni, C. M. Cozzolani, T. Merula, C. Monteverdi (6), G. Rovetta (4), F. Sances, A. Ziani (2)

Profe was organist of the Elisabethkirche in Breslau during the period in which his anthologies were published. Venetian music dominates the collections, with twenty-seven works by Rovetta, fifteen by Grandi, and thirteen by Monteverdi. The anthologies contain only sacred works, but of the thirteen works by Monteverdi, only two were originally composed as sacred works, the other eleven having been supplied with sacred texts by Profe himself.[26] During Profe's time the school of St Elisabeth in Breslau owned a vast collection of Italian publications, obtained perhaps at the initiative of Profe himself. Most of the publications are Venetian, and it seems

---

[26] See A. Adrio, 'Ambrosius Profe (1589–1661) als Herausgeber italienischer Musik seiner Zeit', in *Festschrift Karl Gustav Fellerer* (Regensburg, 1962), 20–7.

likely that they provided much of the music for Profe's own publications.[27] Copies of his anthologies are known to have been owned
by many of the principal courts and churches in the North German
region in the second half of the century. Surviving records of church
and chapel libraries indicate that the anthologies were held not just
by a few major centres, but by many different churches and chapels,
including those at smaller centres, which confirms that the Italian
style was becoming widely known throughout the North German
region at this time. The choir of the Stephanikirche in Helmstedt,
near Wolfenbüttel, for example, owned copies of all four parts of
Profe's *Geistliche Concerten*.[28] The Johanniskirche and Michaeliskirche in Lüneburg also owned these volumes, as well as the
Corollarium geistlicher collectaneorum.[29] Records at the Johanniskirche
indicate that the anthologies were purchased by the cantor M. Jacobi
in 1651. Profe's volumes also travelled to Sweden and to Denmark,
where they provided a useful source of information for the writer
M. H. Schacht, whose manuscript bibliography 'Musicus Danicus'
of 1678 contained the first alphabetical index of famous composers.

Profe's anthologies were not the only German publications containing Italian music which were published around the middle of the
seventeenth century. Other editors, including J. Havemann and
J. Nenning (using the name Spiridio), published anthologies that
became diffused throughout the North German region. Havemann's
*Erster Theil geistlicher Concerten . . . aus den berühmtesten, italiänischen
und andern Autoribus . . .* (Jena and Berlin, 1659) (RISM 1659³), for
example, was owned by the Marienkirche at Elbing, near Danzig.[30]
This anthology, like those of Profe, was dominated by Venetian
composers, including Monteverdi, Rigatti, Rovetta, and Grandi, but

[27] The publications are listed in E. Bohn, *Bibliographie der Musik-Druckwerke bis 1700,
welche in der Stadtbibliothek, der Bibliothek des Academischen Instituts für Kirchenmusik und der
Königlichen und Universitäts-Bibliothek zu Breslau aufbewahrt werden* (Berlin, 1883; repr. 1969).

[28] W. Schmieder and G. Hartwieg, *Kataloge der Herzog-August-Bibliothek Wolfenbüttel*, xii
(Frankfurt am Main, 1967), p. xi. For a fuller picture of the transmission of Italian church
music in the North German region, see ch. 5 of G. Webber, 'A Study of Italian Influence
on North German Church and Organ Music in the Second Half of the Seventeenth
Century, with Special Reference to the Collection of Gustav Düben (D.Phil. thesis,
Oxford, 1988), 135–87.

[29] Walter, *Musikgeschichte der Stadt Lüneburg*, 285–7; W. Junghans, 'J. S. Bach als Schüler
der Partikularschule zu St. Michaelis in Lüneburg, oder Lüneburg einer Pflegestätte kirchlicher Musik', *Programm des Johanneums zu Lüneburg, Ostern 1870* (Lüneburg, 1870), 26–8.

[30] T. Carstenn, 'Katalog der St. Marienbibliothek zu Elbing', *Kirchenmusikalisches
Jahrbuch*, 11 (1896), 40.

Nenning's anthology of 1665 has a different emphasis, made explicit in the title of the volume: *Musica romana D.D. Foggiae, Charissimi, Gratiani, aliorumque excellentissimorum authorum . . .* (Bamberg, 1665) (RISM 1665[3]). His choice of Roman music reflects the increasing importance of Rome as a musical centre around the middle of the century, focused on the figure of Carissimi. His anthology is almost certainly the volume listed simply as 'Musica Romana' that was purchased by the German church in Stockholm, where Gustav Düben was organist, in 1668.[31]

As well as German publications containing contemporary Italian music, Italian publications of church music are also known to have been owned by several churches and chapels in the North German region during the second half of the seventeenth century. These include important publications by major composers as well as more obscure volumes. For example, Monteverdi's *Selva morale e spirituale* (Venice, 1641) was purchased for the Michaeliskirche in Lüneburg sometime between 1656 and 1666,[32] and a volume of motets by the comparatively little-known composer Giovanni Battista Chinelli was present in the library of the Gymnasium at Västeras in Sweden.[33] The largest known collections of Italian publications of church music were those at the Marienkirche in Lübeck, where Buxtehude was organist, and the royal court chapel at Stockholm, where Düben was *Kapellmeister*: thirteen such publications were owned in Lübeck, and fourteen in Stockholm.[34] The Stockholm collection contained single-author publications of church music by G. Carisio, M. Cazzati, C. D. Cossoni, F. della Porta, F. Foggia, G. Legrenzi, C. Ruggieri, O. Tarditi, S. Vesi, and P. A. Ziani, dating from between 1645 and 1665, and three of the anthologies by the famous Roman editor F. Silvestri: RISM 1647[2], 1649[3], and 1649[4].

Besides possessing publications of Italian music, an increasing number of churches and chapels in the region also acquired

[31] See Kjellberg, 'Kungliga musiker i Sverige', Bilaga 6.2, 6.3. The entry says simply 'Musica Romana', but, as Kjellberg has suggested, this almost certainly refers to 1665[3].

[32] Junghans, 'J. S. Bach als Schüler', 26–8.

[33] G. B. Chinelli, *Il terzo libro de motetti* (Venice, 1640). See T. Norlind, 'Vor 1700 gedruckte Musikalien in den schwedischen Bibliotheken', *Sammelbände der Internationalen Musik-Gesellschaft*, 9 (1908), 214.

[34] For Lübeck see Snyder, *Dieterich Buxtehude: Organist in Lübeck*, 493–5, and W. Stahl, *Die Musikabteilung der Lübecker Stadtbibliothek in ihren älteren Beständen* (Lübeck, 1931), 24. The publications owned by the royal chapel in Stockholm are part of the Düben collection now at Uppsala.

manuscript copies of Italian church music. The surviving evidence again shows a wide dispersal of music by both major and minor Italian composers. The manuscript collection belonging to J. Crone, cantor of Wehlau, near Königsberg, contained music by F. Della Porta, I. Donati, C. M. Cozzolani, Monteverdi, Rinaldi, and Rovetta.[35] Most of the collections were formed well into the second half of the century, but one collection is notably early in date, that compiled in Hamburg in 1647, probably by Matthias Weckmann, now housed in the Ratsbücherei in Lüneburg as Mus. ant. pract. K. N. 206.[36] The date is particularly interesting as the manuscript includes copies of works taken directly from Monteverdi's *Selva morale e spirituale* (Venice, 1641), providing evidence that this publication was known in the North German region only a few years after its original publication: the copy of Monteverdi's Psalm setting *Laudate Dominum* carries the inscription 'Claud. Montiv. nella sua Selva morali e spirituali'. The other composers represented in the collection are G. Chillolo, A. Fontana,[37] A. Grandi, T. Merula, B. Rè, S. Todeschi, and G. Valentini.

The quantity of Italian music held in manuscript form at some churches and chapels was considerable, as may be seen from the following lists of the three largest known manuscript collections and inventories from the region, indicating the number of works by each composer (no number indicates a single composition):[38]

The Düben collection
> A. M. Abbatini, A. Accorona, V. Albrici (36), A. Antonelli (2), A. Bertali (4), O. Benevoli (5), S. Bernardi, P. Bettella, G. Bicilli (2), G. A. Bontempi (2), F. Capella, G. A. Capponi, F. Cardarelli, G. Carisio (10), G. Carissimi (37), G. Casati (2), M. Cazzati (2), C. Cecchelli (2), A. Cecconi, R. Cesti, A. Cifra (2), G. Cocci (3), F. Corsi, C. D. Cossoni (2), G. M. Costa, F. Della Porta (5), S. Durante (2), S. Fabri (11), G. P.

---

[35] See J. Müller, *Die musikalischen Schätze der Königlichen und Universitäts-Bibliothek zu Königsberg in Preußen aus dem Nachlasse F. A. Gottholds* (Bonn, 1870), 18–20.

[36] F. Welter, *Katalog der Musikalien der Ratsbücherei Lüneburg* (Lippstadt, 1950), 35.

[37] Fontana was *Kapellmeister* at the Danish court at the time when Weckmann came to Hamburg from Copenhagen in 1647.

[38] This information has been extracted (with some minor alterations and additions) from the following sources: for the Düben collection, F. Lindberg's typed catalogue of the Düben collection in the Carolina Rediviva, Uppsala; for the Lüneburg inventory, M. Seiffert's article 'Die Chorbibliothek der St. Michaelis-Schule in Lüneburg'; and for the Bokemeyer collection, from H. Kümmerling's published catalogue, *Katalog der Sammlung Bokemeyer*. The numbers concerning Carissimi, Foggia, and Albrici in the Düben collection are approximate, since there are a few cases of conflicting attributions.

Finatti (2), F. Foggia (19), C. Giani, V. Giovannoni, A. Grandi, B. Graziani (9), G. A. Grossi (4), R. Honorio, A. Leardini, G. Legrenzi (5), I. Leonarda, F. Lucio (3), F. M. Marini, V. Mazzochi, A. Melani, M. Minozzi (2), C. Monteverdi (4), F. Passerini (3), M. G. Peranda (18), D. Philetari, G. A. Rigatti (6), A. Romani (3), G. Rovetta (14), C. Ruggieri (2), F. Sances, M. Scacchi (3), O. Tarditi (3), P. Tarditi, V. Tozzi, G. B. Trabattone, G. Valentini, P. Vertini, S. Vesi (7), G. B. Viviani, G. Zamponi

The Lüneburg inventory
V. Albrici (7), C. Amadoni (2), J. Augustini, A. Bertali (3), G. B. Bonani, G. A. Bontempi (2), G. Carissimi (5), P. di Carmeni, G. Casati (17), J. Caseli, M. Cazzati (2), F. Della Porta (4), G. P. Finatti (2), N. Fontei (2), A. Giannettini, A. Grandi (5), B. Graziani (4), A. Lazari, F. Lilius (3), T. Merula (3), C. Monteverdi (4), M. G. Peranda (18), S. Posini, S. Reina (4), G. B. Rovetta (3), G. Sabbatini, F. Sances, M. Scacchi (9), R. de Scarsellis, S. Todeschi, Torquati, P. Torri, V. Tozzi, M. Uccellini, G. Valentini, S. Vesi (7)

The Bokemeyer collection
V. Albrici (19), G. Aldrovandini (4), P. F. Alghisi, G. B. Alveri (4), F. A. Arconati (4), G. B. Bassani (69), L. Baseggio, M. E. Biffi, D. Bigalia, G. Carissimi (2), F. Cavalli, M. Cazzati, C. Celini, A. Cesti, S. Cherici, G. Cocci, G. P. Colonna, A. Dalla Tavola, A. B. Della Ciaia (3), R. Fedeli (14), B. Ferrara, F. Foggia (2), F. G. Freschi, A. Giannettini (14), G. Giuliani, C. L. P. Grua, G. Legrenzi (2), A. Lotti (2), L. Mancia, A. Melani, C. Monari (9), C. Monteverdi, S. B. Pallavicini, G. D. Partenio, F. Passarini (4), M. G. Peranda (22), G. A. Perti, Polaroli (2), A. Polaroli (2), C. F. Polaroli (3), G. B. Quaglia, Rossi (3), A. Sartorio (8), M. Scacchi, A. Stradella, F. Tavelli, Torelli, P. Torri (10), Valentini, S. Vesi (2), C. B. Vinacesci, G. B. Vitali (2), G. B. Viviani, L. F. Zey

The Düben collection was compiled in Stockholm between c.1650 and c.1690; the Lüneburg inventory indicates lost manuscripts formerly owned by the church of St Michael in Lüneburg during the period of the cantor F. E. Praetorius (1655–95), and the Bokemeyer collection was compiled for use at the courts of Gottorf and Wolfenbüttel between c.1689 and c.1708.

The evidence of these collections, together with that of other smaller collections, is that the German musicians kept well abreast of the development of Italian church music throughout the second half of the century. Monteverdi is dominant in the Weckmann manuscript of 1647, whilst Carissimi takes centre stage in the Düben collection compiled from the 1650s onwards. The Bokemeyer collection, the latest of the collections, reflects the development of Italian church music in the last few decades of the century, after the death of Carissimi. It includes no works by Grandi and Casati and only one by Monteverdi (composers who were popular in North Germany during the middle of the century), and only two by Carissimi, whose music is so well represented in the earlier Düben collection. After the death of Carissimi, no Italian emerged as the leading composer of sacred music in Italy, and the fame of most Italian composers at this time rested more on their success as composers of opera than of church music. The Bokemeyer collection reflects this situation, since many works are by composers whose operas were performed in the North at this time. Two operas by G. B. Alveri, for example, were performed at Wolfenbüttel in 1691, and three sacred works by him survive in the collection, the only known sacred works by this composer. However, the Italian composer represented by the largest number of sacred works in the collection is Giovanni Battista Bassani, who is not known to have visited Germany. The presence of such a large quantity of his music in the collection is probably explained by the fact that much of his music was available in printed form. Eighteen publications of Bassani's sacred music were printed in the period 1690–1710, a time when publications of church music were considerably more scarce than previously. Two Italian composers deserve special mention, as their music is found in considerable quantity in all three collections: Vincenzo Albrici and Marco Giuseppe Peranda. Both composers worked in Germany for most of their careers. Albrici, a pupil of Carissimi, began his time in the North as the leader of the Roman troupe engaged by Queen Christina of Sweden, but then went on to work, like Peranda, at the Dresden court. Peranda was brought from Rome to Dresden by Bernhard, and succeeded Schütz as chief *Kapellmeister* after the latter's death in 1672. These two composers thus played a very significant part in transmitting the mid-seventeenth-century Roman style to the North.

Thus, although Schütz had complained of the lack of knowledge of Italian music in Germany in 1647 (by coincidence the same year in which Weckmann compiled his manuscript collection in Hamburg), the situation did change rapidly thereafter. Moreover, it is clear that the Italian music was not simply collected by individuals or establishments for academic purposes, but specifically for performance in Protestant services. The title-page of Havemann's *Erster*

Theil geistlicher Concerten states that the music is presented first to the praise and glory of God, but also 'zur Fortpflantzung der Edlen Music; Und zu Erweckung sonderer Andacht bey dem Kirchen-Gottesdienst' (for the dissemination of noble music; and for the cultivation of devotion at church services); Profe's *Vierdter und letzter Theil geistlicher Concerten* was published similarly 'zum Lobe Gottes / in öffentlichen Kirchen-versamlungen zu gebrauchen' (to the praise of God; to be used in public church assemblies). Furthermore, Profe's later anthology *Corollarium geistlicher collectaneorum* contains a dedicatory poem which mentions by name some of the most famous Italian composers of the time, and associates them specifically with performance in German churches and chapels:

> Was *Cremonesius*, was *Grandi*, was *Casat*,
> Was des *Rovettens* Geist mit Kunst gesetzet hat/
> Wird itzt durch seinen Fleiß in unsern Kirch-Capellen/
> Mit Anmuth angehört . . .

(That which Cremonese, Grandi, Casati, and the spirit of Rovetta have set artfully is now heard with beauty, through his [Profe's] diligence, in our churches and chapels.)

The anthologies contain examples of all the major categories of Italian church music: masses, Vespers Psalms, and motets. Both types of mass setting, the complete setting and the *Missa brevis*, were included in Profe's collections, and both types are also found in the manuscript collections of the period. However, as with the North German music of the period, the number of mass settings contained in the collections are relatively few in comparison to the number of settings of Vespers Psalms. These account for almost one-third of the Italian music in the Bokemeyer collection and one-fifth of the Italian works in the Düben collection. Nearly all the categories of texts employed in Italian motets were suitable for the Lutheran liturgy. However, many works designed for Marian feasts or other Marian devotions were not easily adopted by the Lutherans. There was no difficulty with settings of the Song of Songs, since although such motets were used by Catholics in Marian devotions (as, for example, in the motets contained in Monteverdi's Vespers collection of 1610), they could be used by the Lutherans as allegories for other themes, such as the mystical love between the soul and Christ. However, it was not possible for the German Lutheran musicians to perform settings of the Marian antiphons, since these expressly referred to the

Blessed Virgin, invoking her intercession. The solution was either to substitute a completely different text, or to make such alterations as were necessary to redirect the adoration towards Christ rather than the Blessed Virgin. Both solutions were adopted by Profe in his anthologies, and several examples of altered texts are also found in the manuscript collections. The Düben collection contains settings of the *Salve Regina* with altered texts by Carissimi, Rovetta, and Philetari, and the Bokemeyer collection contains two examples from the output of Bassani: *Alma Redemptoris Mater* and *Salve Regina* have been altered to *Alme Rex coelorum* and *Salve Rex Jesu* respectively.

4

Town and Court Musicians: The Composer in Context

◊

THE nature of the output of any seventeenth-century North German composer was determined principally by two related factors, the type of employment he held, and the extent of his exposure to Italian music. The post of cantor at a large town church (sometimes called *Director Musices* or *Kapellmeister*) held great responsibilities in connection with the provision of the regular liturgical music, the leading of the congregational singing, and the instruction of the boys at the adjoining school. Johann Mattheson reports that the Rostock cantor Gottfried Krause was so tied up with school duties that he had little time for composition.[1] Occupants of this type of post did not always concern themselves greatly with the composition of modern concertato sacred music, although this does not mean that they did not compose any music for the church. The most published North German composer of the period, in terms of having the greatest number of individual publications of sacred music to his name, was the Lüneburg cantor Michael Jacobi. However, his output consists mainly of hymn tunes and music for weddings and funerals, reflecting his important town position as cantor of the Johanniskirche. Two particular features of the music by town musicians who did compose concertato church music seem to reflect directly the environment in which they worked: their cultivation of chorale-based works ties in with the regular chorale-leading duties of the cantor, and their use of large instrumental and vocal forces reflects the larger size of the main town churches in comparison with most court chapels. Those composers who held the post of *Kapellmeister* at a court worked in a very different environment than the town cantors. Although subject to

---

[1] Mattheson, *Grundlage einer Ehren-Pforte*, 144.

the usual problems of court employment—most obviously the relative lack of job security—they were free from the sort of school and town responsibilities that took up so much of the cantor's time, and frequently found themselves working alongside virtuoso Italian singers and composers. Thus the output of several composers who worked exclusively at courts consists predominantly of highly Italianate music with virtuosic vocal writing. The third main type of post held by composers was that of a town or court organist, a post that carried no obligations with regard to vocal music. However, many organists wrote music for liturgical performance, presumably either for their own direction or that of the cantor or *Kapellmeister*. Indeed, their compositional efforts often eclipsed those of the other leading musician with whom they worked, as occurred at the Marienkirche in Lübeck, where Buxtehude was organist, and the Catherinenkirche in Danzig, where Crato Bütner was organist. The reputation of these two organist-composers was such that they were both called upon to write occasional works for town dignitaries. Although the use of chorales and German-texted works in general can be associated more with town than court composers, no such clear distinction can be observed concerning the cultivation of strophic arias within larger works. However, Martin Geck and Harald Kümmerling have both suggested that cultivation of the aria can be linked to circles of intense Pietist activity, whether in towns or courts.[2]

The wide circulation of Italian church music in the North German region meant that few composers could escape its influence, but some North German composers fell more completely under the Italians' spell than others. Those who actually travelled to Italy seem to have taken good advantage of their visits. The most completely Italianate North German composer of the period was without doubt Kaspar Förster, who spent much time in Italy. His musical style is indistinguishable from the music of the mid-seventeenth-century Roman school. Other composers had more mixed affiliations. The output of Franz Tunder, for example, contains both chorale works in German and Psalm settings in Latin, the latter composed in a highly Italianate idiom. As already noted, those composers who worked at

---

[2] Geck, *Die Vokalmusik Dietrich Buxtehudes*, and F. Krummacher, 'Das geistliche Aria in Norddeutschland und Skandinavien. Ein gattungsgeschichtlicher Versuch', in D. Lohmeier (ed.), *Weltliches und geistliches Lied des Barock: Studien zur Liedkultur in Deutschland und Skandinavien* (Stockholm and Amsterdam, 1979), 229–64.

the courts had the greatest regular opportunity to come into direct contact with Italian music and musicians, and this proximity is clearly reflected in their music. Such composers include Christian Geist and Christian Ritter at Stockholm, Johann Theile and Martin Köler at Gottorf, and Johann Julius Weiland and Georg Schürmann at Wolfenbüttel. In addition it must be remembered that some of the more prominent town composers of the period had some experience of a court environment, such as Johann Vierdanck, Christoph Bernhard, and Matthias Weckmann, who all began their musical training under Heinrich Schütz at the highly Italianate Dresden court. On the other hand, the more conservative works to have survived from the period are generally by composers who are not known to have come into close contact with Italian music, such as Friedrich Klingenberg, organist at Stettin, and Michael Hahn, cantor at Narva.

COURT COMPOSERS

At the royal Stockholm court, the home of the Düben collection, the principal local composers were Geist and Ritter, but a few works survive by Düben himself. Although Düben apparently preferred to collect and perform the music of others than compose himself, his small number of works does include the only known example from the period of a direct parody of an Italian sacred work by a North German composer. Both Düben and the compiler of the Bokemeyer collection at Gottorf, Georg Österreich, added extra instrumental parts to works by Italian composers, but the case of Düben's *Fadher wår*, a setting of the Swedish text of the Lord's Prayer, is quite different. Rather than simply adding to a pre-existent Italian work, here Düben has composed a new piece which takes its style and some of its content from a specific work by an Italian composer. The model for his work was a setting of the same Swedish text by the main composer of the Italian troupe hired by Queen Christina in the early 1650s, Vincenzo Albrici. At first sight Düben's setting seems quite different from that of Albrici. It is written in the key of A minor and opens with a separate instrumental Sinfonia, whereas Albrici's setting is composed in the key of B flat major and has no such instrumental opening. However, several passages in Düben's work are directly based on Albrici's composition, including the opening tutti section

Ex. 4.1. (*a*) Albrici, *Fader wår*; (*b*) Düben, *Fadher wår*

and the setting of the text 'sckee tin wilie', as illustrated by Ex. 4.1. During the first few years of his appointment as *Kapellmeister* at Stockholm in 1663, Düben had no local composer in his regular company of musicians, but the situation changed with the arrival of Geist in 1670. Geist's fifty-seven works in the Düben collection show a marked preference for Latin texts. Many are settings of Psalm texts and standard liturgical texts such as *Verbum caro* for Christmas and *Veni sancte spiritus* for Pentecost, and there are a number of works with Latin texts in the mystical tradition, such as *Jesu delitium vultus*. Geist is not known to have travelled to Italy or to have studied with an Italian composer, as Kaspar Förster did, yet he had access to the large quantity of Italian music in the Düben collection, and his output is almost wholly Italianate in nature. This was clearly recognized in his own day, since Mattheson reports that when he applied for the post of Hamburg cantor in 1663 (which was given to Bernhard), his fluency in the Italian style was specifically noted.[3] Since most of Geist's surviving compositions date from the 1670s, they provide a useful yardstick for the chronological development of North German sacred music. Aspects of the early seventeenth-century Italian style familiar in the music of Schütz are still present, but there are also many signs of more modern aspects of the Italian style (see pp. 125–6). His music has great vivacity and charm, encompassing a wide expressive range, and the string writing is often demanding, both for the violin and viola da gamba. His finest works include the highly expressive motets *Media vita*, *Seelig, ja seelig*, and *Jesu delitium vultus* and the bravura Psalm setting *Dixit Dominus*.

Geist was replaced at Stockholm by the equally gifted composer Christian Ritter *c*.1681. Some of his works in the Düben collection are brief aria or chorale settings, but the more extended works that survive here and elsewhere show him to have been a composer of the highest calibre. His earliest surviving piece is dated 1666 and comes from his time as an organist at the central German town of Halle. He seems to have had strong central German connections, as he returned there between 1683 and 1688 to work at the Dresden court before resuming work at Stockholm. The 1666 piece, *Herr wer wird wohnen*, inhabits the world of the *Kleine geistliche Konzerte* of Schütz, both in terms of its scoring (voices and continuo only) and style. However, his later works, dating from after his arrival in Stockholm, show that he was also familiar with the more up-to-date Italian styles current at the Dresden court in the 1660s and 1670s. The Italian composers working at Dresden at that time included Albrici, formerly a member of Queen Christina's Italian troupe in Sweden in the early 1650s. The Italianate origins of Ritter's music

---

[3] Mattheson, *Grundlage einer Ehren-Pforte*, 19.

dating from the 1680s is evident throughout, but can be seen perhaps most clearly in his bel canto aria style (see Ex. 8.6*b*), and in the expressive outbursts of impassioned recitative-like passages which, like similar passages in the music of Bernhard, who also worked at Dresden at this time, recall the works of Albrici and Peranda. Typical of this style are brief, ornamental groups of demisemiquavers, as seen in the passage from Ritter's *O amantissime Sponse Jesu* shown in Ex. 4.2.

Ex. 4.2. Ritter, *O amantissime Sponse Jesu*

The Danish royal court at Copenhagen had benefited during the first half of the century from the visits of Schütz, but during parts of the 1650s and 1660s it once again gained from the presence of a leading Italianate German composer, Kaspar Förster. Förster, like Schütz, made trips to Venice, but he also studied in Rome under the leading Italian composer of the mid-seventeenth century, Carissimi. After his Roman education Förster seems to have had no interest whatsoever in displaying his German roots in his compositions. His thirty-five sacred works in the Düben collection are all in Latin, and the handful of secular works have Italian texts. The affinity between his music and that of his teacher Carissimi is particularly apparent in his three dramatic dialogues on Old Testament stories, but his whole corpus is in the purest Italian style. One of his settings of the Vespers Psalm *Confitebor tibi Domine* even contains a passage in *falsobordone* (see p. 140) whilst another makes use of the plainsong Psalm tone. Here, Förster adopts the standard Italian technique of placing the opening of the plainsong tone in long notes over a walking bass in the continuo part, as shown in Ex. 4.3.[4] Many of his motets were probably sung at Copenhagen by Italian singers, for Mattheson reports that he brought back singers from Italy to the Danish court (see p. 48). Over half his works are for between one and three voices only, and they contain many lengthy *passaggi* for solo display. Whereas Schütz began to turn back to his German heritage in the works of his later years, Förster showed no such inclinations. Indeed, he even renounced his Protestantism and became a Roman Catholic; Mattheson reports that he was buried in the Catholic monastery at Oliva, an important Jesuit outpost of Roman Catholicism near his birthplace of Danzig.[5]

Ex. 4.3. Förster, *Confitebor tibi Domine*

The court of the dukes of Schleswig-Holstein at Gottorf, where the early part of the Bokemeyer collection was compiled, did not have the wealth or prestige of the leading German and Scandinavian courts, but Duke Christian Albrecht and his successor Friedrich IV managed to secure the services of an impressive line of musicians during the last three decades of the century, even if war with Denmark sporadically made things extremely difficult. The succession of *Kapellmeister* ran as follows: Augustin Pfleger (1665), Johann Theile (1673), Martin Köler (1675), Johann Philipp Förtsch (1680), and Georg Österreich (1689), who compiled the early part of the Bokemeyer collection. The careers of these composers had many parallels, illustrating the many internal connections that existed within North German musical life at the time. Pfleger, Theile, and Förtsch all came from central Germany; Theile, Köler, and

---

[4] This setting of *Confitebor tibi Domine* is that found in the Düben collection at the catalogue numbers 21:13 and 83:37.

[5] Mattheson, *Grundlage einer Ehren-Pforte*, 76.

Österreich worked for a time at the Wolfenbüttel court; Theile and Förtsch also worked at Hamburg, where they were amongst the leading composers for the Hamburg opera; Theile and Förtsch both wrote contrapuntal treatises, and Österreich was a pupil of Theile.

Augustin Pfleger was a native Bohemian, but his reputation in the North German region began with the publication of a collection of Latin sacred music in Hamburg in 1661 (*Psalmi, Dialogi et Motettae*, Op. 1). A large inventory of lost sacred works dates from the time of his first known post in the North at the court of Güstrow in 1664. In that same year Duke Christian I of Mecklenburg-Schwerin returned from a trip to Paris with a group of six French string-players and restored Catholic services in the Güstrow court chapel.[6] All eighty-nine works in the inventory are in Latin, and they are overwhelmingly liturgical in nature (including a complete setting of the mass), but it is not known whether or not the works were written specifically for the Catholic services at Güstrow. Pfleger then moved to the Gottorf court in 1665, where he remained until 1673, after which he returned to central Germany. His large corpus of works in the Düben collection, including the seventy-one works that make up his *Evangelien-jahrgang*, probably dates from these years at Gottorf. Pfleger's reputation was apparently high throughout the Schleswig-Holstein territory. He composed music for the founding of the University of Kiel in 1665, received payment from the town fathers of Husum in 1672 for sending them some music, and dedicated his *Evangelienjahrgang* to the town council of Flensburg. How Düben procured a copy of the cycle for Stockholm is not known, but his contacts were such that he also acquired copies of many other works by Pfleger, mostly settings of liturgical and mystical texts in Latin. Pfleger's large corpus of surviving and lost works divides almost equally between strictly liturgical music to Latin texts and the increasingly popular Gospel-based works in German, in which composite texts played an important role. The Gospel cycle is a marvel of musical evangelism. The highly developed theology behind the selection of texts (see pp. 97–8) is communicated masterfully. His melodic invention matches perfectly the meaning and accents of the text, and much of the writing is for voices alone. There are many effective dramatic moments, yet the music never comes to dominate the text. Pfleger's recitative-like writing maintains a strong melodic

[6] C. Meyer, *Geschichte der Mecklenburg-Schweriner Hofkapelle* (Schwerin, 1913), 29.

basis, and rarely approaches the almost secco style of recitative found in Förster's dramatic dialogues. His acquaintance with the Italian style is most evident in his Latin church music, though here, as in the Gospel cycle, he shows a typically German interest in mid-texture string parts, either for the viola da gamba or viola da braccio. Of his twenty-four Latin works in the Düben collection, only four have no mid-texture string parts, and seven are scored for violas alone, without violins. This feature of his compositions may possibly have been inspired by the particularly strong tradition of string-playing, especially of the viola da gamba, that existed at the courts of Güstrow and Gottorf in the seventeenth century, established in the early part of the century by players such as the Englishman William Brade.

Johann Theile spent just two years at Gottorf, since war with Denmark in 1675 forced him along with his employer Duke Christian Albrecht to seek refuge in the free city of Hamburg. Theile, like Pfleger, came from central Germany, where he had been a pupil of the aged Schütz. His career took him to many different musical centres in the North German area, including the court at Wolfenbüttel, where he taught the young Georg Österreich. Theile is probably best known for his devotion to counterpoint, as both a theorist and composer, but this represents only one side of the musician whose opera *Orontes* inaugurated the new Hamburg opera-house in 1678. His surviving church music contains not only compositions written in the *stile antico*, but also concertato Latin Psalm settings in the most modern Italian style and German-texted motets with composite texts. Ex. 4.4 contains a particularly imaginative piece of writing in his setting of the Compline Psalm *Cum invocarem*. At the text 'In peace I will both lie down and sleep', Theile creates an atmosphere of stillness and quiet, adding gently undulating triplets as if to lull the listener to sleep.

The relative lack of interest in the use of the chorale found in the works of Pfleger, Theile, and his successor at Gottorf Martin Köler, is typical of court musicians of the time, whilst the almost total domination of German-texted works in the output of Köler and his successor Johann Philipp Förtsch reflects a general trend away from Latin-texted works towards the end of the century. Many of Förtsch's compositions are based on Gospel texts and have title-pages which refer to specific Sundays and other feast-days of the year, recalling the *Evangelienjahrgang* of Pfleger. Förtsch showed a greater interest in the chorale than his predecessors at Gottorf, but chorale

Ex. 4.4. Theile, *Cum invocarem*

melodies still only appear in less than one–fifth of his total output. Stylistically Förtsch's works tend towards the conservative, but this can perhaps be explained by the fact that he had many interests besides music, and was employed as a physician and diplomat after 1690. He retained links with the Gottorf court, but more as a poet than a musician, as can be seen from the settings of his texts by his successor as *Kapellmeister* at Gottorf, Georg Österreich.[7]

Österreich's motets offer the best guide to the development of North German church music during the 1690s and around the turn of the eighteenth century. His arrival as *Kapellmeister* at Gottorf in 1689 coincided almost exactly with the death of Düben in 1690, and it is fortunate that such a substantial quantity of his own music survives. Although Buxtehude was still active as a composer in the 1690s, his surviving music almost all pre-dates this period, since the main collector of his music was Düben. The chief developments found in Österreich's music are the increasingly secco recitative style, the greater prominence given to the instrumental writing in the arias (including the use of violins in unison), the addition of oboes and bassoon to the customary string ensemble, and the continued development of sequential harmony and fugal writing. Österreich's avid acquisition of Italian music kept him well abreast of the latest developments in Italian style, and his motets show him to have been a composer of high creativity and craftsmanship, particularly his dramatic motet *Weise mir Herr deinen Weg* and the *Actus funebris: Plötzlich müßen die Leute sterben.*

When Österreich left Gottorf for Wolfenbüttel in 1702, taking with him his large collection of music, he ceased working as a *Kapellmeister* with regular responsibility for the provision of sacred music. Thus it is not surprising that most of the music by him to survive from his time at the Wolfenbüttel court, where he worked mainly as a singer, is secular in nature, consisting mainly of cantatas. The final stage in the development of North German church music during Buxtehude's lifetime—the adoption of da capo arias—is found in Österreich's output only in his later secular music. However, the cultivation of da capo arias in the realm of sacred music can be seen in the music of one of his contemporaries at Wolfenbüttel, Georg Schürmann. Following his early work as a singer in Hamburg, Schürmann joined the musical staff at Wolfenbüttel in 1697. His main activities were in the field of opera, and his first dramatic composition was performed at Wolfenbüttel in 1700. In 1701 he visited Italy, and his surviving sacred music appears to date from the period immediately after his return to Germany. In 1702 he was granted leave from Wolfenbüttel to take up a temporary

---

[7] See G. Österreich, *Wie eilstu edler Geist.*

post as *Kapellmeister* at the central German court at Meiningen, and it is in the sacred works that he composed at Meiningen in 1705 that the da capo arias can be found. Fortunately, he returned to Wolfenbüttel shortly afterwards, and the scores survive in the Bokemeyer collection.

TOWN COMPOSERS

To explore the difference between the compositional activity of composers in town and court employment, one might compare the output of composers active at the Wolfenbüttel court around the middle of the seventeenth century, Johann Julius Weiland and Johann Jacob Löwe, with that of three of the chief town composers of the same period, Franz Tunder at Lübeck, and Crato Bütner and Balthasar Erben at Danzig. It is at this time, during Buxtehude's youth, that the difference between the town and court composers with respect to the chorale seems to have been most pronounced. None of the total of forty-nine works found in the three publications by Weiland and Löwe published between 1654 and 1660 makes use of chorales, yet it was around this very time that Erben and his fellow town musicians composed their chorale settings. Documents written by Erben reveal that he saw his chorale works as a new form of chorale composition, written for the spiritual edification of the congregation.[8] Certainly in comparison with another Danzig composer of the time, Thomas Strutz, Erben's chorale works are progressive. Those by Strutz are composed in the early seventeenth-century polyphonic style employed by Paul Siefert, but Erben's are composed in the concertato style. To what extent Erben took a lead in the new style of chorale composition is difficult to determine, since similar works by Tunder and Bütner were being composed at about the same time. However, chorale works still form only a small proportion of the total output by all three of these town composers, and much of their best music is to be found in works that were composed more fully under Italian influence, such as their settings of Psalms and mystical texts.

  Danzig was home to many of the finest North German composers of Buxtehude's time. The Catherinenkirche was the workplace of

---

[8] Rauschning, *Geschichte der Musik und Musikpflege in Danzig*, 238.

Christoph Werner, who died young in 1650, and Bütner, whilst the main town church, the Marienkirche, saw an impressive succession of directors of music comprising Kaspar Förster (1655), Balthasar Erben (1658), and Johann Valentin Meder (1687). Manuscripts of fifty-five works by Bütner were destroyed in Danzig during the Second World War, but several published works survive, and Düben fortunately acquired a modest supply of his works. Bütner's surviving music contrasts with that of contemporary court musicians not only because of the composer's use of chorales, but also in his exploitation of large instrumental and vocal forces. The large-scale works are mostly found in manuscript copies, whilst the publications are mostly small-scale concertos (with the exception of a setting of the Te Deum). Bütner's music betrays a thorough familiarity with the North Italian style; the opening vocal phrase of his *Geistliche Concerte* (Hamburg, 1651) recalls the first solo vocal phrase of Monteverdi's Vespers of 1610, as shown in Ex. 4.5. (His predecessor at the Catherinenkirche had already paid homage to Monteverdi's Vespers; see Ex. 8.15.) The surviving music by Erben in the Düben collection is generally more modern in style than that of Bütner, and his most progressive works, such as *Ach dass ich doch in meinem Augen* (copied in 1682) and *Ante oculos tuos*, are notable for their passages of accompanied recitative and use of extended harmonic sequences. Erben's successor at the Marienkirche, Meder, also held posts at

Ex. 4.5. (*a*) Monteverdi, Vespers of 1610; (*b*) Bütner, *Geistliche Concerte* (1651)

(*a*)

S1 Vir - gam vir - tu - tis tu - - - ae

bc

(*b*)

T1 Wirff dein An - lie - - - gen

bc

towns further east than Danzig, in Reval, Königsberg, and Riga. His fifteen surviving motets show a remarkable variety of style and content. Their instrumentation, for example, ranges from a full string ensemble to solo violin and trumpet, and includes one of the earliest recorded uses in North German church music of the trio of two oboes and bassoon in conjunction with strings. The greater range of his music is also apparent in the fact that he made some use of distinct strophic aria sections, notably absent in the works of Bütner and Erben. Mattheson devoted much space to Meder in his *Ehren-Pforte*, in particular dwelling upon his knowledge of Italian music and musicians, a characteristic that is fully reflected in his compositions. A letter written by Meder in 1708, recounted by Mattheson, tells of how he had been in receipt of Italian works from Rome for more than thirty years.[9]

The most flourishing musical city of the North German region in Buxtehude's lifetime was Hamburg. The large number of grand churches and organs in the city was one of Hamburg's obvious advantages, as was the opera-house after its opening in 1678. The Collegium Musicum founded by Weckmann in 1660, which held regular concerts in the refectory of the Cathedral, was another important feature of the city's musical life for a time. The chief cantor at Hamburg around the middle of the century was Thomas Selle (1599–1663), whose large but little-known corpus of extant liturgical church music is rooted in the early seventeenth-century style. However, the arrival of two musicians from the Dresden court, Weckmann and Bernhard, marked a substantial shift in the style of Hamburg church music towards the more modern Italian idioms. Weckmann's early posts at Dresden and in Denmark put him in close contact with Italian musicians, and his interest in Italian music is illustrated clearly by his manuscript collection of sacred music compiled during the 1640s, Lüneburg, K. N. 206 (see p. 56), which contains twenty works by Monteverdi. Only eleven sacred works by Weckmann survive, but they show him to have been one of the finest composers of his day. The Italian style found in his music is principally North Italian rather than Roman, corresponding to the mainly North Italian repertoire found in the Lüneburg manuscript, and to the style of the music of his North German contemporaries Tunder and Bütner. But the greater level of vocal virtuosity

---

[9] Mattheson, *Grundlage einer Ehren-Pforte*, 220.

demanded by his works in comparison with the music of Tunder and Bütner (as, for example, in his solo bass motet *Kommet her zu mir alle*) betrays the direct contact that he had experienced with Italian solo singing. Weckmann's style is at its most bold and expressive in the four works found in the Lüneburg manuscript K. N. 207/6, at least three of which date from 1663. His vocal writing is dramatic and resourceful, and his string-writing creates levels of dissonance unparalleled in the repertoire. One of his finest inspirations occurs in the motet *Zion spricht: Der Herr hat mich verlassen*, shown in Ex. 4.6. The passage of text 'Kann auch eine leibliche Mutter ihres Kindleins vergessen' (can then a natural mother forget her child) is set for bass solo and six-part strings. Weckmann's creativity is apparently in the way he cleverly adapts two standard musical techniques, the *tremolo* style and use of a 7-4-2 chord over a pedal note. The *tremolo* technique is normally employed in an entirely homophonic texture (see pp. 166–9), yet he brings in the strings one after the other, and adds a distinctive, weeping appoggiatura figure. The 7-4-2 chord found in the ninth bar of the extract is not the usual form of this chord, in which the seventh is major, but instead features a minor seventh, creating a rare and beautiful sonority.

Christoph Bernhard, a close friend of Weckmann, succeeded Selle as chief cantor in Hamburg in 1663 and remained there until 1674. Bernhard's fairly large extant output covers a wide range of styles from counterpoint in the *stile antico* to contemporary Italian idioms. His eclectic tastes can be seen in the published collection *Geistlicher Harmonien erster Theil*, published in Dresden but dedicated to his new employer, the Hamburg city council. Virtuoso solo writing can be found here alongside more contrapuntally conceived music, and a small number of works are written in the madrigalian style of Schütz's *Geistliche Chor-Music* of 1648. The Italian element in Bernhard's music is notably different from that found in Weckmann's. The difference stems from the fact that whereas the Italian influence on Weckmann was principally Venetian, that on Bernhard was principally Roman. Weckmann moved to Hamburg in 1655, just before a period of Roman domination at the court brought about mainly through the efforts of Bernhard himself, who was sent to Italy to recruit musicians. Bernhard was thus closely in touch with Roman composers, in particular Albrici, Bontempi, and Peranda, and this is reflected in his music most clearly in the rhapsodic and declamatory nature of the recitative-like passages (as, for example, in

Anima sterilis), and the flowing melodic style of the triple-time aria sections (see Ex. 8.7).

Something of the excitement of the musical scene in Hamburg during the 1660s can be gained from the accounts given by Mattheson of the meetings of Weckmann's Collegium Musicum. He

Ex. 4.6. Weckmann, *Zion spricht: Der Herr hat mich verlassen*

Ex. 4.6. *cont.*

records how music from Venice, Rome, Vienna, Munich, Dresden, and elsewhere was performed and studied, and how German composers from as far afield as Stockholm and Leipzig sent their compositions to the society.[10] Some composers were able to visit Weckmann and Bernhard in person and take part in their music-making; one such was Förster, then working at the Danish court. But the situation changed considerably after Weckmann's death in 1674. Bernhard returned almost at once to Dresden, and the city council appointed as his replacement a cantor of a markedly more conservative disposition. However, Hamburg's importance as a centre for modern music remained, mainly due to the establishment of the opera-house in 1678. This attracted many musicians to the city, both established composers and young musicians seeking their first employment, and the most progressive church music composed by Hamburg composers in the last two decades of the century was written by those who had close connections with the opera-house, notably Nicolaus Strungk, Johann Franck, and Georg Bronner.

The Hamburg city council's replacement for Bernhard was a theology graduate from the University of Wittenberg, Joachim

---

[10] Mattheson, *Grundlage einer Ehren-Pforte*, 397–8.

Gerstenbüttel. His surviving output of thirty-one works in the
Bokemeyer collection, and the list of forty works in the Lüneburg
inventory exemplify the work of a more traditionally minded North
German cantor. Gerstenbüttel had no interest in the opera-house,
and indeed was openly critical of the way in which opera had turned
many people's minds away from the church.[11] His compositional
style is conservative, evident in his use of the increasingly obsolete
3/1 time signature and the undemonstrative nature of his vocal writing, and a substantial proportion of his works features the chorale.
Gerstenbüttel's position as overall director of the city's church musicians is reflected in the high number of works composed for large
forces, and his lack of interest in vocal virtuosity is evident from the
fact that only three of his seventy-one works in the Bokemeyer collection and Lüneburg inventory are solo motets. Gerstenbüttel was
chief cantor in Hamburg for forty-six years, and he is rather noticeable by his absence in Mattheson's *Ehren-Pforte*, which includes
entries on his predecessor, Bernhard, and his successor, Georg
Philipp Telemann, both of whom shared Mattheson's own enthusiasm for Italian music. However, Mattheson does report in *Der
vollkommene Capellmeister* that Gerstenbüttel was renowned for his
dialogues, a small number of which survive in the Bokemeyer collection.[12] In what sounds rather like a back-handed compliment,
Mattheson notes that they were greatly appreciated by the common
man, since the text was set with the greatest clarity. During
Gerstenbüttel's lengthy tenure as cantor many more progressive and
imaginative composers spent time in the city. Although only a handful of sacred works survive by Johann Wolfgang Franck, for example, it is clear that little stylistic gap existed between his Italianate
operas and his church music. His extended chorale-based work *Herr
Jesu Christ du höchstes Gut*, which survives without its violin parts in
a Wolfenbüttel manuscript, opens with a straightforward harmonization of the chorale in minims, but then proceeds immediately with a
dramatically contrasting outburst of expressive writing, shown in Ex.
4.7. The most up-to-date Italian style is also evident in the few surviving sacred works of another operatic composer, Nicolaus
Strungk, who worked in both Hamburg and Hannover in the period

---

[11] See G. Jaacks (ed.), *300 Jahre Oper in Hamburg* (Hamburg, 1977), 46.
[12] Mattheson, *Der vollkommene Capellmeister*, 220.

Ex. 4.7. Franck, *Herr Jesu Christ du höchstes Gut*

1665–85.[13] In stark contrast to the static career of Gerstenbüttel, Strungk's travels took him to Vienna and Rome as well as several German courts and cities. He eventually succeeded Bernhard as *Kapellmeister* at Dresden and founded the opera-house at Leipzig. His solo Psalm setting *Laudate pueri Dominum* is in the purest Italian style, and contains a vigorous concertato opening, a walking-bass aria section ('Sit nomen Domini'), and a typically extravagant melismatic section at the start of the Gloria Patri, shown in Ex. 4.8. Mattheson acknowledges the modernity of Strungk's church music in his *Ehren-Pforte*, noting that 'Im heutigen Kirchen-Styl . . . hat er herrliche Proben abgeleget' (he has composed excellent works in today's church-style).[14] Georg Bronner, who also had close connections with the Hamburg opera-house, was some twenty years younger than both Strungk and Franck, and most of his mature work, dating from after 1700, has been lost. His modest collection of six *Geistliche Concerten* for one or two voices, two instruments, and continuo dates

---

[13] See F. Berend, *Nicolaus Adam Strunck, 1640–1700: Sein Leben und seine Werke. Mit Beiträgen zur Geschichte der Musik und Theaters in Celle, Hannover und Leipzig* (Freiburg, 1915).

[14] Mattheson, *Grundlage einer Ehren-Pforte*, 354.

Ex. 4.8. Strungk, *Laudate pueri*

from 1696, and contains an interesting mixture of old and new musical features. The style and structure of the music is in some ways fairly conservative for the date, suggesting that the young composer was starting out by trying his hand at the style of his older, established contemporaries, but the collection also displays up-to-date characteristics, such as the instrumental scoring of two oboes and bassoon, and the appearance of a brief passage of secco recitative (see Ex. 8.4).

The two nearest large towns to Hamburg, Lüneburg and Lübeck, both maintained strong musical traditions throughout the seventeenth and early eighteenth centuries. Lüneburg had two particularly active musical establishments, the Johanniskirche and Michaeliskirche, although the principal musicians at these churches during the second half of the seventeenth century do not seem to have included many composers. Although the chief cantors Michael Jacobi and

Friedrich Funcke at the Johanniskirche and Friedrich Praetorius at the Michaeliskirche confined themselves as composers to occasional works (such as Funcke's *Danck- und Denck-Mahl* written after the tower of the Johanniskirche was partially destroyed in a thunderstorm in 1666; see Ex. 8.12), their activities as collectors of manuscript and printed sacred music for use at their churches is well documented.[15] The only Lüneburg cantor who is known to have composed a substantial quantity of church music is August Braun, who succeeded Praetorius at the Michaeliskirche in 1695 and was cantor during the young Bach's time there. None of his music survives, but the Lüneburg inventory, compiled at the Michaeliskirche, shows him to have favoured large-scale music, like many cantors. At least two of the town organists of this period were active as composers of sacred vocal music, Christian Flor and his successor as organist at the Johanniskirche, Georg Böhm. Only a few works by Flor survive, showing a melodious but harmonically rather limited style, but Böhm's extant output is slightly larger and considerably more impressive in content. Although Böhm took up his post in 1698 and lived until 1733, the sacred works that are attributed to him in the Bokemeyer collection are similar in style and content to the works of Buxtehude and Bruhns.[16] It seems quite likely, therefore, that they may date from the period of five years that he spent in Hamburg (1693–8), before his move to Lüneburg. Two sacred vocal works by Böhm which survive (SW 8 and 9) appear to pre-date even his Hamburg years. Found in central German sources only, they are examples of the central German polyphonic motet style and thus probably date from his early years at Gotha.

As at Lüneburg, compositional activity at Lübeck during the period lay more with the organists than the cantors. Tunder and Buxtehude were successive organists at the main town church, the Marienkirche. Tunder's establishment of regular concerts in the church on Saturday afternoons was one of the most significant developments in the musical life of the city. It has been suggested that he composed his surviving church music for performance at these concerts rather than at the church services, but there is no concrete evidence to support this view, and it is likely that Tunder, along with

[15] Walter, *Musikgeschichte der Stadt Lüneburg*, 143–7.

[16] One work included in the collected edition of his works, *Warum toben die Heiden* (SW 11), is much more 18th-c. in style but is anonymous in the source, and thus not necessarily by Böhm.

the large number of other organist-composers of the period, occasionally directed performances of their works in church services.[17] His few chorale-based works show a common interest with his contemporaries in Danzig, Bütner and Erben.[18] Like the Psalm settings by the Danzig composers, Tunder's Latin motets and Psalm settings are highly influenced by the North Italian style. Indeed, one work ascribed to Tunder in the Düben collection reposed quietly in his collected works for many years until it was discovered to be a contrafactum of a work by Giovanni Rovetta.[19] Mattheson claimed that Tunder studied in Italy with Frescobaldi, but most scholars have rejected this claim in the absence of corroborating evidence. However, it is clear from the music itself that Tunder's knowledge of the contemporary Italian style was considerable. This is particularly apparent in his lively concertato Psalm settings and in expressive solo motets such as *Salve coelestis Pater*, a setting of a Protestantized version of the *Salve Regina*.[20]

In his study of Buxtehude's church music, the Danish scholar Søren Sørensen makes the following observation:

Wir kommen zu dem Schluß, das Buxtehudes Kantatenkunst eher als Endphase einer Stilentwicklung (die Kulmination des Carissimi-Stils in der norddeutschen Schule) anzusehen ist denn—wie bisher—als Vorläufer der hoch-barocken Kantate . . .[21]

(We come to the conclusion that Buxtehude's cantata style is to be seen rather as the end-phase of a stylistic development (the culmination of the Carissimi style in the North German school) than—as up to now—as the prototype of the high Baroque cantata . . .)

Buxtehude's extant church music dates mainly from the 1670s and 1680s, and Sørenson rightly points out that it belongs more to the tradition of Rome-influenced music by composers such as Förster and Geist than to the emerging recitative–aria pattern of early eighteenth-century church music seen in the works of Österreich and

---

[17] See the entry on Tunder by Karstädt in *The New Grove*.

[18] Karstädt's entry on Tunder in *The New Grove* claims that his chorale-based vocal works 'initiated the development of the Lutheran church cantata that culminated in the work of Bach', but similar works by Danzig composers of the same generation (Bütner and Erben) suggest that no single composer can be credited with the establishment of the genre.

[19] See J. Roche, 'Rovetta and Tunder: An Interesting Example of Plagiarism', *Early Music*, 3 (1975), 58–60.

[20] It remains possible that such works may also in fact be by Italian composers, and are wrongly attributed to Tunder in the Düben collection.

[21] S. Sørenson, *Diderich Buxtehudes vokale kirkemusik* (Copenhagen, 1958), 324.

Schürmann. Moreover, it should also be noted that his extant church music is not as thoroughly Italianate in style as the church music of some of his North German contemporaries. After all, Buxtehude is not known to have visited Italy; neither apparently did he travel in Germany a great deal, though he certainly had close connections with the Hamburg musical scene. He did not work alongside Italian musicians, as Bernhard and Weckmann had done at Dresden, or Förster in Rome, Venice, and Copenhagen. This conservative element in his output can be illustrated by his Latin Psalm settings. There are only two settings of complete Vespers Psalms in his output: *Dixit Dominus* (BuxWV 17) and *Laudate pueri* (BuxWV 69). The first of these shows little advance on the early seventeenth-century North Italian style found in Tunder's Psalm settings, whilst the second is based on a highly idiosyncratic ostinato bass, rather than on one of the typical Italian formulas employed by other North German composers. Other non-Italian features in his music include his often virtuosic writing for the viola da gamba, as in *Jubilate Domino* (BuxWV 64), and his comparatively limited use of harmonic sequence. But Buxtehude did keep pace with much of the development of Italian church music around the middle of the century and later. Some of his most modern Italianate writing is found in his aria settings. In particular, the aria sections of his cycle of motets *Membra Jesu nostri* (BuxWV 75), dedicated to 'his most noble and honoured friend' Gustav Düben, show a complete assimilation of the Roman aria style. This style is not so much that found in the music of Foggia and Carissimi, but rather that of the slightly later group of Roman musicians whose music survives in the Düben collection, such as Giovanni Bicilli (see p. 154).

Unfortunately, we have very little evidence of how Buxtehude's church music developed in the 1690s and early years of the eighteenth century, if indeed he continued to write church music during this time, but there is some evidence to suggest that as in his earlier music he continued to cultivate a blend of old and new features. The use of oboes in *Ich suchte des Nachts* (BuxWV 50), which survives outside the Düben collection, is in line with the general trend during the 1690s, but the work is not as modern in style as the music of Georg Österreich dating from around this time. Similarly, the surviving libretti of his famous *Abendmusik* concerts in 1705 contain evidence of his use of the new type of unison violin-writing, but it is notable that all the arias are of the strophic rather than da capo type.

Buxtehude's surviving church music, like that of Bach, is thus more notable for its high musical quality than for its progressive elements. With respect to his choice of texts, he appears to have had a particular interest in German aria texts, either set as separate works, as found in two of Tunder's works, or as part of a textual compilation of the sort increasingly favoured in the 1670s and 1680s, as found in the works of Pfleger, Theile, Köler, Meister, and others.

Other North German composers active in towns across the region whose music survives in some quantity include Johann Sebastiani at Königsberg, Johann Martin Rubert at Stralsund, Johann Meister at Flensburg, and Nicolaus Bruhns at Husum. Of these, only Sebastiani worked as a cantor, a fact that is reflected in his large output of published occasional works, now mostly lost, and the four large-scale works in the Düben and Bokemeyer collections. (He states in the foreword to the publication of his Passion setting of 1672 that he had composed, like Pfleger, an *Evangelienjahrgang*, a setting in German of Gospel texts with the inclusion of 'Kirchenliedern', but this unfortunately does not survive.[22]) By contrast, the output of the Stralsund organist Johann Rubert consists of a single collection of small-scale concertos. They follow very much in the tradition of the publications of the earlier Stralsund organist Johann Vierdanck (*Geistliche Concerten*, two volumes: 1641, 1643), whose works combine the early seventeenth-century North German instrumental tradition and the style of the small-scale concertos of Schütz, under whom he had worked for fifteen years at the Dresden court.[23] Rubert's *Musicalische Seelen-Erquickung* (Stralsund, 1664) continues Vierdanck's interest in varied instrumental scoring and mainly German texts, and the works are notably conservative in style in comparison with the publications of contemporary composers such as Bernhard and even Weiland, who died in 1663. The works by Meister and Bruhns are close in style and content to Buxtehude's church music. Bruhns had studied with Buxtehude in Lübeck, and both he and Meister found employment in the Schleswig-Holstein region close to Lübeck. Of the two, Bruhns was certainly the more inspired composer, whose work benefited in particular from his own expertise as a violinist and the

---

[22] See J. Sebastiani, *Das Leyden und Sterben unsers Herrn und Heylandes Jesu Christi nach dem heiligen Matthaeo* (Königsberg, 1672), (Denkmäler deutscher Tonkunst, 17; 1904, repr. 1958), [5].

[23] See A. Kirwan-Mott, *The Small-Scale Sacred Concertato in the Early Seventeenth Century* (Ann Arbor, 1981), 159–78.

talent of his fellow musician at the town church at Husum, the cantor Georg Ferber, who according to Mattheson was a fine bass. The Ferber–Bruhns partnership is suggested in particular by *Mein Herz ist bereit*, scored for just bass, solo violin, and basso continuo. The most modern aspect of his music is his extensive use of harmonic sequences, as, for example, in the opening section of *Die Zeit meines Abschieds ist vorhanden*, and it is greatly to be regretted that this excellent composer died so young at the age of 32.

5

Texts

◊

THE nature of the texts employed in North German church music in the Baroque period reflected directly the principal concerns of Lutheran teaching. The first priority of worship was the praise of God. In addition, the church encouraged the faithful to nurture a personal relationship with God, and sought to elucidate the Scriptures through its teaching. *Lob*, *Andacht*, and *Erbauung* (praise, devotion, edification)—these three words appear time and again in the religious literature of the period, and often in specific relation to the role of music in church. The first two ideals, *Lob* and *Andacht*, were priorities from the very beginnings of the Lutheran Reformation, but the third, *Erbauung*, became particularly central during the age of Buxtehude. By serving the cause of *Erbauung*, church music became involved in the evangelism of the church, taking part in the education and moral instruction of the people.

The praise of God is nowhere expressed more eloquently than in the Book of Psalms, and this remained the single most popular source of texts for church music throughout the seventeenth century. Many works are settings of complete Vespers Psalms with doxology, but a larger number are settings of the opening few verses or a short passage from within a single Psalm. In the earlier part of the period the importance of the Psalms can be seen in Christoph Bernhard's *Geistlicher Harmonien, erster Theil* of 1665 and J. J. Löwe's *Neue geistliche Concerten* of 1660, in which ten of the twelve works are settings of Psalm texts, and towards the end of the century the continued importance of Psalm settings may be observed in the works of composers such as Nicolaus Bruhns and Georg Bronner, whose six concertos in his *Geistliche Concerten* of 1696 all contain verses from the Psalms. Owing to their central liturgical function, settings of complete Vespers Psalms generally had Latin texts, whereas those of other Psalm texts mostly were in German.

Turning to the second ideal, *Andacht*, Latin texts again played an important role, since the tradition of mystical poetry and prose in Lutheran circles came about largely through the influence of Catholic writers, both German and Italian, who wrote in Latin.[1] The four main sources or themes of Catholic mysticism that were employed for musical compositions were the hymn *Jesu dulcis memoria*, attributed to St Bernard of Clairvaux, the theme of *vanitas*, the Song of Songs, and the traditional Marian antiphons.[2] Many Italian compositions based on these themes were in circulation in the North German region during the seventeenth century, and they provided models for the North German composers, both regarding the choice of texts and the musical idioms associated with them. Among the anthologies of Profe and Havemann and the manuscripts of the Düben collection we find two settings of *Jesu dulcis memoria*, by Carisio and Albrici; two works on the *vanitas* theme, Carissimi's *Vanitas vanitatum* and Albrici's *Quo tendimus mortales*; two settings of the *Salve Regina*, both turned into addresses to Christ, by Rovetta (*Salve Rex Christe*) and Cocci (*Salve mi Jesu*); and two works on Song of Songs texts, *Descende dilecti mi* by Casati, and *Per rigidos montes* by Peranda.

The appeal of the hymn *Jesu dulcis memoria* was based on the intensity of the devotion it expressed between Christ and the believer. Both Catholic and Protestant composers made use not only of the opening verses but also of strophes taken from later in the poem. The 1656 publication of the Wolfenbüttel composer J. J. Weiland (*Deuterotokos*) contains almost entirely Latin devotional poetry, including a total of five works with texts taken from *Jesu dulcis memoria*. The second, fourth, and ninth works in the collection are settings of strophes 1–5 of the poem; the fifth contains strophes 27–9, and the twelfth has strophes 1–5 and 45. The complete list of contents of the collection is as follows:

---

[1] See K. O. Conrady, *Lateinische Dichtungstradition und deutsche Lyrik des 17. Jahrhunderts* (Bonn, 1962).

[2] For further reading on the place of mysticism in 17th-c. German literature see G. Hoffmeister (ed.), *German Baroque Literature: The European Perspective* (New York, 1983), in particular ch. 6, 'Neo-Latin Tradition and Vernacular Poetry' (L. Forster), and ch. 16, 'The Mystical Quest for God' (J. B. Dallett).

J. J. Weiland, *Deuterotokos: Hoc est Sacratissimarum odarum partus* (Bremen, 1656)

    à 3

1   *O Nomen Jesu*
2   *Jesu dulcis memoria*
3   *Amor Jesu dulcissime*
4   *Jesu dulcis memoria*
5   *O Jesu mi dulcissime*
6   *Puer qui natus nobis*
7   *Adsunt festa jubiloea*

    à 4

8   *Ego sum vitis illa vera*
9   *Jesu dulcis memoria*
10 *Ad te Domine levavi*

    à 4 and 5

11 *O anima mea suspira*

    à 5

12 *Jesu dulcis memoria*
13 *Salve, O Jesu mi*
14 *Veni sancte spiritus*

    à 6

15 *Factum est proelium magnum*

(16 Sonata à 3)

Other North German composers who made use of the text *Jesu dulcis memoria* were Buxtehude, Tunder, Weckmann, Förster, and Georg Stübendorff. The text was also employed in a free manner and as a basis for new poetry and prose that was used for musical compositions. The motet *Amor Jesu dulcissime* by the Italian composer Antonelli consists of a free compilation of individual lines of the poem (many of which have been slightly altered) taken from five different strophes. Stübendorff's *O Jesu dulcissime* consists of a single strophe from the poem followed by an apparently new passage in prose inspired by the language of the poem. The full text of the motet is as follows:

> O Jesu mi dulcissime
> Spes suspirantis animae
> Te piae quaerunt lachrymae
> Et clamor mentis intimae

Sed a periculis cunctis libera nos Jesu / amantissime Jesu dulcissime Jesu suavissime sit nomen tuum benedictum in saeculum seculi

(O Jesus my dearest
You are the hope of my yearning soul
My tears of contrition
And the cry of my conscience seek you out

But deliver us, Jesus, from every danger; most beloved Jesus, dearest Jesus, may your name most pleasingly be blessed, world without end)

Amongst the many other examples of works by Italian and North German composers whose texts were inspired by the hymn are Francesco Della Porta's motets *O amantissime Jesu* and *O dulcissime Jesu*, and Geist's *O Jesu amantissime* and *O Jesu dulcis*.

The classical themes of *fortuna*, *vanitas*, and *mors* may have struck a particular chord with the German people during the seventeenth century on account of the widespread suffering experienced during the Thirty Years War. The most famous German novel of the century, Grimmelshausen's *Simplizissimus* (1669), tells of the hardships of the war years; it underlines the vanity of human existence and stresses that hope for the future should be based on thoughts of the afterlife rather than a better world on earth. Mystical writers again turned to the writings of St Bernard, in particular his *Rhythmus de contemptu mundi*. The general tenor of the writing may be gleaned from the following passage of verse, taken from Meder's motet *Sufficit nunc Domine*:

Vale mundi vanitas
Salve coeli suavitas
Tecum, munde, sum deceptus
Sed in coelo iam repletus

(Farewell, empty world
Welcome, enchantments of heaven
By you, O world, I was deceived
But now in heaven I have all things received)

The most extended treatment of the theme by a North German composer is probably that by Förster in his Latin dialogue *Vanitas vanitatum*, a setting of the parable of the rich man and Lazarus.

Settings of Marian antiphons by Italian composers were performed with altered texts in Protestant worship, and the popularity of settings of the *Salve Regina* was such that some North German composers appear to have composed their own settings of the texts in altered form. Some merely borrowed the incipit of the antiphon and then developed independently, as with Bernhard's *Salve mi Jesu* and

Weiland's *Salve o Jesu*, but other texts followed the antiphon more closely. The text of Erben's *Salve suavissime Jesu* is based on an altered version of the opening and closing passages of the antiphon. Instead of the final phrase of the antiphon 'O clemens, O pia, O dulcis Virgo Maria', his motet ends with the text 'O clemens, O dulcis Fili Redemptor'. However, there remains the possibility that works containing texts based on the complete *Salve Regina* may in reality be misattributed Italian compositions. This has been shown to be the case with the *Salve mi Jesu* attributed to Tunder in the Düben collection,[3] and may perhaps be true of another work attributed to Tunder, his *Salve coelestis Pater*.

The Song of Songs was one of the most popular sources for texts amongst Italian composers of the seventeenth century. The text was highly prized in Germany as well, where it was frequently printed in German translation in the course of the seventeenth century: at least thirteen different translations are known, many of which were reprinted several times. The most popular version was that by the Dresden court preacher and poet Martin Opitz. First published in Breslau in 1627, it was printed eight times within the next twenty years, including twice at the North German city of Danzig. The popularity of the text rested on the suitability of its highly emotional love poetry for expressing the yearning for mystical union between the individual soul and Christ. It was thus used as an allegorical form of the love expressed in the hymn *Jesu dulcis memoria*. This association is made explicit in some of the titles of the seventeenth-century German translations of the poem. The translation by Johann Dilherr published in Jena in 1640, and dedicated to certain noble ladies at the Brandenburg and Braunschweig-Lüneburg courts, is entitled: 'Christliche Andachten / Gebet und Seufftzer / Uber das Königliche Braut-Lied Salomonis / darinnen ein Gottseeliges Hertz / fürnemlich zu eiveriger Betrachtung der unverschulden Liebe Christi / und seiner schuldigen Gegenliebe / wird angemahnet' (Christian devotions, prayer, and sighs on the royal bridal song of Solomon, in which a devout heart is exhorted principally to eager contemplation of the spotless love of Christ and his own sinful love in return).[4] Most of the North German motets set to devotional texts were in Latin, but because of the popularity of contemporary German translations of the Song of Songs, motets with texts from this source were more

---

[3] See above, p. 82.
[4] M. Göbel, *Die Bearbeitungen des Hohen Liedes im 17. Jahrhundert* (Halle, 1914), 38.

often than not in German. Bütner's *Musicalische Concerte* (Danzig, 1652) is one such work. The title-page of the publication proclaims that the text, beginning 'Ich suchte des nachts in meinem bette', is taken from the third chapter of the Song of Solomon.

Besides these four main categories of devotional texts, many other texts set by the North German composers fall within the category of devotional or mystical literature. In the realm of Latin writing another poem attributed to St Bernard was popular with both Italian and North German composers, the *Rhythmica Oratio*. This meditation on Christ's crucifixion is employed in the Roman composer Giovanni Bicilli's *Gloriosum diem colimus* and Buxtehude's cycle of motets *Membra Jesu nostri* (BuxWV 75). Moreover, there is a notable similarity of musical style between the settings of Bicilli and Buxtehude (see p. 154). Towards the end of the century settings of devotional texts in the vernacular came to outnumber those in Latin. Most common was the German aria (or ode) text, a poetic form widely known through the popularity of printed songbooks. Although the famous Latin text *Jesu dulcis memoria* is a strophic form, the musical settings by both Italian and North German composers were generally through-composed, but because of the prominence of the German songbooks, aria texts in German were nearly always set to strophic musical forms. The texts were often related in spirit to the Latin devotional literature, sharing the theme of the union between Christ and the believer or the theme of *vanitas*. The latter was understandably popular for aria texts written for use at funerals. Sebastiani's aria *Jesu, Jesu du mein Licht*, for example, was published under the title *Parnaß Blumen* (Königsberg, 1672), and Österreich's *Wie eilstu edler Geist*, a setting of a text written by the composer Johann Förtsch, was composed for a funeral in 1694.

The principle of *Erbauung* was closely connected with the readings of the Sunday Gospel and the ensuing sermon at the weekly *Gottesdienst*. This was the part of the service where the people were to be given instruction in the faith, firmly based on the words of Holy Scripture. Many works by North German composers of the period are simply settings of the Gospel texts themselves, and were probably sung immediately after or during the sermon. One of the two pieces by Michael Hahn of Schleswig in the Lüneburg inventory is listed with no incipit, simply as 'Evangelium am 14 Sont. nach Tr.'. The regular demand for musical pieces which fitted in with the Gospel of the day led some composers to set whole cycles of Gospel texts, either in pure or troped form. A complete cycle by the Gottorf court composer Augustin Pfleger survives in the Düben collection, whilst another by the Königsberg composer Johann Sebastiani referred to in the foreword to his published St Matthew Passion of 1672 is lost. Because of the narrative nature of the Gospel texts, many works were composed as dialogues, a technique that had long been popular in both Italy and Germany, but which gained a new lease of life with the advent of the dramatic possibilities of the _stylo recitativo_.[5] Italian examples of the genre which reached North Germany include G. Casati's Epiphany dialogue _Quid vidistis o Magi_ and Stefano Bernardi's six-voice dialogue on Christ's first miracle, _Non habemus vinum_. Casati's work, originally published in 1640, was included in Profe's anthology _Cunis solennibus_ (RISM 1646[3]), and was copied into manuscript for the Catharinenkirche in Danzig,[6] and Bernardi's dialogue was included in Profe's _Vierdter und letzter Theil geistlicher Concerten_ (RISM 1646[4]) and copied into manuscript by Düben for use in Stockholm. Förster's dialogue on the parable of Dives and Lazarus, _Vanitas vanitatum_, was probably composed under the influence of his teacher Carissimi, whose dialogues were amongst his most famous works. Musicians in central Germany, notably Schütz, Andreas Hammerschmidt, and Wolfgang Briegel, cultivated the form with particular relish around the middle of the century, and their influence may also have been important in the spread of the genre in the North German region, particularly concerning the use of texts in German. One of Hammerschmidt's most popular volumes was his 1655 collection of Gospel dialogues in German, _Musicalische Gespräche über die Evangelia_ (Musical Dialogues on the Gospels). Weckmann may well have been inspired to write his touching dialogue for the Annunciation _Gegrüsset seist du_ by Schütz's own Annunciation dialogue _Sei gegrüsset, Maria_ from his _Ander Theil kleiner geistlichen Concerten_, which was published at Dresden in 1639 when he was working there as court organist. The genre remained in use throughout the Buxtehude period, as is shown by several works in the Bokemeyer collection, such as Österreich's dialogue _Und Jesus ging aus_, headed 'Dom: Reminiscere' and dated 1693.

[5] For a full examination of the 17th-c. Latin dialogue, see F. Noske, _Saints and Sinners: The Latin Musical Dialogue in the Seventeenth Century_ (Oxford, 1992).

[6] See O. Günther, _Die musikalischen Kirchenbibliotheken von St. Katharinen und St. Johannis in Danzig_ (Katalog der Handschriften der Danziger Bibliothek, 4; Danzig, 1911), 55–60.

But the principle of *Erbauung* went far beyond the simple setting of Gospel texts. The composite text was born out of the desire to elucidate and interpret the Scriptures by juxtaposing different texts on a single theme, rather in the way in which the New Testament writers themselves called upon the writings of the Old Testament to demonstrate the fulfilment of prophecy. Although the Lutherans certainly came to revel in the creation of composite texts, it would be misleading to understand it as an exclusively Lutheran phenomenon, for the Italians cultivated this type of text at a relatively early stage in the century, and may have been in part responsible for the development of such texts in Protestant countries. The spirit of the Counter-Reformation found amongst the Jesuits and Oratorians in particular was as much devoted to the cultivation of a close understanding of the Scriptures as that of the Lutheran Reformation. As with the case of the dialogue, Carissimi was a leading figure in the use of composite texts, working under the Jesuits at the German College in Rome. Andrew Jones's study of Carissimi's motets has shown that only around 22 per cent of his output is based on strictly liturgical texts, whilst the largest single category of texts, accounting for 32.5 per cent of the corpus, consists of composite texts in which scriptural and non-scriptural texts are combined.[7] Some motets contain composite texts which are purely scriptural, and these often take the form of expanded Gospel dialogues. One such work, *Ecce nos reliquimus omnia*, contains the unusually high number of fourteen different scriptural texts taken from both the Old and New Testaments, some of which have been modified to fit into the form of the dialogue. The work was copied into manuscript for Düben in Stockholm, and is based on the theme of the trials and ultimate rewards of a Christian life. North German composers who employed composite texts taken purely from the Bible include Pfleger, Weiland, and Bernhard, whose *Heute ist Christus von den Toten auferstanden* contains texts from 1 Corinthians, The Book of Revelation, 2 Timothy, and Colossians. The care that was taken over the selection of texts can be seen in the manner in which texts were sometimes displayed in publications of individual works. Michael Jacobi's *Timor Domini*, published in 1663, exhibits the text separately at the start of the publication, with clear indications of the sources used. The compiler of the text had brought together Old and New Testament verses based on the theme of the

---

[7] A. V. Jones, *The Motets of Carissimi* (Ann Arbor, 1982), i. 130.

fear of the Lord (*timor Domini*), using Psalms 3, 25, and 34 and ch. 3 of the Letter to the Ephesians.

Like Carissimi, most North German composers enjoyed the greater contrast of both style and content afforded by the juxtaposition of biblical and non-biblical texts, particularly when the latter was in poetic form. The mixture of prose and poetry was already established at Rome during the 1640s in the music of Foggia and Carissimi, usually in works of a strongly devotional or penitential nature, and there can be little doubt that Förster's use of this type of composite text was influenced by the Roman masters. His dependence on Roman models is made even clearer by the fact that his compositions include secular works with Italian texts which also combine prose and poetry, for example his *Sotto la luna*, preserved in the Düben collection.[8] Foggia's motet *Excelsi luminis*, which survives in the Düben collection in a manuscript probably copied in Italy in 1646,[9] opens with the prose text 'Excelsi luminis cultores inditi' and contains a three-verse aria, the first verse of which is as follows:

> Ergo nostri miserere
> Peccatorum filium
> Ac nos fortiter tuere
> Contra hostis impetum
>
> (Therefore have mercy upon us
> The children of sinners,
> And strongly defend us
> Against the assault of the enemy)

In the same manner, Förster's motet *Quanta fecisti Domine* opens with prose, but also contains poetic passages such as the following couplets:

> Tu nos regis tu nos moves
> Tu nos nutris tu nos foves
> Sic da tecum congaudere
> Te potiri te videre
>
> (You rule us, you guide us,
> You nourish us, you care for us,
> Grant therefore that we may rejoice with you,
> Possess you, and look upon you)

---

[8] Düben collection, vok. mus. i hdskr. 22:17.
[9] Düben collection, vok. mus. i hdskr. 23:6.

Composite texts with prose and poetry also feature prominently in the works of the influential Italian composers Albrici and Peranda. Albrici's *Cogita o homo*, a work on the *vanitas* theme, contains both prose and the aria 'Homo Dei creatura'. Its popularity was such that it appears in all three major North German collections of the period: the Düben collection, the Lüneburg inventory, and the Bokemeyer collection.

Two of the earliest datable examples of the combination of prose and poetry by North German composers can be found in two publications, Weiland's *Deuterotokos* (Bremen, 1656) and Pfleger's *Psalmi, Dialogi et Motettae* (Hamburg, 1661). One of the settings of part of the hymn *Jesu dulcis memoria* in Weiland's publication (no. 9), contains strophes 1–5 of the hymn, but concludes with the following passage of free prose: 'Omnis terra adoret te, Deus, et psallat tibi psalmum dicat Nomini tuo Domine Jesu'. Pfleger's dialogue *O pulcherrima mulier* is based on the first six verses of the third chapter of the Book of Genesis, but also contains three poetic sections. A. Nausch has pointed out the similarity of the text of this work to a dialogue by the little-known Venetian *maestro di cappella* Niccolò Gibellini, published six years earlier in 1655.[10] Two of the three poetic sections used by Pfleger are found in Gibellini's work.

North German composers such as Geist, Buxtehude, and Meder continued to set composite Latin texts after Italian models through to the 1680s. The poetry used often bore the same eight-syllable lines as *Jesu dulcis memoria*, but shorter lines were also in common use, sometimes with as few as four syllables. The motet *O quam terribilis*, ascribed to both Albrici and Carissimi in the Düben collection, contains the following burst of short phrases revealing a typical play on words:[11]

> illa fecit
> ista curat
> illa fugat
> ista petit
> illa fremit
> ista durat

[10] See Nausch, *Augustin Pfleger*, 40.
[11] For a discussion of this style of Latin poetry see Conrady, *Lateinische Dichtungstradition*, 164.

Christoph Bernhard's *Salve mi Jesu* exhibits the same literary technique:

> O grandis amor
> o fortis amor
> tibi divus
> mihi pius
> tibi crudelis
> mihi vitalis

Such brief rhyming passages also often appear as if spontaneously within texts that are otherwise written in prose.

During the last two decades of the seventeenth century there was a marked decrease in the use of composite texts in Latin, as the emphasis in general moved ever more towards the use of the vernacular. One of the earliest known composite texts involving prose and poetry in German is the final work of Bernhard's *Geistlicher Harmonien, erster Theil* (Dresden, 1665), the dialogue *Euch ist's gegeben*. Like Pfleger's Latin dialogue *O pulcherrima mulier*, Bernhard's work underlines the importance of the dialogue in the early history of the composite text. The most direct stimulus for the composition of composite texts in German appears to have come from the central German composer Wolfgang Briegel. The first two parts of his *Evangelische Gespräche*, which contain Gospel dialogues enriched with aria verses, were published in 1660 and 1662. As with the equivalent Latin works, the poetry acts as a gloss to the biblical text, allowing interpretation and reflection. Most of the works in Pfleger's complete Gospel cycle, the *Evangelien Jahrgang*, contain aria verses in the manner of Briegel's publications, and the use of such composite German texts became increasingly popular during the last two decades of the century. Pfleger himself was of central German origin, and was taught by another central German composer of dialogues, Johann Kindermann.

In addition to aria texts, chorale texts were also used as part of composite texts in German. The particular advantage of employing chorale texts was that, since they were known to the congregation, the combination of a chorale text with, say, a biblical story formed a compelling way in which to bind together the traditional Gospel message with the contemporary Lutheran church. Some of the earliest known examples of the combination of prose and chorale texts texts may be found, as in the case of the combination of prose and aria texts, amongst the Gospel publications of the central German composers. Chorales are employed in Andreas Hammerschmidt's *Musicalische Gespräche über die Evangelia*, published in 1655 and 1656, and these publications, like those of Briegel, were owned by many North German churches and chapels during the second half of the century. Initially, the North German composers seem to have favoured the setting of chorale texts as separate works. Tunder, who died in 1667, composed five independent chorale works. However, the combination of chorales with other texts appears in works dating from the 1670s and 1680s, by composers such as Pfleger, Buxtehude, and Förtsch. By this time the tradition of composite texts was well established, and so the stage was set for the final phase in the development of composite texts: the amalgam of biblical prose, aria texts, *and* chorale texts. With this development the principle of *Erbauung* is seen at its most complex and in its most obviously Lutheran form. In this way the Word of God is presented to the congregation with the addition of both a personal and a collective response, the personal element coming from the contemporary devotional aria texts, and the collective element from the traditional chorales of the Lutheran church. Immense care went into the selection of appropriate texts, as can be seen in the following example from Pfleger's Gospel cycle. *So spricht der Herr* is based on the Gospel for the First Sunday in Lent, Matt. 4: 3–10. The Gospel text, concerning the temptation of Christ in the wilderness, is expanded by means of further biblical passages as well as an aria text and chorale. Although the Gospel deals with the temptation of Christ, the clear objective of the compiler of the text is to throw the emphasis on the individual, encouraging each believer to consider his own response to temptation. Two of the additional biblical passages contain the word *Versuchung* (temptation): 'Wachet und betet, daß ihr nicht in Versuchung fallet' (Watch and pray that you may not enter into temptation, Mark 14: 38a), and 'Gott ist getreu, der euch nicht läßt versuchen über euer Vermögen, sondern machet, daß die Versuchung so ein End gewinne, daß ihr's könnt ertragen' (God is faithful, and he will not let you be tempted beyond your strength, but with the temptation will also provide the way of escape, that you may be able to endure it, 1 Cor. 10: 13b). The aria begins with a reminder of man's first submission to temptation, the Fall, and then considers the protection against sin given by Christ, the Word of God. The chorale used is the seventh verse of Luther's chorale on the Lord's Prayer, *Vater unser im Himmelreich*, which opens with a further reference to *Versuchung*: 'Führ uns Herr in Versuchung nicht' (Lead us not Lord into temptation). The texts which have been added to the Gospel text are not simply tacked on at the end, but are mixed into the Gospel text in an imaginative and effective manner:

Text of Augustin Pfleger, *So spricht der Herr*
(a) Joel 2: 13
(b)   ARIA, vv. 1–2
(c) Isa. 43: 24b
(d)   GOSPEL text
(e)   ARIA, v. 3
(f) Isa. 43: 24b repeated
(g)   GOSPEL text
(h)   ARIA, vv. 4–5
(i)   CHORALE verse, first line only
(j)   GOSPEL text
(k)   CHORALE verse, complete
(l)   1 Cor. 10: 13b
(m)   ARIA, v. 6

Elaborate textual structures such as this, in which biblical texts, arias, and chorales are combined, found favour amongst many late seventeenth-century North German composers, including Buxtehude, Meister, Johann Hanff, Ritter, Österreich, Schürmann, and Georg von Bertuch. Sometimes the biblical element is quite brief, and Gospel texts are not the only source used. Meister's *Unser Wandel ist im Himmel* contains only the first two verses of the Epistle for the 23rd Sunday after Trinity, Phil. 3: 20–1, together with another biblical passage which is a combination of Ps. 84: 1 and Phil. 1: 23b: 'Wie lieblich sind deine Wohnungen, Herr Zebaoth; ich habe Lust, abzuscheiden und bei Christo zu sein' (How lovely is thy dwelling place, O Lord of Hosts; my desire is to depart and be with Christ). This theme of the final communion of the believer with Christ in heaven is also present in the aria text 'O seliger Wandel zur Wohnung' and the chorale 'Herzlich thut mich verlangen', also employed in Meister's composition. As with Pfleger's *So spricht der Herr*, key words link the various passages employed, in this case *Wandel* and *Wohnung*, and the different texts are carefully intermingled.

It is not clear to what extent composers themselves made up these complex amalgams of texts, which sometimes draw on several dif-

ferent literary sources, including the Bible, contemporary prose and
poetry, non-biblical liturgical texts, and chorale texts. Whilst there
seems little reason to suppose that composers were not capable of
such text compilations, it also seems likely that the clergy may have
put together some of these texts. The case of Erdmann Neumeister's
cantata texts of 1700 is well known, and since many Lutheran pastors
acknowledged the power of music to convey the meaning of texts it
is not difficult to imagine a pastor encouraging his cantor or organist to set a particular selection of texts that he had made, perhaps
specifically for use after or before his sermon.

The development of this kind of complex composite text with its
emphasis on illuminating the Scriptures in the manner of a sermon
was perhaps the major cause of the gradual eclipse of Latin composite texts by those in German. The chorale texts were of course in
German, and elaborate textual structures in Latin would have been
understood only by a handful of people. But this shift in favour of
German texts was also part of a general swing in this direction in
North German church music as a whole. The proportion of
German-texted to Latin-texted works in North German church
music of the 1650s and 1660s is roughly 3 to 2, whereas the equivalent proportion concerning music from the 1680s and 1690s is about
4 to 1. The continued use of Latin towards the end of the century,
albeit in a reduced quantity, was in part due to its central position in
Orthodox Lutheranism, particularly in education. Even as late as
1703, cantor Georg Motz defended the use of Latin in church music,
citing Luther's aim to preserve Latin in worship alongside the use of
the vernacular.[12] But its use was also in part connected with the continued influence of Italian church music, regularly performed in
Lutheran worship at the time. Latin works composed towards the
end of the century tended to be based on either traditional liturgical
texts such as the Vespers Psalms, or the more popular Latin devotional texts. The eight Latin works by Georg and/or Michael Österreich, for example, comprise three Psalm settings, four settings of the
Sanctus, and one containing a devotional text, *Ubi eras, o bone Jesu*,
which is in fact a reworking of a motet composed several decades
earlier by Francesco Della Porta.

If one takes an overall view of the texts set by the North German
composers in the age of Buxtehude, it is tempting to draw conclusions

---

[12] G. Motz, *Die vertheidigte Kirchen-Music* (n.p., 1703), 49–52.

about the use made of different types of texts by the various different groups of composers, such as those that worked in town and
court environments. But the difficulty with using the surviving corpus of music in this way is that our knowledge is at best patchy, and
there are only a very few composers whose surviving output is large
enough to enable one to draw any meaningful conclusions about
their choice of texts. However, a few vague general impressions can
be gained from surveying the corpus as a whole. It would appear that
the use of German texts, and in particular chorale texts, was more
common in the towns than in the courts. This impression supports
the thesis that Latin texts were more suited to the more cosmopolitan atmosphere at the courts than to the largely uneducated and
parochial congregations at the churches. Only in the output of three
North German composers from the period whose total number of
extant compositions for the church exceeds twenty is the number of
Latin-texted works higher than that of German-texted works. Two
of these composers, Förster and Geist, worked mostly at courts, but
the third, Erben, worked at the Catherinenkirche in Danzig. Erben's
output also includes five chorale settings, and the only extant chorale
settings dating from the 1650s and 1660s are by composers active in
towns: Tunder in Lübeck, Bütner and Strutz in Danzig, and
Melchior Schildt in Hannover. Towards the end of the century the
number of extant chorale works by court and town composers
becomes more equal, but it should be remembered that the numbers
involved are small. In contrast to the early part of the century, when
chorale settings played a very significant part in the output of most
important North German composers, the total proportion of North
German works dating from the second half of the seventeenth century which contain chorales, either as independent chorale settings
or as part of a larger composite text, is only about 13 per cent. The
proportion of works which contain aria texts is higher, but it is even
less possible here to make judgements concerning the social contexts
in which they were used. Buxtehude, who was organist of the
Marienkirche in Lübeck, appears to have employed aria texts with
particular enthusiasm, but then so did Pfleger and Förtsch, who both
worked as *Kapellmeister* at the Gottorf court.[13] Even in cases where a
composer's extant output shows a preference for a particular type of

[13] A full examination of the place of the aria in North German church music has been
carried out by Krummacher in his article 'Das geistliche Aria in Norddeutschland und
Skandinavien'.

text, as with Buxtehude's cultivation of the aria, it is not clear to what extent these represent the interests of the composer concerned or the interests of the clergy or nobility for whom the composer worked.

Throughout the repertoire, the musical structures and styles employed by the composers were closely allied to the texts themselves. Devotional texts in Latin, for example, were nearly always set for solo voice, using a highly expressive style. Directly influenced by Italian models, this scoring reflected the importance of the individual in the texts themselves. Gospel texts which contained reported speech were generally set as dialogues, and poetry was usually set in strophic form. Composite texts provided a clear structure for a composer, as well as implying the use of specific musical styles for the various sections of the text, and the freedom of approach used in the selection of composite texts accounts for many of the multifarious musical structures encountered in the late seventeenth-century repertoire. In the early eighteenth century this flexibility gave way to the more rigid pattern of alternating recitatives and arias found in contemporary Italian music, but for most of Buxtehude's lifetime it meant that composers wrote much more to prescription than to formula. The ingenuity and unpredictability of works based on the principle of *Erbauung* constitute one of the most fascinating as well as idiosyncratic features of late seventeenth-century North German church music.

6

Scoring and Structure

◊

THIS chapter is concerned with what might be described as the external characteristics of individual compositions, that is, their vocal and instrumental scoring, and overall musical structure. The study of scoring brings to light a highly pragmatic and adaptable approach on the part of the seventeenth-century musicians, one that tends to undermine any modern attempts to determine a single 'authentic' manner of performance, whilst an examination of structure reveals in particular the wide range of techniques adopted by composers to lend unity and coherence to a composition.

SCORING

The protracted hardship of the Thirty Years War inevitably restricted German cultural activity during this period. Johann Vierdanck observed in the foreword to his *Geistliche Concerten* (Rostock, 1643) that in many thousands of places the usual sacred music had been replaced by nothing but weeping and wailing. Although musical activity was far from extinguished altogether, the waning of resources in many towns and courts brought about a reduction in the musical forces available for church music. Large-scale works were avoided, and small-scale church music became the norm in places where resources were scarce. However, after the war there was a sharp increase in the quantity of large-scale church music composed, and the increase in its popularity continued right through to the end of the century, as can be seen from comparing the surviving music in the Düben and Bokemeyer collections. Of the North German church music in the Düben collection, the proportion between the number of works scored for one to three voices and works scored for four or more voices is approximately equal, but in the later Bokemeyer collection, almost two-thirds are scored for four or more voices. In the Düben collection the most favoured vocal scoring is for three voices, whereas in the Bokemeyer collection it is for four voices. A similar pattern can be observed concerning instrumentation. In the Düben collection the proportion of North German works with instrumental forces greater than the trio texture of two violins and continuo is approximately one-half, but this has increased to about two-thirds in the repertoire of the Bokemeyer collection.

However, too great a distinction between large-scale and small-scale church music can be misleading. One of the most remarkable features of the repertoire is the way in which the scoring of a work could be changed to suit the forces available, so that a small-scale work could be enlarged to become a large-scale work and vice versa. The Hamburg cantor Thomas Selle comments on this flexibility in the introduction to his manuscript 'Opera Omnia', written only a few months before his death in 1663. In the following passage he explains why he provided extra parts to his small-scale works:

Die kleinen Concerten mit wenig stimmen, die in etlichen Ohren in grossen Kirchen allzu bloß klingen wollen, hat der Autor vermehret mit Capellis fidiciniis und Vocalibus, damit sie desto völliger hereintretten u. die Musici Instrumentales, deren hier in Hamburg eine Zimbliche anZahl, neben den übrigen Vocalisten auch mögen zu thun haben.[1]

(The small concertos with few voices, which in large churches sound too bare to some ears, the author has strengthened with string and vocal choirs, so that these join in the more fully, and the instrumentalists, of whom there are a fair number here in Hamburg, might also have something to do, as well as the other singers.)

The three normal methods of expanding a small-scale work into a large-scale one were as follows: (i) the addition of a secondary choir, usually called the 'Capella', which serves to reinforce the principal vocal group at full sections; (ii) the addition of a secondary instrumental group, usually named the 'Ripieno', which functions in the same way as the vocal 'Capella'; (iii) the addition of string parts to the middle of the instrumental texture (normally for either viola or viola

---

[1] The foreword can be found in the 'Liber primus TABULATURA' containing 'Concertuum Latino Sacrorum' which forms part of Selle's Opera Omnia, housed in the manuscript department of the Staats- und Universitätsbibliothek, Hamburg.

da gamba), so that the basic trio texture is fleshed out into one of
either four or five parts. The first method is described by Fuhrmann
in his *Musicalischer-Trichter* of 1706. He states that the function of a
Capella is to provide 'Pracht und Stärckung' (splendour and
strengthening), adding that it can be omitted in the absence of sufficient personnel. The tailoring of vocal and instrumental forces to suit
the time and place also took place in contemporary Italian church
music. The provision of an extra choir is suggested by I. Donati in
the preface to his *Salmi boscarecci* of 1623,[2] and examples of the practice can be found in the Psalm settings of Foggia in the Düben collection. Optional string parts in the middle of the instrumental
texture appear in Rigatti's *Messa e salmi* of 1640.[3]

   The optional addition of a 'Capella' is indicated clearly in the
manuscript of the concerto *Ad sacram mensam* by Johann Sebastiani of
Königsberg. The work is scored for the vocal forces of SSATB 'con
la Capella se piace a 5'. A more complex arrangement is found in
some works. Bütner's *Frohlocket mit Händen* is described on its title-
page as 'A 8 voci con li stromenti e 6 capella'. The '8 voci' are
divided into two groups—SSA, 'Basetto', and ATTB—and the
Capella comprises SSATTB. Many works survive in the Düben collection in parts as well as in tablature scores, and the use of additional
vocal parts is verified through the presence of several such Capella
parts in the collection. The Bokemeyer collection consists chiefly of
scores in modern staff-notation, but here the use of Capella parts is
indicated by the appearance of the word 'Capella' at the tutti sections
of several works as well as on title-pages.[4] The use of an additional
instrumental group may be illustrated by Förtsch's concerto *Ich
vergeße was dahinten ist*. The title-page refers to both a strengthening
vocal group (here described as 'pro Ripieno') and a reinforcing
instrumental group, to be used 'se piace', 'if desired':

Ich vergeße was dahinten ist.

à 10, 15 et 20.

2 Violini ⎫
2 Viole ⎬
Fagotto ⎭

et

---

[2] Roche, *North Italian Church Music*, 132.   [3] Ibid, 138.
[4] See e.g. the score of Johann Theile's *Beatus vir* in the Bokemeyer collection.

2 Violini ⎫
2 Viole ⎬ pro sopplemento se piace
Violoncino ⎭

2 Canti ⎫
Alto ⎪
⎬ in Concerto
Tenore ⎪
Basso ⎭

2 Canti ⎫
Alto ⎪
⎬ pro Ripieno
Tenore ⎪
Basso ⎭

con
Organo.

The varying ways in which the work could be performed are underlined by the numbers given underneath the title of the work.

The addition of string parts to the middle of the texture can be
found in several works in the Düben collection. Düben himself
added them to many works in his collection, both German and
Italian, for example, to Weiland's motet *Salve o Jesu*, which contained
an instrumentation of just 2 violins and continuo in the original publication,[5] and to two motets by Foggia, *Excelsi luminis* and *Laetantes
canite*, both originally scored for SSB, two violins, and continuo. The
latter work is headed by Düben 'Laetantes canite complimente'. The
extra string parts, either for violas or violins low in their register, are
always simple in nature, designed to fill out the texture rather than
add melodic or motivic interest to the work, as can be seen in the
opening instrumental phrase of Foggia's *Laetantes canite*, shown in Ex.
6.1. That such middle parts were intended to be optional, like those
in Rigatti's *Messa e salmi* of 1640, is suggested by his use of the phrase
'ad placitum' in connection with his added string parts to the motet
Cogita o homo by Albrici.

The relatively few publications of concertos by North German
composers in the age of Buxtehude contain mostly works for small-
scale forces, probably on account of the cost of printing and the
desire to maximize sales. Moreover, the composers also sometimes
indicated that some vocal or instrumental parts of the larger-scale
works in a collection could be omitted in the absence of a sufficient

[5] J. J. Weiland, *Deuterotokos: Hoc est Sacratissimarum odarum partus* (Bremen, 1656).

Ex. 6.1. Foggia/Düben, *Laetantes canite*

number of musicians. Two of the works in Rubert's *Musicalische Seelen-Erquickung* (of 1664) contain alto and tenor viola parts marked 'si placet', and one of the works, *Ich weis mein Gott*, even contains a non–Capella vocal part that is indicated as optional, so that the vocal scoring could be either SSB or just SS.[6]

In a few isolated works the flexible approach to scoring even went as far as the addition of instrumental parts to works that were originally for voices and continuo alone, or the removal of string parts from works originally for voices, instruments, and continuo. In the case of Förster's *In tribulationibus*, which exists in the Düben collection in two versions, one with instrumental parts and one without, it is not clear which represents the original scoring of the piece. Ex. 6.2 shows a typical passage given to voices alone in one version, and divided between voices and instruments in the other. A manuscript in the Bokemeyer collection, dated 1701, contains a version of Della Porta's motet *Ubi eras, o bone Jesu*, originally for two voices and continuo, in which Österreich has added three string parts. The reverse process can be seen in a manuscript of unknown origin in the Düben collection. In this case, one of Monteverdi's settings of *Nisi Dominus*, originally for STB, 2 violins, and continuo, has had its instrumental parts removed.[7]

String instruments formed the core of the instrumentation of North German church music of the late seventeenth century. Some 80 per cent of the North German works in the main part of the Bokemeyer collection have instrumental scorings of strings and

---

[6] See also the remarks in the foreword to Johann Vierdanck's *Geistliche Concerten* (Rostock, 1643).

[7] Vok. mus. i hdskr. 35:9b, incorrectly ascribed to Rovetta. The alteration of the work has been carried out in a rather clumsy manner. The *Nisi Dominus* by Monteverdi is that for STB, 2 violins, and basso continuo in his *Messa a quattro voci, et Salmi* . . . (Venice, 1650).

Ex. 6.2. Förster, *In tribulationibus*: (*a*) version for voices and b.c. only; (*b*) version for voices, instruments, and b.c.

continuo alone. The standard Baroque trio texture of two violins and continuo was popular throughout the period, particularly around the middle of the seventeenth century, and this texture was at times expanded to give a richer sonority by the addition of simple fill-in parts in the middle of the texture. But a significant minority of works was scored for a full five- or six-part string texture in which the middle string parts are contrapuntally as well as harmonically active, thus forming an important musical component of the work. Such works were often, though not exclusively, based on devotional texts and featured a solo singer. Closely based on Italian models, the full string texture added an appropriate sense of *gravitas* to the overall sonority of a work. One of the earliest Italian examples of this type of texture is found in a work based on the most popular of all devotional texts, the *Jesu dulcis memoria*, by F. Marini, published in the collection *Concerti spirituali* (Venice, 1637).[8] Italian examples which survive in the Düben collection include Rigatti's *Ave Regina coelorum*, copied with the altered text *Ave Regnator coelorum* found in Profe's anthology RISM 1646[4], and Rovetta's *Salve Regina*, copied as *Salve mi Jesu* under the name of Franz Tunder,[9] both scored for solo voice and five-part strings. North German composers who imitated this type of scoring include Erben, Pfleger, Meder, and Ritter, whose devotional motet *O amantissime sponse* is scored for soprano solo and five-part strings (see Ex. 4.2).

Perhaps the most significant change that occurred in the use of strings during Buxtehude's lifetime was the introduction around the turn of the eighteenth century of the Italian unison manner of violin-playing, whereby several violins play the same part. Buxtehude himself used the technique late in life,[10] and a number of examples can be found in the Bokemeyer collection. Italian precedents can be seen in works by composers such as Bassani, Polaroli, and Pistocchi,[11] and the earliest examples of the use of this type of violin-grouping amongst the North German composers include Österreich's 'Motetto concertato' *Alle Menschen müßen sterben* (dated 1701), where the indication 'NB Violini 1 et 2 in Unisono' may be found, and Schürmann's *Es wird ein Stern aus Jacob auffgehen*.

Around the middle of the seventeenth century the traditional

---

[8] Roche, *North Italian Church Music*, 87.   [9] See p. 82.

[10] See Snyder, *Dieterich Buxtehude*, 382–3.

[11] See e.g. the works numbered 104, 725, and 758 in Kümmerling, *Katalog der Sammlung Bokemeyer*.

ensemble of cornetts and trombones was still in common use in large-scale Italian and German church music. Large-scale works by Venetian composers were often scored with a five-part instrumental texture for either two cornetts and three trombones (the third of which being a 'trombone basso'), or two violins and three trombones, and many North Germans imitated these scorings. The copy of Rovetta's *Laudate Dominum* in the Düben collection, for example, calls for either violins or cornetts for the top two parts and three trombones beneath. A similarly flexible approach can be seen in the large-scale works by the mid-seventeenth-century Danzig composer Cratone Bütner, many of which call for the use of either trombones or violas for the lower instrumental parts, as in *Ei du frommer und getreuer Knecht*. However, the use of cornetts and trombones became increasingly rare towards the end of the seventeenth century, and in the early decades of the eighteenth century the horn came to replace the trombone as the normal alternative to the viola, as can be seen in the later additions to the Bokemeyer collection. By contrast, trumpets and timpani played an important role in the instrumentation of large-scale works throughout the period. They were almost exclusively used in response to the text being set, either to add splendour and brilliance to texts of praise such as the Sanctus or Te Deum, as in Bütner's *Te Deum* (Danzig, 1662), or to depict scenes of battle such as that appropriate to the celebration of the feast of St Michael and All Angels, as in Werner's *Es erhub sich ein Streit*, or to the setting of Ps. 2 with its reference to warring nations, as in Theile's *Warum toben die Heyden*. At the Dresden court, sacred works were often performed with large numbers of trumpets and drums, presumably borrowed from the ranks of the military musicians at the court. The court diaries record that Peranda's *Herr Gott dich loben wir* was performed with twenty trumpets and three pairs of timpani on the feast-day of the Birth of John the Baptist in 1674.[12] Although there are no surviving records of the use of such huge forces in church music in the North German region, the use of smaller numbers of trumpets and timpani in the North was common in towns and courts alike. Fifteen large-scale North German works in the Lüneburg inventory are listed as having parts for trumpets and timpani, and a further nine with parts for trumpets without timpani. Most of these works are by

---

[12] M. Fürstenau, *Zur Geschichte der Musik und Theaters am Hofe zu Dresden* (Dresden, 1861; repr. 1971), 183.

the Hamburg cantor Joachim Gerstenbüttel and the Lüneburg cantor August Braun.

Some aspects of the instrumentation of North German church music of the period illustrate an independence from Italian models. First, the German musicians made greater use of instruments in general, and of woodwind instruments in particular. Second, the developments in instrumentation that took place towards the end of the century came largely from French, rather than Italian, influence. Where resources allowed, North German composers continued the tradition of large-scale works employing multiple groups of instruments found in the music of Michael Praetorius (who died shortly after the outbreak of the Thirty Years War). The largest instrumental forces tended to arise from the addition of both the trumpet and drum grouping and the cornett and trombone ensemble to the basic string texture, as in Ritter's *Gelobet sey der Name des Herren* (dated 1672), Buxtehude's *Benedicam Dominum in omni tempore* (BuxWV 113) and Theile's *Herr unser Herrscher*, the rousing opening of which is shown in Ex. 6.3. The traditional German love of woodwind instruments can be seen in the importance of the recorder in the repertoire. Recorders, generally called either 'flauti' or 'fleute doux', appear in only one Italian work in circulation in the North German region in this period,[13] whereas they are found in twelve North German works in the Düben collection alone. They are often used by the German composers in connection with pastoral references, as in Förster's Christmas motet *Ah peccatores*, which contains the angel's announcement to the shepherds concerning the birth of Christ. Ex. 6.4 shows the beginning of a passage from this work clearly influenced by the Italian pastorale style.

French influence on the instrumentation of North German church music can be seen in the use of the transverse flute, the oboe, and the bassoon. Although all three instruments had their antecedents in German instruments, the crucial developments that led to the use of these three instruments in late Baroque music all took place in France, a fact that was acknowledged unashamedly by Johann Quantz in his *Versuch einer Anweisung die Flöte traversiere zu spielen* (Berlin, 1752).[14] The transverse flute is indicated in the score

[13] G. Casati, *Laudate Dominum*, listed in the Lüneburg inventory. See Seiffert, 'Die Chorbibliothek der St. Michaelis-Schule in Lüneburg', 602.

[14] See ch. 1, paras. 4–7 in this publication. For a translation, see the edition by E. R. Reilly, *On Playing the Flute* (London, 1966), 30–1.

Ex. 6.3. Theile, *Herr unser Herrscher*

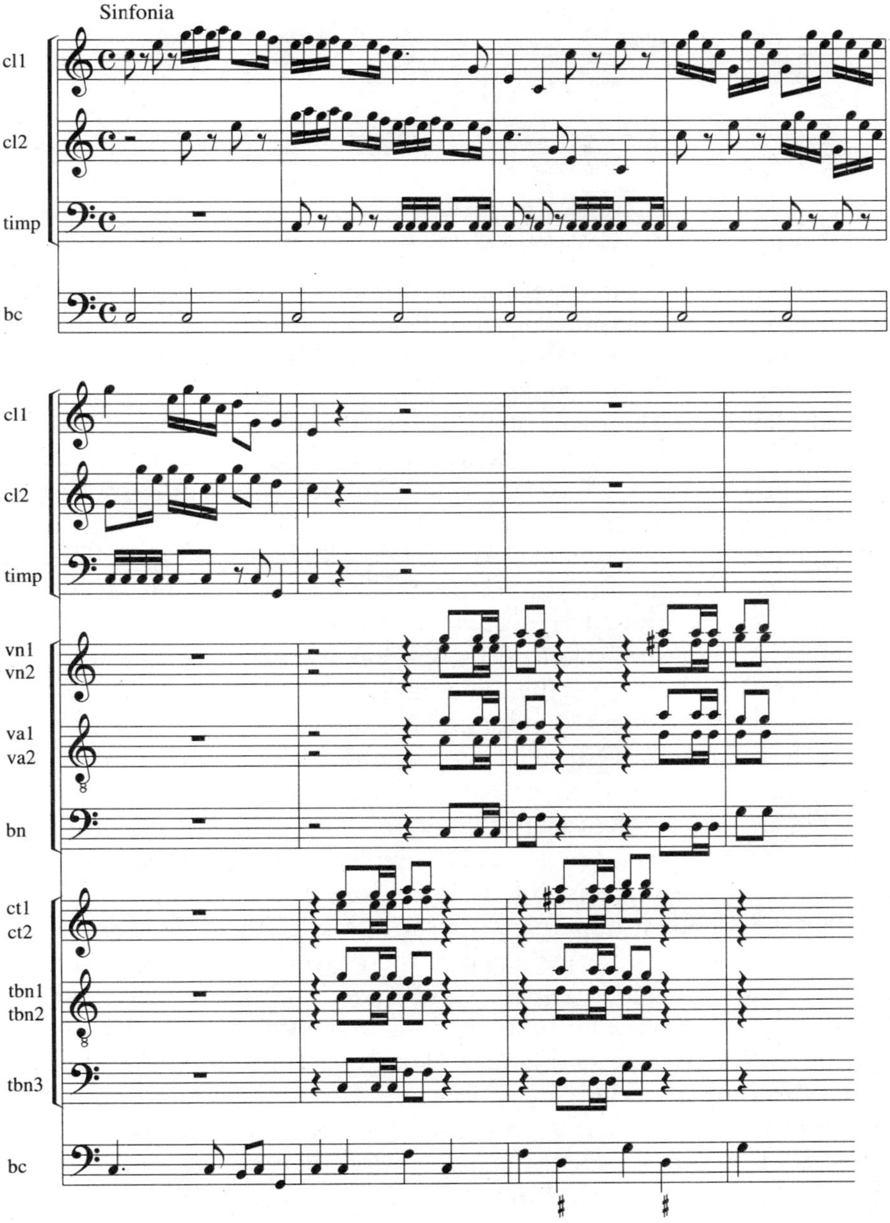

Ex. 6.4. Förster, *Ah peccatores*

of a motet by the itinerant opera composer Johann Kusser, a musician of Hungarian descent who styled himself Jean Cousser following a period of study with Lully in Paris. Before moving to North Germany in 1690 he was famed for his introduction of the French style of playing at the court at Ansbach. The French influence in Kusser's *Quis det oculis* is evident in the use of French terms in the score: '2 Fl. trav., Haute Contre, Taille, Quinte'. Much more widespread than the use of the transverse flute was the use of the newly developed French instrumental trio of two oboes and bassoon. The French *hautbois* came into use in the North German region during the 1690s. It is mentioned in just two works in the Düben collection, Buxtehude's *O clemens, o mitis* (BuxWV 82) and Meder's *Gott! mein Hertz ist bereit*. In both cases the oboes merely double the violin parts. However, the instrument appears much more frequently in the collection assembled by Österreich at Gottorf, and it is here in the Bokemeyer collection that we see the oboes gaining instrumental parts that are independent from the violins. The earliest dated work in the collection to refer to oboes is Österreich's dialogue *Und Jesus ging aus*, dated 1693, in which the oboes also just double the violins, but fully independent oboe parts appear in his *Weise mir Herr deinen Weg*, dated 1695. Further evidence of the introduction of the oboe in the 1690s is provided by Georg Bronner's *Geistliche Concerten*, published in Hamburg in 1696, in which the concerto *Lobet den Herren alle Heyden* is headed 'con 2 Hau[t]bois è Fagotto'. Another Hamburg composer, the cantor Joachim Gerstenbüttel, suggested the use of the new trio of instruments as an alternative to trumpets in his work *Lobet den Herrn ihr seine Engel*, despite the difficulty caused by the different pitch and ranges of the instruments:

NB. Dieses Stück ist gesetzet mit 4 Voci 2 Clarini Tamburi und 4 Voci. Es kan auch an Stad der Clarinen mit 4 oder 3 Hautboi gemacht werden,

wenn solche ein ton höher transponirt werden und kan man an den Ort
wo die Hautbois sogar tieff hinunter gehen ein 8 höher blasen

(NB. This piece is scored for 4 voices, with 2 trumpets and drums. It can
also be performed with 4 or 3 oboes instead of the trumpets, if these are
transposed up a tone and can be played an octave higher when the oboes
go low.)

The French *basson* was a more versatile instrument than the German
Fagot, and the North German composers were quick to see that the
potential of the instrument lay beyond the mere continuo function
that the German instrument had supplied throughout the seventeenth century. The earliest dated obbligato use of the bassoon in the
Bokemeyer collection also appears in Österreich's *Weise mir Herr
deinen Weg* of 1695. This special use of the bassoon is acknowledged
by the composer in his title-page for the work, which lists the instrument as 'Bassono obligato'. During a tenor 'arioso' section in the
work, scored for 'Oboi solo', 'Bassono solo', and continuo, the bassoon plays mostly in the tenor register, above the continuo part, as
illustrated by Ex. 6.5. Österreich went one stage further in his
Alle Menschen müßen sterben, dated 1701, for this work contains two

Ex. 6.5. Österreich, *Weise mir Herr deinen Weg*

obbligato bassoon parts, heard together in a passage for two basses, two bassoons, and continuo.

Buxtehude's lifetime spanned the development from the multi-sectional structures of the early Baroque to the emergence of the distinct recitative and aria pattern of the late Baroque period. This development went hand in hand with the evolution of modern tonality and other compositional techniques, all of which enabled composers to produce more extended musical movements within a single work. As befits the music of a period of transition, the structural techniques employed by the composers of Buxtehude's time are characterized by diversity rather than conformity. Many of the more complex structures occur as a direct reflection of the careful and imaginative selection of composite texts, but others exist as purely musical inventions, designed to provide an extended work with both shape and coherence. The North German composers adopted all the structural techniques of their Italian contemporaries, but also possessed an extra potential ingredient in the form of the chorale, which allowed them to develop unusually elaborate and varied structures.

Although some very short works comprise but a single section with no change of time signature, the normal structural design of late seventeenth-century North German church music consisted of a succession of short sections in contrasting time signatures, in which the changes of signature corresponded to the sentence structure of the text. A typical short work had a rounded tripartite structure, in which two duple-time sections surrounded one in triple time, or vice versa. In these short works there was very often no repeated material, and this was sometimes also the case in more lengthy works. But throughout the period composers were absorbed with the concept of musical repetition. Even short works based on a brief text from a single source (such as Psalm extracts) were sometimes given shape through repetition, as can be seen in a number of works in Bernhard's *Geistlicher Harmonien, erster Theil. Das ist ein köstlich Ding*, for example, a setting of three verses from Ps. 92, has the structural pattern ABA (3/2– C –3/2), brought about by the repetition of the opening 3/2 section at the conclusion of the work.

The concept of musical repetition was applied to both instrumental and vocal writing. In most works which open with an independent instrumental section, usually entitled either 'Sonata' or 'Sinfonia', the movement stands as a separate entity, merely setting the scene, as it were, for what was to follow. However, opening Sinfonias, when not too protracted, were sometimes repeated once or more during the course of a work. The bipartite Sinfonia at the start of Buxtehude's *Singet dem Herrn* (BuxWV 98) is repeated towards the end of the work, whereas the opening Sonata of Georg Böhm's *Nun komm der Heyden Heylandt* is heard again at the midpoint of the work, and the opening Lamento of Georg Bronner's *Gott hilff mir* from his *Geistliche Concerten* of 1696 is repeated very soon after the start of the work. But the most common form of repeated instrumental sections was that often labelled Ritornello—a brief passage heard several times between vocal sections such as verses of an aria or chorale. Such ritornellos appear as distinct, closed sections, as a conclusion to a vocal section, or as part of a lengthy continuous movement. In some longer works, more than one ritornello may be found. Bernhard's *Currite pastores* has two closed ritornellos, the first sounded twice and the second heard three times. The same pattern can be found in an Italian work that survives in the Düben collection, C. Cecchelli's *Per rigidos montes*. Ritornellos which occur as the final passage in a vocal movement are common in aria sections. Again, Italian composers provided the models for the North German composers, with works such as Albrici's *Cogita o homo*. The use of instrumental ritornellos within a continuous movement is most normally encountered in settings of long Psalm texts, but Buxtehude also employed the technique in a number of his chorale works. Rather than setting each verse as a distinct section, he sometimes set several verses as a continuous movement in which simple chordal settings of the chorale verses are separated by instrumental ritornellos, as in *Nun laßt uns Gott* (BuxWV 81).

The use of recurring vocal phrases within a work arose either from purely musical factors or from the desire to highlight a particular phrase of the text. In the early seventeenth-century Italian motet *Non habemus vinum* by S. Bernardi, included in Profe's anthology RISM 1646[4] and copied into manuscript in the Düben collection, the desire for more wine on the occasion of Jesus's first miracle at the wedding in Cana is given dramatic emphasis by the threefold repetition of the setting of the opening text. Later Italian composers continued to use this type of vocal refrain, and the North Germans followed suit, as can be seen by comparing the structures of two works in the Düben collection, Cossoni's *Morior misera* and Bernhard's *Jubilate Deo*:

C. Cossoni, *Morior misera* (SSB, bc)	C. Bernhard, *Jubilate Deo* (STB, bc)
SSB, bc 'Morior misera'	STB, bc 'Jubilate Deo'
SSB, bc	T, bc
SSB, bc 'Morior misera'	STB, bc 'Jubilate Deo'
S1, bc	B, bc
SSB, bc 'Morior misera'	STB, bc 'Jubilate Deo'
B, bc	S, bc
SSB, bc 'Morior misera'	STB, bc 'Jubilate Deo'
S2, bc	STB, bc
SSB, bc 'Morior misera'	STB, bc 'Jubilate Deo'

In both works the opening portion of text is employed for the refrain, and since this encapsulates the mood of the text as a whole, the refrain fits comfortably when used at any stage during the course of the work. The sombre mood of Cossoni's refrain is created through the use of chromatic movement and echos, whilst the joy of Bernhard's is enhanced by the use of syncopation, as shown in Ex. 6.6. Pfleger made particularly good use of refrain structures in his textually elaborate cycle of Gospel settings. His setting of the story of the Transfiguration, *Und Jesus ward verkläret*, based on Matt. 17, is illuminated by the addition of two Old Testament texts, one from Isa. 6 and the other from Ps. 16. Pfleger employs his setting of these two texts as refrains and states the Isaiah text three times and the Psalm text twice, thus successfully integrating the Old Testament texts into the work as a whole. Similarly, Förster's setting of the parable of Dives and Lazarus, *Vanitas vanitatum*, gains dramatically from the repetition of the setting of the famous dictum 'Vanitas vanitatum et omnia vanitas', also encountered in Albrici's *Quo tendimus mortales*.

The use of repeated vocal and instrumental material was particularly beneficial in the setting of long texts such as complete Psalms composed for liturgical use at Vespers. The most common techniques used by the North German composers in imitation of their Italian contemporaries were the return of the opening instrumental Sinfonia at a later stage in the work, as in Erben's *Dixit Dominus*, the return of the opening vocal phrase, together with its text, as in Nicolaus Strungk's *Laudate pueri*, or the return of the opening vocal music during the Gloria Patri with new words. This latter technique

Ex. 6.6. Bernhard, *Jubilate Deo*

was particularly common, providing a satisfying overall symmetry to the work. In certain works where the Gloria text fitted well under the notes of the opening vocal music of the Psalm the repeat was exact, but in other works the return of the general style of the opening music sufficed. The return of the opening music took place either at the start of the Gloria Patri, as in Förster's *Beatus vir*, or, more usually on account of the textual pun, at the words 'Sicut erat in principio' (as it was in the beginning), as in one of the settings of the Psalm *Nisi Dominus* by Tunder.[15]

The more structurally elaborate works of the period employ the repetition of both instrumental and vocal material. Intricate patterns emerge, especially when strophic arias are involved. One particular structural pattern employed in aria settings deserves to be singled out

[15] This particular setting is the one found in the Düben collection at vok. mus. i hdskr. 36:8, 81:69, 86:56.

because of its apparent popularity. The typical juxtaposition of a brief prose text (usually biblical) with a contemporary poem gave a particular problem to the composer. Since the weight of text tended to lie so heavily within the aria, a setting of the texts was in danger of becoming rather unbalanced, with the prose text receiving insufficient emphasis. The solution was to begin the work with the prose text and to repeat this section at the conclusion of the work after the last aria verse, thus achieving structural symmetry in the process. The opening section might also appear at the mid-point of the work as well as at the end. The Italian Albrici wrote several works in this form which survive in the Düben collection. Among the earliest examples by North German composers are Bernhard's funeral piece *Ich sahe an alles Thun* (Hamburg, 1669), and a secular work by Förster, *Sotto la luna*, one of the few secular works to survive in the Düben collection.[16] The Italian text of the work only serves to underline the ultramontane origin of this type of structure. The North German composers continued to make use of it right through the second half of the seventeenth century. Buxtehude wrote several works in this form, as did younger composers such as Österreich and Förtsch. Albrici's *Sive vivimus* and Österreich's *Du Tochter Zion freue dich*, composed in 1689, have this structure:

Albrici, *Sive vivimus* (SAB, 3vn, bc)	Österreich, *Du Tochter Zion freue dich* (SATB, 2vn, 2va, bc)
Sinfonia: 3vn, bc	Sinfonia: 2vn, 2va, bc
'Sive vivimus': SAB, 3vn, bc	'Du Tochter Zion': SATB, 2vn, 2va, bc
Aria verse 1: S, 3vn, bc	Aria verse 1: S, 2vn, 2va, bc
Aria verse 2: A, 3vn, bc	Aria verse 2: A, 2vn, 2va, bc
Aria verse 3: B, 3vn, bc	Aria verse 3: T, 2vn, 2va, bc
'Sive vivimus': SAB, 3vn, bc	Aria verse 4: B, 2vn, 2VA, bc
	'Du Tochter Zion': SATB, 2vn, 2va, bc

In works written for a single voice, arias are often set in a straightforward strophic manner. But when strophic aria verses are set for each of a group of different voices in turn, the situation is more complex because of the different ranges of the voices. In this event the solution was either to give each voice a different vocal line over the same bass, or to allot the same vocal part to the soprano and tenor verses and another to the alto and bass verses. In the aria of Albrici's

---

[16] Vok. mus. i hdskr. 22:17.

Sive vivimus the basso continuo line remains the same for each verse but the vocal parts are different each time. In Österreich's *Du Tochter Zion freue dich* the other technique can be observed. The instrumental participation in the aria is the same in both works: each verse concludes with the same instrumental ritornello.

Buxtehude showed particular inventiveness in his use of elaborate aria and ritornello structures. In *Wie schmeckt es so lieblich* (BuxWV 108), scored for SAB, 2vn, bc, he extends the idea of an identical instrumental ritornello at the conclusion of each verse of an aria to the use of repeated vocal material as well. Each voice is given a solo aria verse containing different though similar music, and this leads directly into a passage for all the voices which is the same in each verse but with different words; this in turn leads directly into an instrumental ritornello which concludes each verse. The structure of his nine-strophe aria *Jesu, komm, mein Trost und Lachen* (BuxWV 58) is particularly fascinating. Each verse has the same six-bar basso continuo line. Moreover, this same basso continuo line also serves for the Sinfonias that separate the verses, but with the last bar repeated. Over this seven-bar basso continuo the upper instrumental parts are different each time. The result is something approaching a set of variations, but two of the verses are brought back to act as refrains.

Chorale settings of the period show the same variety of structural patterns as encountered in aria settings, involving the repetition of both instrumental and vocal passages. A type of structural pattern similar to that illustrated above was also applied to some chorale settings, as can be seen in Gerstenbüttel's setting of the chorale *Wohl dem der in Gottes Furcht steht*. Here, verse 1 of the chorale is set for full voices, SSATB; verses 2 to 5 are given to solo voices, and then the music of verse 1 is repeated at the conclusion of the work with the text of verse 6 of the chorale. In addition, the Sonata which opens the work is repeated between verses 3 and 4. A more complex design can be seen in Österreich's fifteen-verse 'Corale concertato' *Herr Jesu Christ meins Lebens Licht*, composed in 1698. The chorale melody is employed in the opening Sinfonia and sporadically throughout the work, and he maintains interest by setting the chorale in both duple and triple time and by placing in relief the main key of the work, A major, by setting verses in F sharp minor and D major. The music of verses 1–6 is repeated for verses 7–12; the complete structural pattern of the work is as follows:

G. Österreich, *Herr Jesu Christ meins Lebens Licht*
(SATB, 2vn, 2va, bc)

Sinfonia: 2vn, 2va, bc			a	A major
Verse 1:	Tutti		b	A major
Verse 2:		S, 2va, bc	c	F sharp minor
Verse 3:		BB, 2vn, 2va, bc	d	D major
Verse 4:	Tutti		e	A major
Verse 5:		T, 2vn, 2va, bc	f	A major
Verse 6:		A, bc	g	A major
Sinfonia: 2vn, 2va, bc			a	A major
Verse 7:	Tutti		b	A major
Verse 8:		S, 2va, bc	c	F sharp minor
Verse 9:		BB, 2vn, 2va, bc	d	D major
Verse 10:	Tutti		e	A major
Verse 11:		T, 2vn, 2va, bc	f	A major
Verse 12:		A, bc	g	A major
Verse 13:	Tutti		h	A major
Verse 14:	Tutti		e	A major
Verse 15:	Tutti		i	A major

The structural use of chorales in long works based on composite texts took a variety of forms. The simplest manner was to present a chorale verse or group of verses at the conclusion of a work, but some composers sought to integrate the chorale more fully into the work as a whole. In *Herr Jesu Christ du höchstes Guth*, attributed to J. W. F. (probably J. W. Franck) in a manuscript at Wolfenbüttel, the chorale is used at the outset of the work and again during the work's 'secunda pars'.[17] Österreich employs a chorale to break up an aria in his Concerto *Aller Augen warten auf dich*, which otherwise has a structural outline like that of his *Du Tochter Zion freue dich* shown above. In Georg von Bertuch's *Gott der Herr, der mächtige redet* the composer states the first verse of the chorale 'Wachet auf, ruft uns die Stimme' as a cantus firmus in the soprano part during the opening section for bass solo, and subsequently utilizes the second and third verses at the conclusion of the work, following a four-verse aria.

Towards the end of Buxtehude's life, Italian vocal music moved gradually towards the final clear demarcation of recitative and aria styles. Recitative sections became more secco in style, and arias tended to be through-composed rather than strophic in structure.

[17] The manuscript is no. 294 in E. Vogel, *Die Handschriften der Herzoglichen Bibliothek zu Wolfenbüttel, 8: Die Handschriften nebst älteren Druckwerken der Musik-Abtheilung* (Wolfenbüttel, 1890), 61–2.

Although the older patchwork type of structure remained in vogue for Psalm settings, motets came to be composed increasingly as a succession of separate recitatives and through-composed arias. The solo motet *Ecce jubar* by Giovanni Colonna, who died in 1695, contains at the heart of the work an alternation of recitatives and arias, and this new format can also be seen in works by Polaroli and Giovanni Bassani which were probably copied before Österreich's departure from Gottorf in 1702.[18] The final development of the form came with the introduction of the da capo aria, and the establishment of the following structural pattern: aria, recitative, aria, concluding Alleluia or Amen. The solo bass motet *Volate nubila* by Giuseppe Aldrovandini (1672/3–1707), containing two da capo arias, exhibits this plan, and this work may also have been copied at Gottorf before 1702. In the Italian tradition the structural intricacy of individual works had thus shifted from overall construction of a piece consisting of many distinct sections, to the organization of individual aria movements, as seen in contemporary secular vocal music. Instrumental writing became more integrated with the vocal writing, and ritornellos became part of the aria structure rather than an addition to it, and solo vocal display became ever more prominent. The development also further enlarged the difference between Psalm settings and motets. The former, normally set for an ensemble of voices, retained a diverse multi-sectional structure, whereas the motet, usually for a solo voice, followed the structural outline just described, employing da capo arias.

The North German composers continued to feed in general on the structural and stylistic developments of the Italian composers, and thus abandoned the strophic aria in favour of the through-composed aria, and adopted the alternation of aria and recitative as the basic structural pattern of their works. But their affinity for spiritual *Erbauung* and composite texts including chorales bred a more flexible and varied approach to structural matters, and less interest in extended vocal exhibition (which had always been strongly denounced by the Pietists). Although short works based on a text from a single source continued to be written around the turn of the

---

[18] The manuscripts of these works (see Kümmerling, *Katalog der Sammlung Bokemeyer*, nos. 67 and 758) carry the so-called Gottorf-numbering identified by Kümmerling. Österreich left Gottorf in 1702, and judging from the dates which survive in some of the manuscripts it would seem likely that most if not all of the works with Gottorf numbers were copied before 1702. See Kümmerling, ibid. 10–12.

eighteenth century, the pride of a composer's output was without doubt the large-scale work based on a composite text with distinct recitative, aria, and tutti movements. The clearer divisions that came to exist between individual sections of a work in the period around the year 1700 also allowed the introduction of independent fugal sections. The Italians tended to compose a fugue for the final movements of their compositions, both in Psalms and motets, but the German composers often made use of fugue at various places during the course of a work. All these structural developments can be observed in the later works of Österreich, but they appear more consistently in the works of Georg Caspar Schürmann, who worked in Hamburg before moving to Wolfenbüttel in 1697. His Christmas motet *Siehe, eine Jungfrau ist schwanger* will serve as an illustration of the new type of structure:

G. Schürmann, *Siehe, eine Jungfrau ist schwanger*
(SATB, 2vn, 2va, bc)

Free section:	B, 2vn, 2va, bc
Recitative:	S, bc
Aria:	S, 2vn, 2va, bc
Fugue:	Tutti
Aria:	A, vn, bc
Recitative:	B, bc; T, bc
Duet:	TB, 2vn, bc
Free section:	A, bc; Tutti
Chorale:	Tutti

The typical Italian alternation of aria and recitative can clearly be seen, but there are other sections included according to the demands of the text, and a substantial fugue in the first half of the work. The final part of the work is taken up with the Christmas chorale 'Vom Himmel hoch'. Schürmann's output contains the earliest dated da capo arias in the work of a North German composer, found in a group of compositions written for the feast of Pentecost whilst the composer was working temporarily at Meiningen in 1705, following his trip to Italy in 1701.

7

Compositional Techniques

◊

THE compositional techniques that can be observed in the North German church music of Buxtehude's era include both the new seventeenth-century Italian techniques that were adopted by German composers in all fields of composition, and older Italian techniques that were maintained specifically in the realm of church music. An examination of the sacred repertoire thus provides a case study in the development of techniques such as the growth of harmonic sequence, new patterns of tonal organization, and the cultivation of different rhythmic metres, whilst also revealing the continued use of techniques such as polyphony and *falsobordone*. In addition, specifically German techniques can be identified in relation to the setting of chorales.

HARMONY AND TONALITY

Buxtehude's lifetime covered most of the period of transition between the use of modes and modern tonality. As noted in Chapter 1, books on the modes were still being published in Germany as late as 1652, but in 1706, a year before Buxtehude's death, Fuhrmann's *Musicalischer-Trichter* signalled the death of the modal system by asserting that only two, the Ionian and Dorian, remained in common use. However, Fuhrmann's comment also reminds us that the complete systematic working out of major and minor keys had yet to take place, and explains why composers of the period continued to write in what we now call D minor with no flat in the key signature, in G minor with only one flat, and so on. A further reminder of the lingering presence of modes is provided by the continuing use of the Phrygian cadence, in which the bass line descends by semitone from

F to E. All four of the motets by Matthias Weckmann contained in a Lüneburg manuscript dated 1663, for example, contain a Phrygian cadence at the entry of the voices.[1] The use of particular keys for composition was naturally dependent on tuning. During the early part of Buxtehude's life only a comparatively small number of keys was available for comfortable use. A. V. Jones has noted that the most frequently used major key in the motets of Carissimi is F major and the most frequently used minor key is G minor,[2] and the same is true of the motets by Carissimi's North German pupil Kaspar Förster. The rarest keys employed at this time were those which would require three flats or sharps in modern notation. Of these the two most common were C minor and A major, though in the second half of the century the keys of F sharp minor and E flat major also began to be used. Towards the end of the century the keys that would require four sharps or flats in modern notation were occasionally used. Of these the key of E major was the most common (notated usually with three sharps in the key signature),[3] as found in von Bertuch's motet *Du Tochter Zion freue dich.*

One of the clearest features in the development of tonal writing during the seventeenth century is the changing structural role of keys. In the early part of the period, the tonality within the various short sections that made up a work was not stable; thus it was not necessary for a particular section to end in the same key that it had started in. The only factor governing tonal planning was that the work as a whole should contain enough brief excursions to other key centres to throw the main tonal centre in relief, thus avoiding monotony. A representative example is one of Tunder's settings of *Nisi Dominus*:[4]

	Opening key	Closing key
Sonata	C major	C major
Nisi Dominus (soli)	C major	C major
Nisi Dominus (tutti)	A minor	C major
Vanum est vobis	C major	D major
Ecce haereditas	D major	F major

[1] The manuscript is Mus. ant. pract. K. N. 207/6 in the Ratsbücherei, Lüneburg, and the works have been edited by A. Silbiger: Matthias Weckmann, *Four Sacred Concertos* (Recent Researches in the Music of the Baroque Era, 46; Madison, 1984).

[2] Jones, *The Motets of Carissimi*, i. 149.

[3] Meder's motet *Vox mitte clamorem*, also in the key of E major, is notated in the Düben collection with just two sharps in the key signature.

[4] Düben collection, vok. mus. i hdskr. 36:8, 81:69, 86:56.

	Opening key	Closing key
Sicut sagittae	F major	C major
Beatus vir	E major	C major
Gloria (soli)	G major	C major
Gloria (tutti)	A minor	C major

Other than the home key of C major there is no clear hierarchy in the tonal centres employed, and in parts of the work it is not at all clear which tonal centre, if any, is prevalent. In multi-sectional works in general the cadence at the conclusion of one section might prepare the listener for the tonal centre of the ensuing section, whilst in other places the listener might be taken by surprise by an unexpected chord. But such surprises are normally the result of only superficial changes of tonal centre, as can be seen at the start of the 'Beatus vir' section in Tunder's *Nisi Dominus*. The previous section ends in C major and the 'Beatus vir' is announced by a chord of E major, but within eight bars the music has cadenced back in the home key of C major. One of the striking features of the tonal plan of works such as Tunder's *Nisi Dominus* is that apart from sections in the home tonal centre, no other sections begin and end on the same chord. By the time of Buxtehude's death, however, free-standing sections within a single key had become a standard feature of tonal organization. At the heart of this change lay the cultivation of more extended and distinct sections such as through-composed arias. The dramatic motet by Österreich *Weise mir Herr deinen Weg* (dated 1695), for example, is in the key of A minor, but separate, closed sections are contained within the work in the keys of C major and E minor.

This change in the overall tonal organization of works was facilitated by the development of harmonic practice at a more fundamental level of musical composition. In the music of Buxtehude's youth, the use of harmonic sequence was for the most part limited to the repetition of short phrases based on root-position triads, but during Buxtehude's lifetime the cultivation of longer themes with their own sense of harmonic direction, and the development of more elaborate forms of harmonic sequence allowed composers to construct movements on a broader canvas. The earlier technique can be seen in the music of composers of the generation of Tunder (born 1614), Förster (born 1616), and Bütner (born 1616), but signs of change are clearly evident in the music of the next generation of composers, including Buxtehude (born c.1637) and Christian Geist (born c.1640). Ex. 7.1 contains the opening bars from two compositions by Geist copied

Ex. 7.1. (*a*) Geist, *Alleluia. Virgo Deum*; (*b*) Geist, *Domine qui das salutem*

into the Düben collection in the early 1670s: *Alleluia. Virgo Deum* and *Domine qui das salutem*.[5] The first extract consists of a typical early seventeenth-century harmonic progression based mainly on simple root-position chords, which opens with the repetition of a short phrase up a whole tone. However, the second extract shows Geist rushing headlong into the new type of sequence based on the use of suspended sevenths. North German composers of the next generation show a complete mastery of the harmonic sequence, which was becoming an increasingly important tool in the composer's armoury. The opening section of *Die Zeit meines Abschieds ist vorhanden* by Nicolaus Bruhns (1665–97), for example, is dominated by the sequence based on a circle of fifths with seventh chords. Ex. 7.2 con-

---

[5] Geist began work as a musician at the court in 1670, and the manuscripts of these two works are dated 1672 (*Verbum caro factum est*) and 1679 (*Jesu delitium vultus*), though it is not clear whether these dates also represent the dates of composition.

Ex. 7.2. von Bertuch, *Gott der Herr, der mächtige redet*

(Alla breve)

tains three excerpts from the basso continuo part of the concluding section of von Bertuch's *Gott der Herr, der mächtige redet*, illustrating three of the harmonic sequences employed in this section, an extended fugal working out of the chorale 'Wachet auf'. Although this particular work is not musically of the highest quality, it is interesting to note the way the composer has employed the harmonic sequence as the principal means of composing a work of considerable length. The copyist has noted the overall length of the piece by adding '837 T.' at the end of the composition.

Suspensions and passing notes dominated the forms of diatonic dissonance employed during Buxtehude's lifetime. In addition to the regular suspensions employing a suspended fourth, seventh, or ninth, some composers indulged in the double suspension 11–9 (or 9–7) to 10–8 (8–6). This was a characteristically French rather than Italian form of dissonance, and was used by composers active in the 1670s and later, such as Buxtehude, Geist, and Ritter. Passing notes were of particular importance amongst North German composers in their writing for string instruments in the middle of the texture, either the viola or viola da gamba. Diatonic dissonance also played an important part in cadential formulas, either through the use of a minor or major seventh added to the triad based on the fourth degree of the scale, or by the use of two vocal parts which clash a tone or semitone apart. One particular form of dissonance which was a characteristic element of the recitative style also found its way into the general harmonic language. This consisted of the chord progression 5-3, 7-4-2, 5-3 over a sustained bass note. Ex. 7.3 contains a passage from the

Ex. 7.3. Ritter, *Miserere Christe mei*

opening section of Ritter's motet *Miserere Christe mei*, written for a funeral in 1681, demonstrating the typically French double suspension as well as the dissonant 7-4-2 chord over a pedal.

The chromatic harmony employed by the North German composers of Buxtehude's time can all be traced back to Italian models. Early seventeenth-century Italian techniques, such as the juxtaposition of chords a minor or major third apart, appear in the music of North German composers active around the middle of the seventeenth century, as can be seen in the change between the sections 'Sicut sagittae' and 'Beatus vir' in Tunder's *Nisi Dominus* (see above). Förster makes effective use of this particular technique in his dramatic motet *Congregantes Philistei*, which tells the story of the young David slaying the Philistine Goliath. Immediately after the stone that kills Goliath is thrown, the chorus sings the text 'O mutatio, o vindicta dexterae excelsi' to block chords, and he illustrates the word 'mutatio' (change) with a sudden shift from the chord of A major to a chord of F major. But more common in the music of Buxtehude

and his contemporaries was the chromatic harmony developed by
the mid-seventeenth-century Roman composers. Some specific
chromatic turns of phrase were directly imitated by the North
German composers, as illustrated by Ex. 7.4, which contains identical progressions from Carissimi's *Surrexit pastor* and Förster's *In tribulationibus*, but in general chromatic pasages were usually built on
either a rising or descending chromatic bass line, over which 5-3 and
6-3 chords might be decorated through the use of suspensions. Less
common was a chromatic progression using root-position chords
over a leaping bass line, as seen in the opening Sinfonia of
Weckmann's *Weine nicht*, which contains sequences of root-position
triads such as C–A–d–B–e and D–g–E–a–F♯–b (upper case letters
indicating major triads and lower case minor). The first of these progressions, heard at the very beginning of the work, is identical with
that found at the text 'quoniam non repellet' in Carissimi's motet
Jubilemus omnes. Two particular chromatic chords found in the music
of Förster, the diminished seventh and so-called Neapolitan sixth,
betray clearly the composer's period of study in Italy under Carissimi.
Both chords are used only sparingly and for expressive texts. In
Gentes redemptae the diminished seventh chord appears at the text

Ex. 7.4. (*a*) Carissimi, *Surrexit pastor*; (*b*) Förster, *In tribulationibus* 'mori dignatus est', and in the setting of the parable of Dives and Lazarus, *Vanitas vanitatum*, the Neapolitan sixth chord is used during the phrase 'quia crucior in hac flamma'. The next generation of composers made greater use of the two chords, and the diminished seventh became part of the general musical vocabulary, though it was still used to good effect as a means of textual expression. At the start of Geist's motet *Media vita*, the composer employs the chord to emphasize our mortality. The innocent opening melody in triple time is cut short by a diminished seventh chord, reminding the listener that 'Media vita in morte sumus' (In the midst of life we are in death), as shown in Ex. 7.5. The key of E flat major is thus interrupted by a Gb. This conflict between the major and minor third can be linked to a more widespread technique of introducing the minor third note of the tonic chord shortly before a cadence, without the use of a diminished seventh chord. Italian examples of the technique abound in the Düben collection, and include Mauritio Cazzati's *Carissime frater*. Written, like Geist's *Media vita*, in the unusual key of E flat, Cazzati's piece includes the melodic use of a Gb before a cadence in E flat major and a Db before a cadence in B flat major.

Ex. 7.5. Geist, *Media vita*

COUNTERPOINT

The principal categories of counterpoint employed by the North German composers of Buxtehude's time were the *stile antico*, in which sixteenth-century techniques were perpetuated, exercises in learned counterpoint, and fugue. The *stile antico* was used only by a relatively small group of composers, most of whom had a particular interest in music theory, and was mainly reserved for use in mass settings and funeral motets. Schütz had turned back to a more contrapuntal style towards the end of his life, and his pupil Bernhard

composed a motet for Schütz's funeral specifically in the style of
Palestrina (the piece has not survived). Bernhard himself had carefully set out the parameters of what he called the *stylus gravis* in one
of his music treatises, and his own expertise in the style can be best
observed in his five-part *Missa brevis*. Bernhard's successor as theorist
and practitioner of the *stile antico* was Johann Theile, who wrote several mass settings in this style. Buxtehude's contribution to the genre
includes a *Missa brevis* (BuxWV 114), though this work contains a
number of passages that owe more to the *stile moderno* than the *stile
antico*. The maintenance of the *stile antico* by such composers was not
a German peculiarity since the style had several champions in Italy at
the same time, but a specifically German tradition existed in the use
of chorale melodies for contrapuntal compositions, either mass settings or exercises in learned counterpoint. The chorale-mass had
flowered in the early decades of the seventeenth century, for example in the works of the prolific North German composer Michael
Praetorius, but in the second half of the century its only known
exponent was Bernhard, who wrote two such works, the *Missa
Christ unser Herr zum Jordan kam*, and *Missa Durch Adams Fall*.
However, the tradition of using a chorale melody as the basis for an
exercise in strict counterpoint appears to have been more widespread. Some examples were composed and printed as musical
memorials for worthy figures, friends, or relations, whilst others
appear to have had no external prompting. The former category
includes Bernhard's *Prudentia prudentiana* (Hamburg, 1669),
Buxtehude's setting of *Mit Fried und Freud ich fahr dahin* (BuxWV 76-
1; composed in 1671 and published in Lübeck in 1674), and
Christian Flor's lost setting of *Auf meinen lieben Gott* (Hamburg,
1692). Bernhard's counterpoint is highly complex, as befits the work
of an avid theoretician, and the four verses which make up the work
include voice exchange, inversion, retrograde, and canon.
Buxtehude seems to have known Bernhard's work, since the counterpoint of his two-verse setting of *Mit Fried und Freud ich fahr dahin*
is exactly the same as the first two verses of Bernhard's *Prudentia prudentiana*, composed two years previously.[6] Only the title of Flor's
funeral piece survives, but this indicates that the work was written
with invertible counterpoint. It is not clear how such works were
intended to be performed. The publications of the works by

---

[6] See Snyder, *Dieterich Buxtehude*, 215–16.

Buxtehude and Bernhard include text under the chorale melody itself, and it is thus possible that the chorale melody may have been sung, with various instruments or the organ providing the other (textless) voices, but it is equally possible that they may have been performed as purely instrumental pieces. The title of Flor's publication indicates that the chorale was 'fürs Clavier . . . gesetzt' (set for the keyboard), though this does not necessarily exclude the possibility that the chorale melody itself might have been sung.[7] More obviously vocal in conception are a collection of thirty-two canons by Johann Förtsch for from two to eight voices on the chorale *Christ der du bist der helle Tag*, together with a four-part contrapuntal setting.

Inextricably bound up with developments in harmonic practice, the development of fugal writing during Buxtehude's lifetime consisted of the gradual adoption of longer and more tonally oriented themes. Around the middle of the seventeenth century the contrapuntal technique of the canzona was still widespread, as can be seen in the opening Sinfonia of the motet *Quanta fecisti Domine* by Förster. Headed 'Canzona' in the manuscript,[8] the section is built on a short motif employing the characteristic canzona rhythm of a long followed by two shorts. Although this type of theme died out with the generation of Förster and Bütner, the composers of the next generation continued to write substantial imitative sections based on short motifs, generally either as part of an instrumental Sinfonia or as a concluding vocal 'Amen' or 'Alleluia'. Some typical themes are given in Ex. 7.6, in which two North German examples—taken from Bernhard, *Fürchtet euch nicht*, and Weckmann, *Gegrüsset seist du*—can be compared with typical Italian models, from Peranda, *Dedit abyssus*, and Carisio, *Benedicam Dominum*.

A more ambitious approach can be detected in the increasing use of double or even triple themes, creating more intricate contrapuntal textures, such as that found in the 'Alleluia' section of Geist's *Resurrexi et ad huc tecum sum*, in which two themes are shared out between the solo soprano and the two violins. But soon composers were beginning to experiment with longer themes and take advantage of the developments in sequential harmony, as can be seen at the

---

[7] The repertoire of strict counterpoint for keyboard is examined in F. W. Riedel, 'Strenger und freier Stil in der nord- und süddeutschen Musik für Tasteninstrumente des 17. Jahrhunderts', in *Norddeutsche und nordeuropäische Musik* (Kieler Schriften zur Musikwissenschaft, 16; Kassel, 1965), 63–70.

[8] Düben collection, vok. mus. i hdskr. 54:13.

Ex. 7.6. (*a*) Peranda, *Dedit abyssus*; (*b*) Bernhard, *Fürchtet euch nicht*; (*c*) Carisio, *Benedicam Dominum*; (*d*) Weckmann, *Gegrüsset seist du*

(*a*)

al-le-lu - ia——

(*b*)

al - le - lu - ia——

(*c*)

al   -   le- lu - ia——

(*d*)

al   -   - le - lu- ia

opening of the Sinfonia to Erben's motet *Ante oculos tuos*, given in Ex. 7.7. His theme shows a characteristically mature Baroque construction of a head-motif followed by a long tail contingent upon a chain of suspensions, together with a regular and stylistically contrasting counter-subject. Long fugue subjects were essential to the

Ex. 7.7. Erben, *Ante oculos tuos*

independent fugal sections that became popular around the turn of the eighteenth century. The fugue subject in Österreich's 'Motetto concertato' *Ich bin die Auferstehung* (composed in 1704) modulates to the dominant, prompting the use of a tonal answer, as shown in Ex. 7.8. The effectiveness of this fugal movement as a whole lies not just in musical factors such as the use of a chromatic counter-subject, but also in the careful way in which the musical characteristics of the

Ex. 7.8. Österreich, *Ich bin die Auferstehung*

themes reflect their texts. Österreich breaks up the single biblical sentence 'Und wer da lebet und gläubet an mich der wird nimmermehr sterben' (And whosoever liveth and believeth in me will never die) between subject and counter-subject, providing the word 'lebet' (liveth) with a semiquaver melisma, underlining the word 'nimmermehr' (never) with a repeated dotted rhythm, and supplying a chromatic melisma for 'sterben' (die). Composers particularly interested in counterpoint, such as Theile, explored the possibilities of writing fugues with two or three themes, following the example of Italian composers. Such movements often appeared as the conclusion of complete Psalm settings. A. Gianettini's *Dixit Dominus* and Theile's *Beatus vir*, for example, both conclude with a triple fugue. Towards the end of the seventeenth century, fugal movements were often composed in the 'alla breve' metre, thereby allying the modern contrapuntal technique with the old contrapuntal technique of the *stile antico*. The technique can be seen in Ritter's *Wie lieblich sind deine Wohnungen* (dated 1681), where a short theme is employed, but examples from later decades display more lengthy subjects, often based on chorale melodies, as in several works by Förtsch.

METRE

During Buxtehude's lifetime the time signatures **C** and **₵** were at times used interchangeably, as is evident from the fact that they are sometimes found simultaneously in different vocal or instrumental parts of the same section. But the **₵** time signature was often used to denote a faster tempo than **C**. Thus within a single work the specific change from one to the other might indicate a change of tempo (see p. 190). The **₵** time signature was also closely allied with the *stile antico*, and appears in most of the works composed in this deliberately archaic style, such as Buxtehude's *Missa alla brevis* (BuxWV 114), the title of which seems to underline the metric nature of the piece.[9] In addition, the **₵** time signature was normally used for fugal movements headed *alla breve*, although even here the **C** time signature was sometimes employed.

The change that took place during the second half of the seventeenth century in the use of time signatures indicating triple time can

---

[9] See Snyder, *Dieterich Buxtehude*, 223–6. It is possible that Düben's title may have been intended as a pun on the Latin term 'missa brevis' and the Italian term 'alla breve'.

be illustrated by comparing three publications: Vierdanck's *Geistliche Concerten*, published in 1643, Bernhard's *Geistlicher Harmonien* of 1665, and Bronner's *Geistlicher Concerten*, published in 1696. Vierdanck uses only 3/1; Bernhard uses predominantly 3/2, with one instance of 3/1 and one of 3/4, whereas Bronner regularly employs 3/2 and 3/4, and occasionally 3/8. The frequent use of 3/1 time signatures by many of the earlier composers of the period, such as Vierdanck (born *c.*1605), Tunder (born 1614), and Bütner (born 1616), contrasts strongly with the almost complete absence of this time signature in the music of Förster (born 1616)—a difference that can be traced to the contrasting types of Italian influence on these composers. The music of Tunder and Bütner in particular is heavily dependent upon the music of North Italian composers such as as Rovetta and Monteverdi, whereas Förster was subject to Roman influence. Although the time signature 3/1 was ubiquitous in the music of the North Italian composers, it was used less frequently by the Roman composers that influenced Förster, and this difference shows up clearly in the surviving Italian music in the Düben collection. It is particularly noticeable that 3/1 is completely absent from the group of manuscripts of Italian origin containing music by the Roman composer Francesco Foggia copied in the 1640s. As occurs in most of the music by Foggia, Carissimi, Albrici, and other Roman composers, the large majority of Förster's sections in triple metre are written in 3/2. In both 3/1 and 3/2, black notation was employed by the Italian and North German composers for hemiolas and related rhythmic patterns. During the second half of the century North German composers continued to follow the Italian lead by gradually adopting shorter time-values for sections in simple triple metre, as well as exploring the different possibilities afforded by compound time signatures. 3/4 is found occasionally in the music of Carissimi and Förster (often indicated simply by the number 3), but it becomes increasingly prominent towards the end of the century. 3/8 appears in a small number of works by Buxtehude amongst those in the Düben collection copied in the early 1680s (see BuxWV 11, 35, and 83), and continues to be used sporadically after this time. The earliest compound time signature to be used regularly was 6/4, but this was gradually usurped by 6/8. An early instance of the use of 6/8 in the Düben collection occurs in a secular work with an Italian text by Förster, *Sotto la luna*,[10] and it also appears in some of the later additions

---

[10] Vok. mus. i hdskr. 22:17.

to the collection, including works by Alessandro Melani and Buxtehude, but it only becomes a frequent time signature amongst the music collected by Österreich towards the end of the century. 9/8 and 12/8 also appear in the later works of the Düben collection, but become more common in the music composed in the 1680s and 1690s: 6/8, 9/8, and 12/8 are all found, for example, in the works of Nicolaus Bruhns (1665–97). The earliest datable use of 12/8 in the repertoire occurs in Geist's O caeli sapientia, the copy of which is dated 1670. Its novelty is underlined by the fact that the composer thought fit to write '3' above each group of three quavers in the vocal part.

An extremely rare and fascinating case of the simultaneous use of two time signatures occurs in Weckmann's motet Weine nicht, one of a group of four motets written in 1663. All the triple-time sections in these works are written in 3/1. This is in itself slightly surprising for the date in question, but it should be remembered that Weckmann had not come directly into contact with Roman musicians (as Förster had), and that the manuscript of Italian sacred music copied by him in 1647 contains predominantly North Italian music by Grandi and Monteverdi.[11] In one passage of Weine nicht, vocal writing in 3/1 is combined with instrumental writing in 9/8. Weckmann's desire was to provide a lively concertato instrumental accompaniment to the jubilant vocal passage, but his imagination required the triple sub-division of each semibreve. His solution was to use 9/8, thereby beaming together the notes in the instrumental parts that fitted within each semibreve of the vocal parts. Like Geist, Weckmann also clarified the situation by writing '3' above each group of three quavers.

OSTINATO BASSES

The ostinato bass was, of course, a popular technique amongst North Italian composers during the seventeenth century, and several examples survive in the Düben and Bokemeyer collections, most of which are Psalm settings. One Italian work in the Düben collection, Laudate pueri by Casati, contains specimens of the three main types of ostinato bass used by Italian composers of the period: a 'walking' bass, a rhythmically syncopated theme, and a stepwise descending four-note

[11] See M. Seiffert, 'Matthias Weckmann und das Collegium Musicum in Hamburg', Sammelbände der Internationalen Musik-Gesellschaft, 2 (1901), 76–132.

phrase.[12] All three types of ostinato were employed by the North German composers of the period. The most commonly used type was the 'walking bass', whose exponents included Bütner, Buxtehude, Geist, and Österreich. Monteverdi's six-voice *Beatus vir*, which survives in Weckmann's Lüneburg manuscript as well as the Düben collection,[13] contains a more extended version of Casati's 'walking' bass, the second half of which was employed by Geist in *Quis hostis in coelis* and by Österreich, in the minor, in *Ach Herr wie sind meine Feinde*, as illustrated by Ex. 7.9. The syncopated type of ostinato bass was employed in a typically inventive manner by Weckmann in a section of his motet *Weine nicht*. He states the traditional diatonic form of the ostinato only halfway through the section, having before this employed two versions of the theme that have been chromatically altered by the use of a diminished fourth. The themes used by Casati and Weckmann are shown in Ex. 7.10. The third type of ostinato, a descending four-note phrase, can be found in Pfleger's *Laudate Dominum* and Geist's motet *Seelig, ja seelig*. Like Weckmann, Pfleger and Geist both imprinted their own identity on the tradition by using a slightly adapted version of the traditional theme, as can be seen in Ex. 7.11. Pfleger links together three four-

Ex. 7.9. (*a*) Monteverdi, *Beatus vir* (*Selva morale e spirituale*, a 6 voci); (*b*) Geist, *Quis hostis in coelis*; (*c*) Österreich, *Ach Herr wie sind meine Feinde*

---

[12] See Roche, *North Italian Church Music*, 103.   [13] See p. 56.

Ex. 7.10. (*a*) Casati, *Laudate pueri*; (*b*) Weckmann, *Weine nicht*

(*a*)

(*b*)

Ex. 7.11. (*a*) Casati, *Laudate pueri*; (*b*) Pfleger, *Laudate Dominum*;
(*c*) Geist, *Seelig, ja seelig*

(*a*)

(*b*)

(*c*)

note themes beginning on different pitches, using duple metre, whilst Geist extends the four-note theme down through a complete octave. The most elaborate ostinato bass to be found in the North German church music of the period is probably that in Buxtehude's *Laudate pueri* (BuxWV 69). Rather than merely copying a standard Italian type of theme, Buxtehude invents an eight-bar theme in 4/4 time, employing an unusually high level of rhythmic variety.

FALSOBORDONE

A further Italian compositional technique that found its way to the North German region was the practice of *falsobordone*. This common method of chanting Psalms or Canticles was sometimes used by Italian composers to lend variety to their concertato Psalm settings, as is well known from the Psalms of Monteverdi's celebrated Vespers of 1610. Although the technique can be found in a number of early seventeenth-century North German Psalm settings, such as the *Dixit Dominus* by Selle,[14] it appears to have been used extremely rarely later in the century. The Düben collection only contains one example of the device, found in a setting of *Confitebor tibi Domine* by Förster, who would without doubt have experienced the technique during his stays in Italy.[15] This example is particularly interesting as one of the three verses set in this manner is marked 'Solo falso Bordone'. There are no written-out vocal parts for this verse, suggesting that the verse was intended to be improvised by a soloist. A further example of the technique exists, not in a Psalm setting, but in one of the few published motets of the period, Weiland's *Nun dancket alle Gott* (Wolfenbüttel, 1661). Weiland worked at the court of Wolfenbüttel, and it is possible that he may have learned of the technique from Schütz, who had close connections with the Wolfenbüttel court at this time. There is one passage of *falsobordone* in the work in which a single phrase of text is repeated, as shown in Ex. 7.12.

TECHNIQUES OF CHORALE SETTING

Chorale melodies offered composers the opportunity of exploring many different compositional techniques, ranging from strict cantus firmus to free paraphrase and polyphony. Most settings by Buxtehude and his contemporaries of a chorale melody used as a solo cantus firmus contain non-imitative textures in which the driving force was either expressive dissonance or lively concertato writing. One of the most favoured textures for expressive writing was the use of the soprano voice for the chorale melody pitted against a full four-

---

[14] Contained in the second book of Selle's Opera Omnia, housed in the manuscript department of the Staats- und Universitätsbibliothek, Hamburg.

[15] This setting of *Confitebor tibi Domine* is that found at vok. mus. i hdskr. 21:12.

Ex. 7.12. Weiland, *Nun dancket alle Gott* (1661)

or five-part string texture. Ex. 7.13 contains the opening of Erben's setting of the chorale *Erbarm dich mein o herre Gott*. The contemporary string tremolo style, in which a group of string instruments perform slow-moving expressive harmony using repeated-note quaver patterns (see Ch. 8), was also used as an accompaniment to a chorale cantus firmus, as can be seen in works such as Buxtehude's *Nimm von uns, Herr, du treuer Gott* (BuxWV 78) and Meder's *Ach Herr mich armen Sünder*.[16] The simplest form of concertato accompaniment to a chorale cantus firmus comprised nothing more than an animated basso continuo line, as in verse one of Böhm's setting of the Advent chorale *Nun komm der Heyden Heilandt*, but other settings contain considerably more elaborate concertato writing for either voices or instruments, or both. In Erben's setting of *Herr Christ der einige Gottes Sohn* the concertato string parts in verse 2 of the chorale, set as a cantus firmus in the second soprano part, return in verse 5, where they are used as vocal as well as instrumental parts. Schürmann introduces the chorale 'Vom Himmel hoch' into his Christmas motet *Siehe, eine Jungfrau ist schwanger* with a short introduction for instruments alone. He places the chorale melody untypically in the bass of the texture, which precipitates the harmonic shift from D major to F sharp major at the end of the second phrase, as shown in Ex. 7.14. Some composers, notably Buxtehude, wrote concertato instrumental parts in

[16] For a description of Meder's work, see Rauschning, *Geschichte der Musik und Musikpflege in Danzig*, 290–1.

Ex. 7.13. Erben, *Erbarm dich mein o herre Gott*

conjunction with a setting of the chorale melody for voices in simple four-part harmony. In several of his chorale settings the instrumental writing occurs between each line or pair of lines of the chorale,[17] but the most common technique towards the end of the seventeenth century and at the beginning of the eighteenth was the setting of concertato instrumental parts against the four-part harmonization itself, as can be seen in works such as Meister's *Wie schön leuchtet der Morgenstern* and Schürmann's *Es wird ein Stern aus Jacob auffgehen*. In a few isolated works a chorale cantus firmus is employed in the instrumental parts only, whilst the text is sung by the voices to free parts. This occurs, for example, in Buxtehude, *Gott hilf mir, denn das Wasser geht mir* (BuxWV 34) and verse 4 of Meder's *Ach Herr mich armen Sünder*.[18]

---

[17] See Snyder, *Dieterich Buxtehude*, 189–91.

[18] Rauschning, *Geschichte der Musik und Musikpflege in Danzig*, 291.

Ex. 7.14. Schürmann, *Siehe, eine Jungfrau ist schwanger*

Other settings of chorale melodies were more free in nature, ranging from lightly embellished settings of a cantus firmus to paraphrase
settings in which the chorale melody is almost wholly obscured. It
was these techniques that gave life to the more extended chorale
works of the period, where the uninterrupted use of cantus firmus
techniques might have resulted in monotony. Mild forms of chorale
embellishment were brought about through the application of
Figuren, ranging from simple patterns to more modern effects associated with the recitative style, as illustrated by Ex. 7.15. The former
can be seen at the opening of Bütner's setting of *Vom Himmel hoch*
(Ex. 7.15*a*), which contains three similar four-note patterns, and the
latter at the start of Tunder's setting of *An Wasserflüssen Babylons* (Ex.
7.15*b*), which exhibits the snapped rhythm commonly found in passages of recitative (the crosses indicate the chorale melody). In his
six-verse setting of the chorale *Wend' ab deinen Zorn, lieber Herr, mit*

Ex. 7.15. (a) Bütner, *Vom Himmel hoch*; (b) Tunder, *An Wasserflüssen Babylons*

Gnaden, Tunder alternates between cantus firmus and paraphrase techniques. The first verse of the chorale is set as a cantus firmus, but in the second verse the chorale melody is paraphrased as a duet for two tenors and basso continuo. After another cantus firmus verse the melody is once again heard in paraphrased form, set for two sopranos, alto, and basso continuo, but here the paraphrasing is much freer than in verse 2. A similarly cumulative effect is provided by Böhm in the three verses of the chorale 'Wachet auf, ruft uns die Stimme' included in *Das Himmelreich ist gleich einem Könige*. Verse 1 is set as a solo cantus firmus against a basso continuo accompaniment, verse 2 as a lightly paraphrased chorale duet for alto, tenor, two violas, and basso continuo, and verse 3 as a more freely paraphrased chorale movement for all voices and instruments.

Chorales also formed the melodic basis of imitative movements. In many strict cantus-firmus settings each line of the chorale melody is pre-figured by imitative entries in the other voices (a technique common in organ settings of chorales). In some works the fore-imitation appears in instrumental parts, as in verse 1 of Tunder's *Wend' ab deinen Zorn, lieber Herr, mit Gnaden*, whilst in others it appears in the vocal parts, as in verse 1 of Österreich's multi-verse setting of *Herr Jesu Christ meins Lebens Licht* (dated 1704). But chorale melodies were also used in a freer manner as the material for polyphonic settings, in a tradition that remained little altered from the sixteenth century. Each line of a chorale forms a point of imitation for the entry of all the vocal parts. In the early part of the period this technique can be found in Johann Schop's *Erster Theil geistlicher Concerten* (Hamburg, 1643–4), a publication that shows little stylistic advance on the chorale settings of Michael Praetorius, and in the later part of

Ex. 7.16. Gerstenbüttel, *In dich hab ich gehoffet*

the seventeenth century the technique tended to be employed by the more conservative composers such as Joachim Gerstenbüttel. Such movements were often headed 'alla breve', as in Gerstenbüttel's setting of *In dich hab ich gehoffet*, the opening of which is given in Ex. 7.16. Composers who wished to use a chorale melody in a more modern stylistic context took an individual chorale phrase and used it as the basis for a fugal movement. This often occurs as the final section of a chorale setting for the 'Amen', as in Buxtehude's *Nimm von uns, Herr, du treuer Gott* (BuxWV 78), in which he employs the last line of the chorale melody. A more unusual instance occurs in *Hemmt eure Thränenflut* by Bruhns, in which the final chorale fugue is the only appearance of a chorale melody in the entire work. Headed 'Madrigale' in the manuscript source, the work was clearly intended for use on Easter Day. Rather than incorporating an Easter chorale into the work in an orthodox manner, he merely used the melodic incipit of the chorale for the final 'Amen'. The listeners would have instantly recognized the melody as belonging to one of the best-known of Easter chorales, 'Christ lag in Todesbanden'.

8

Compositional Styles

◊

TOWARDS the end of the seventeenth century the principal stylistic development in vocal music was the gradual polarization of recitative and aria; as the dominant recitative style became increasingly *secco*, consisting of short, formulaic passages, so the aria became more extended and elaborate. But during Buxtehude's youth the demarcation between the two styles was much less clear, allowing composers to move more readily from one to the other and explore the shades of musical possibilities in between them, responding rapidly to the demands of the text. This fluidity of style was recognized by some contemporary theorists, who sought to identify a style unique to church music, part way between recitative and aria.

'ETWAS RECITATIVISCHES'

Christoph Bernhard, writing in his treatise 'Tractatus compositionis augmentatus', states that the true home of recitative is in the theatre. Although his detailed analysis of different forms of recitative includes one entitled the *stylus oratorius*, it is likely that this refers to the more narrative style of recitative that he probably experienced firsthand in the Roman oratories during his stay in Rome, rather than to normal liturgical church music. However, he does refer to the frequent use in church music of 'something recitative-like' ('etwas recitativisches').[1] A similar but more detailed attempt to distinguish between theatrical recitative and the style used in church music can be found in the treatise *Breve discorso sopra la musica moderna* (Warsaw, 1649) by the famous Italian *Kapellmeister* at Warsaw, Marco Scacchi, who had

---

[1] Müller–Blattau, *Die Kompositionslehre Heinrich Schützens*, 43.

close connections with musicians working in Danzig. Scacchi's discourse was written to refute those who complained that modern church music is indistinguishable from the style used in the theatre. He identifies a simple representational type of recitative ('semplice rappresentativo') that is accompanied by acting in the theatre, and a mixed style in which the recitative is interrupted by other styles, which he describes as follows:

il secondo si chiama imbastardito; id est stile mischio, il quale va qualche volta rappresentando l'orazione con lo stile recitativo et in un subito varia con passaggi, e con altra modulazione[2]

(the second is called hybrid, that is, mixed style, which will go on for a while representing the text in the recitative style and then, all of a sudden, will be varied with *passaggi* and other melodic effects)[3]

Referring directly to church music he writes as follows:

ma quello che usano i moderni nella Chiesa alcuna volta, secondo l'occasione, e il luogo che lo ricerca, et anco l'orazione, è un modular variato a differenza del rappresentativo, cioè non è in tutto e per tutto lo stile che s'usa nei teatri.[4]

(What the moderns sometimes use in church, according to the demands of the occasion, the place and also the text, is a varied kind of vocal line as opposed to the representational recitative. Thus it is not altogether the same style as is used in theatres.)[5]

Scacchi and Bernhard thus both refer to a style employed in church music that is similar but not exactly the same as the simple representational style used in theatres. This similarity between the theatrical and church styles is evident in the many passages of solo vocal writing in the North German church music of the time that clearly owe their stylistic origin to the theatrical style of recitative. Such glimpses of the Italian representational style often took the form of simple triadic figures over held chords. Ex. 8.1 shows the two most common shapes, a descending phrase outlining a tonic triad, here taken from Buxtehude's *Singet dem Herrn* (BuxWV 98), and an ascending phrase

[2] Z. M. Szweykowski, 'Stile imbastardito i stile rappresentativo w systemie teoretycznym Marka Scacchiego', *Muzyka*, 19/1 (1974), 21, and Palisca, 'Marco Scacchi's Defence of Modern Music (1649)', in *Studies in the History of Italian Music and Music Theory* (Oxford 1994), 106, 108.

[3] English version from Palisca, 'Marco Scacchi's Defence', 107, 109.

[4] Szweykowski, 'Stile imbastardito i stile rappresentativo', 21, and Palisca, 'Marco Scacchi's Defence', 108.

[5] Palisca, 'Marco Scacchi's Defence', 109.

Ex. 8.1. (*a*) Buxtehude, *Singet dem Herrn* (BuxWV 98); (*b*) Förster, *Et cum ingressus*

which outlines a second-inversion triad, taken from Förster's *Et cum ingressus*. Many passages in the recitative-like style contain *Figuren* listed by Bernhard as being part of the 'stylus luxurians communis', that is, the normal modern style common to all forms of music, both sacred and secular.[6] But the overlap that existed between the theatrical and church styles of recitative was so great that even some of the *Figuren* described by Bernhard as belonging solely to the theatrical style of recitative can also be found in some sacred works of the period, including many of Bernhard's own compositions. Ex. 8.2 shows instances of the use of three of the theatrical *Figuren* described by Bernhard: (i) *heterolepsis* (a leap to a dissonant note that might be in another voice), from Buxtehude, *Canite Jesu nostro* (BuxWV 11); (ii) *ellipsis* (the omission of a normally required consonance), from Meder, *Wie murren denn die Leute*; (iii) *tertia deficiens* (the interval of an augmented second between melody and bass), from Erben, *O Domine Jesu Christe*.

The recitative-like passages in North German church music of the mid-seventeenth century can be broadly divided into two types, corresponding to the categories outlined by Scacchi. Some passages comprise a simple juxtaposition of the representational style with melismatic writing, as in Scacchi's 'recitativo imbastardito', whilst other passages contain more of a blend of styles, recalling his 'varied

---

[6] Examples include the *subsumptio* and *prolongatio*.

Ex. 8.2. (*a*) Buxtehude, *Canite Jesu nostro* (BuxWV 11); (*b*) Meder, *Wie murren denn die Leute*; (*c*) Erben, *O Domine Jesu Christe*

vocal line'. Ex. 8.3 illustrates the two types of recitative with passages from the music of Weckmann. In Ex. 8.3*a*, taken from *Weine nicht*, he opens with a simple parlando style and then breaks into a melisma for 'David', whilst in Ex. 8.3*b*, showing the opening of the Annunciation dialogue *Gegrüsset seist du*, a more melodic style is employed. Although the slow-moving bass line and broken-up vocal line at the start of the dialogue are reminiscent of the theatrical style of recitative, the vocal line itself is much more melodically inspired, and there is a brief passage of motivic interplay between the voice and continuo line. At times the 'varied vocal line' style became highly impassioned and virtuosic in nature, as can be seen in Bernhard's *Anima sterilis*. He probably encountered this idiom at Dresden, where he worked alongside Albrici and Peranda in the late 1650s and early 1660s. Works such as Albrici's *Quo tendimus mortales* and Peranda's *Te solum aestuat* exhibit the same style of recitative, which is characterized by the repetition of phrases to heighten

Ex. 8.3. (*a*) Weckmann, *Weine nicht*; (*b*) Weckmann, *Gegrüsset seist du*

tension, the use of rapid demisemiquaver patterns, and many of the theatrical *Figuren* described by Bernhard.

The closest any North German composer came to the pure representational style of recitative was Förster in his dramatic Latin works that belong to the Roman oratorio tradition, such as *Vanitas vanitatum* and *Viri Israelite*, but most composers preferred to explore the endless possibilities afforded by the 'varied vocal line' and the 'recitativo imbastardito'. Even Pfleger's cycle of Gospel dialogues, which by its nature gave plenty of opportunity for the adoption of a parlando style, contains a negligible amount of such writing. Melodic freedom was essential to the style of mid-seventeenth-century church music, and the lack of a clear distinction between aria and recitative at this time gave the composers liberty to switch rapidly from style to style, responding directly to the demands of the text. However, towards the end of the century the stylistic delineation between recitative and aria became ever more apparent. The varied kind of vocal line of the mid-seventeenth century began to disappear, and distinct passages of recitative purely in the representational style became more common, together with the designation of such passages in the sources by the abbreviation 'Recit.'. One of the earliest Italian examples of the secco style in church music to be found in the North German sources occurs in the Wolfenbüttel manuscript 294.[7] Although its origins are obscure, the manuscript and its contents point to production in the North German region around 1690. It contains mainly church music by North German composers, but also includes an anonymous work in Italian and Latin works by the Italian composers Antonio Rigatti and Giovanni Bassani. Rigatti's music dates from the first half of the seventeenth century, but the inclusion of a work by Bassani, born *c.*1657, shows that the compiler of the manuscript also had copies of the most up-to-date Italian church music. The motet by Bassani, *Quid arma quid bella*, contains two separate passages of secco recitative, both eight bars in length. Although German imitations of this type of recitative are absent from the Wolfenbüttel manuscript, many can be found in the Bokemeyer collection and other sources dating from the 1690s and after. Georg Bronner's *Geistliche Concerten* of 1696 contains just one passage of secco recitative, found in the first motet, *Gott sey mir gnädig*, shown in Ex. 8.4. This short passage demonstrates many of the characteristics of the style, including the beginning of a passage over a first-inversion chord, the lack of melismas, and the conclusion of the passage by the continuo alone, after the voice has ceased.

Some of the most poignant writing to be found in the North German church music of Buxtehude's time occurs in passages of *recitativo accompagnato*. The style appears in a few works by North German composers born in the second and third decades of the century, such as Förster and Bernhard, but becomes more common in those born after *c.*1640, notably Geist, Ritter, and Meder. Like other forms of recitative, the style originated in Italian opera, where a

---

[7] Vogel, *Die Handschriften der Herzoglichen Bibliothek zu Wolfenbüttel*, 61–2.

Ex. 8.4. Bronner, *Gott sey mir gnädig*

single line of recitative was at times accompanied either by violins in the lower part of their range, or by viola da gambas, often at 'ombra' scenes where an especially dark or lugubrious atmosphere was required.[8] Probably the earliest examples of this style in North German church music are those found in the music of Förster. The opening of his motet *Repleta est malis anima*, marked 'Un poco piano e tutto adagio', is scored for alto solo, two violins pitched low, and basso continuo, and there can be no doubt that the texture was employed here to illustrate the grave nature of the text. But the most common texture for accompanied recitative was that using lower stringed instruments, as can be found in Erben's *Ach dass ich doch in meinem Augen*, where the two gamba parts are marked 'per accompagnam.', or violins and lower stringed instruments in combination. One of the finest passages of *recitativo accompagnato* in the repertoire occurs in Geist's *Media vita*, shown in Ex. 8.5, in which the style is of the 'varied' type described by Scacchi. Note the omission of a normally required resolution in the vocal part in the second bar of the extract (Bernhard's *syncopatio catachrestica*), the breaking up of the vocal line with rests at 'sancte fortis' (Bernhard's *abruptio*), and the diminished seventh interval between melody and bass at 'salvator' (Bernhard's *sexta superflua*). Although *recitativo accompagnato* seems to have been most popular amongst North German composers in the 1670s and 1680s, it remained in use well into the next century.

---

[8] See, for example, Act II, Sc. xii of Antonio Cesti's *La Dori*, first performed at Innsbruck in 1657; facs. edn. H. M. Brown (New York, 1981), 153–4.

Ex. 8.5. Geist, *Media vita*

However, as with unaccompanied recitative, the vocal style tended to become more secco and formulaic in nature, as can be seen in the section headed 'Recitativo con Accompag[n]ement de Viol:' in Österreich's *Actus Funebris* of 1702.

THE ARIA STYLE

Strophic arias, whether independent works or subsections of more extended compositions, were closely allied to the contemporary German tradition of aria or song publications for solo voice and accompaniment. Song publications were intended for both church and domestic use, and relied on a simple, popular idiom, with accompaniment nearly always restricted to a basso continuo. Within the sphere of more ambitious church music the style was often very similar, but greater attention was given to the participation of instruments, whether playing within or between the verses, and to the nature of the melodic style, which took its inspiration from contemporary Italian music. Some of the earliest Italian motets found in the Düben collection contain strophic arias. Foggia's motet *Excelsi luminis*, for example, contains a three-verse strophic aria in which two of the most important musical characteristics of the North German strophic aria style can be seen: regular phrase-lengths and motivic consistency. But the influence of the Italian strophic aria style can be seen at a very detailed melodic level, as is demonstrated by the next group of examples, which involve two of the latest Italian works found in the Düben collection, composed by the Roman composer Giovanni Bicilli. The first aria section in *Gloriosum diem colimus* demonstrates a smoothly flowing 3/2 idiom based on four-bar phrases. In Ex. 8.6 the first three phrases of the aria may be compared with the opening of an aria section in Ritter's *Miserere Christe* composed in 1681. Not only is the flow of the melody very similar in the two extracts, but the cadence points at the end of each phrase are the same: half-close on the dominant, cadence in the relative major, and cadence in the dominant. Ex. 8.7 demonstrates specific melodic and rhythmic ideas that migrated from Italian to German soil: a triple-time melodic figure from Bicilli's *Perge curre sequere* found in Bernhard's *Salve mi Jesu*, and a duple-time rhythmic pattern from the same work by Bicilli found in Buxtehude's *Surge anima mea* (from the cycle *Membra Jesu nostri*, BuxWV 75).

Other common Italian aria techniques found in the North German repertoire include the use of fore-imitation by the basso continuo part, hemiola (particularly at cadence points), instrumental participation between the vocal phrases (usually repeating the end of the previous vocal phrase), a *moto perpetuo* basso continuo line (usually quavers in 4/4 time), the use of extended melismas towards the end of an aria, and the so-called 'motto' technique at the opening of an aria. This last procedure, in which the first few notes of the vocal part are repeated after a short break, is perhaps best known in the context of the later da capo aria, but its origins were in the through-composed or strophic aria of the late seventeenth century. Ex. 8.8 shows similar passages in 6/8 metre from Alessandro Melani's motet *Exultent concinant* and Buxtehude's *Jesulein, du Tausendschön* (BuxWV

Ex. 8.6. (*a*) Bicilli, *Gloriosum diem colimus*; (*b*) Ritter, *Miserere Christe mei*

(*a*)

(*b*)

63), in which the accompanying strings also repeat the motto phrase. Strophic arias constructed from short, equal-length vocal phrases remained in use after the turn of the century, as can be seen in Böhm's motet *Wie lieblich sind deine Wohnungen*, composed, according to the manuscript source of the work, in 1709. However, during the 1690s the increasing polarity of recitative and aria led to the development of a fundamentally different type of aria composition, found in the music of Italian composers of the generation of Bassani. In the earlier strophic style the instrumental participation was only of secondary musical importance, and the vocal phrase-lengths

Ex. 8.7. (*a*) Bicilli, *Perge curre sequere*; (*b*) Bernhard, *Salve mi Jesu*; (*c*) Bicilli, *Perge curre sequere*; (*d*) Buxtehude, *Surge anima mea* (*Membra Jesu nostri*, BuxWV 75)

(*a*)

(*b*)

(*c*)

(*d*)

remained more or less constant, only varied by the extension of a phrase by a melisma before the final cadence. In the newer type of aria, based on non-strophic verse, the instrumental participation became of equal musical importance with the vocal part, and the regular phrase-lengths disappeared in favour of free melodic extension and development. The earliest examples of this new type of aria were through-composed, for example 'Ich dancke dir Herr' in Österreich's *Weise mir Herr deinen Weg*, dated 1695. The change in balance

between voice and instruments is apparent at the outset. In the older
form of aria the voice generally began immediately at the beginning,
and the instruments were used mainly to echo the last phrase of the
voice between lines of the text. However, Österreich's section
begins with a lengthy 34-bar instrumental introduction, scored for
oboe, bassoon, and basso continuo (see Ex. 6.5). After presenting the
main theme of the aria the instrumental introduction contains much
motivic and sequential development before the entry of the voice.
The instrumental writing in the new type of aria was thus more independent from the vocal style than before, and many more specifically
instrumental idioms crept into aria writing. The beginning of the aria
'Beherrscher aller Welt' in Schürmann's *Siehe, eine Jungfrau ist
schwanger*, for example, contains a typically incisive Italianate motif
for the violin solo with leaps of an octave, sixth, and seventh respectively, followed by a more restrained entry for the voice, as shown in

Ex. 8.8. (*a*) Melani, *Exultent concinant*; (*b*) Buxtehude, *Jesulein, du
Tausendschön* (BuxWV 63)

(*a*)

Ex. 8.8. *cont.*

(*b*)

Ex. 8.9. These changes in style paved the way for the da capo aria, found in many Italian works in the Bokemeyer collection dating from around the turn of the eighteenth century, but which only became a standard feature of North German church music after Buxtehude's death.

TEXTUAL ILLUSTRATION

Whether setting Latin or German, the North German composers of Buxtehude's time showed an exhaustive preoccupation with correct word setting, both in terms of emphasis and interpretation. Even the most musically uninspired works in the North German repertoire generally show great care on the part of the composer in the setting of the text. Textual illustration, or *hypotyposis*, as Burmeister named

Ex. 8.9. Schürmann, *Siehe, eine Jungfrau ist schwanger*

it in his *Musica Poetica* (1606),[9] took many different forms. Individual words might be illustrated in a single vocal part, for example, or the sense of an entire phrase could be portrayed in the music; in some places only the voice or voices might be involved, but in others the instruments might take the lion's share of the illustration. Obvious examples of word-painting, such as animated melismas for words indicating praise, singing, or victory are ubiquitous, but other examples show a more inventive approach or are associated with specific musical styles. Interrogatives such as 'quis?' and exclamations such as 'O!' or 'Ach!' are usually set as single off-beat notes or chords, and words expressing length of time such as 'semper', 'lange', or 'expectas' are often given held notes or chords. Texts that describe the penitent sinner crying out to God are illustrated by ascending musical phrases, whilst those concerned with earthly things are given low notes. The opening soprano phrase of Bernhard's *Aus der Tiefe ruf' ich Herr, zu dir* (Out of the deep have I cried unto Thee, O Lord) rises from c' to d'', whilst Förster sends his bass soloist down to BBb, for the word 'deficiat' (become weak) in his motet *O bone Jesu*. Settings of words meaning weeping or sighing frequently produced an imaginative response from the composer. The Latin verbs 'fleo' and 'lacrimo' (weep) often provoked a sudden use of the minor third in a major key, not in the form of a minor chord at a cadence but by

---

[9] See M. Ruhnke, *Joachim Burmeister* (Schriften des Landesinstituts für Musikforschung Kiel, 5; Kassel, 1955), 163.

introducing a minor third just before a cadence in the major, creating a bitter-sweet effect. Ex. 8.10 contains a typical Italian example of the effect, taken from Albrici's Psalm setting *In convertendo Dominus*, together with a more elaborate working of the technique by Erben from his motet *Ante oculos tuos* in which the composer takes the effect even further by using an extended undulating vocal line and a diminished seventh chord. An equally impressive though different technique is used by Weckmann for the equivalent German verb 'weinen' in his motet *Wie liegt die Stadt so wüste*, where snapped rhythms and echoes are used to create a sobbing effect.[10] For the verbs meaning to sigh, rests were employed during the word itself, no doubt encouraging the singer to fill the gaps with audible sighing noises. The technique was so common that the term *suspiratio* was adopted by Bernhard and others in their discussion of rhetorical

Ex. 8.10. (*a*) Albrici, *In convertendo Dominus*; (*b*) Erben, *Ante oculos tuos*

Figuren. Geist adopts the *suspiratio* for the concluding passage of his *Jesu delitium vultus*—a setting of a highly emotional text in the mystical tradition. At the final phrase of text, 'Vale ad Jesum aspiro' (Farewell, to Jesus I aspire), Geist acknowledges the derivation of the verb 'aspiro' from 'spiro' (breathe), and employs off-beat chords and an echo to enhance the sighing effect, as shown in Ex. 8.11. Like other Italian techniques that grew up in association with particular Latin words or phrases, the *suspiratio* was adopted for works with German texts. Buxtehude inserts rests, for example, into his setting of the verb 'seufzen' (to sigh), in *O Gottes Stadt* (BuxWV 87).

Ex. 8.11. Geist, *Jesu delitium vultus*

Many instances of *hypotyposis* are bound up with military metaphors. The call to arms was set with a repeated rising fourth (a technique described by the theorist Athanasius Kircher),[11] as at the start of Förster's motet *Ad arma fideles*. Other cases draw upon the *stile concitato* tradition established by Monteverdi in his *Madrigali guerrieri et amorosi* (1638) and subsequently transferred to sacred music. Biblical battle scenes afforded the most obvious opportunities for the use of this style, consisting of repeated-note quavers and semiquavers for the strings, as can be seen in Förster's *Congregantes Philistei*, a

---

[11] Kircher, *Musurgia Universalis*, ii. 144.

setting of the story of David and Goliath. However, looser connections with military matters were often exploited in the same way. Many Psalm settings contain examples of the style employed for phrases referring to the judgement or rule of God. Settings of 'Dixit Dominus' almost invariably adopt the style, for example those by Erben, at the text 'judicabit in nationibus' (he will judge among the nations), Geist, at the text 'conquassabit capita' (he shall smite the heads), and Buxtehude (BuxWV 17), at the word 'dominare' (subdue). The *stile concitato* is used by Bütner in his chorale setting *Du heilige Brunst süsser Trost* for the word 'ritterlich' (knightly), and as late as 1699 by Österreich in his motet *Ach Herr, wie sind meiner Feinde* at the text 'mit deiner Macht' (with thy might), whilst other composers employed the style in a rather different manner simply to depict joy, as in Dietrich Becker's *Schaf in mir Gott* for the text 'und der freudige Geist' (and the joyful spirit). More unusual cases of the use of the style include the depiction of thunder, shown in Ex. 8.12, found in Friedrich Funcke's *Danck- und Denck-Mahl*, composed and published in 1666 in commemoration of a storm that damaged the tower of the Johanniskirche in Lüneburg, and the depiction of wedding revellers calling for more wine in the Gospel dialogue by Pfleger that sets the story of Christ's first miracle, *Und es war eine Hochzeit zu Kana*. A particular vocal form of the *stile concitato* was developed by the Italian composers for three-syllable imperatives such as 'surgite' and 'fugite'. These words were set to a rising scale in the rhythm quaver–semiquaver–semiquaver. The device was particularly popular amongst Roman composers such as Carissimi and Foggia, and early examples in the North German repertoire include one of Tunder's settings of *Nisi Dominus*,[12] at the word 'surgite' (rise up) and Förster's motet *Ah peccatores* for the text 'surgite timidi', marked 'presto'.

A number of specific types of *hypotyposis* in the North German repertoire were associated with settings of Vespers Psalms, following the example of Italian composers. These include the dramatic juxtaposition of slow and fast for the text 'sanctum et terribile' (holy and terrible) in the Psalm 'Confitebor tibi Domine', as can be seen in the setting by Erben. Such instances probably gave rise to the use of this contrast in other contexts, such as Meder's *In tribulatione*, which opens with a slow-moving expressive passage using first a chromatic bass and then a chain of suspensions for the words 'In tribulatione'

---

[12] Düben collection, vok. mus. i hdskr. 36:8, 81:69, 86:56.

Ex. 8.12. Funcke, *Danck- und Denck-Mahl* (1666)

(in tribulation), and then suddenly bursts into a vivace section at the text 'invocavimus Dominum' (we have called to the Lord). Another technique developed in Vespers Psalm settings is the musical depiction of words such as 'peribit' (perishes), as occurs at the end of the Psalm 'Beatus vir'. Many composers followed the example of Monteverdi in his six-part setting in the *Selva morale e spirituale* (1640) by using several repetitions of the relevant word to create the effect. The technique can be seen, for example, in Förster's setting of *Beatus vir*, although instead of the gradual disintegration of the texture employed by Monteverdi, Förster uses echo effects. As with the *hypotyposis* associated with the text 'Sanctum et terribile', that associated with 'peribit' was also transferred from Psalm settings to other contexts. It can be seen in Buxtehude's *Ich habe Lust abzuscheiden*

(BuxWV 46) at the words 'zu sterben' (to die), a phrase that has the same stress pattern as 'peribit', and in Förster's *Intenderunt arcum* at the word 'pereunt', where a different rhythmic pattern was required.

Many individual examples of *hypotyposis* could be cited, but amongst the more interesting are the use of a hemiola by Förster in the voice part but not in the basso continuo part to emphasize the repetition of the word 'non' in his Psalm setting *Lauda Jerusalem*, the use of an abrupt cut-off for the word 'plötzlich' (suddenly) at the end of *Ach Herr, strafe mich nicht* by Bernhard (see also the later setting of the same text by Meder), and the depiction of the word 'wandert' (wandered) in Österreich's motet *Alle Menschen müßen sterben*, as shown in Ex. 8.13. Here the composer may be implying an actual sliding between the notes, if not some sort of shaking of the sound, indicated by the wavy lines above the voice parts.

Ex. 8.13. Österreich, *Alle Menschen müßen sterben*

INSTRUMENTAL WRITING

The strong tradition of instrumental participation in church music that existed already in the early decades of the seventeenth century in the music of Praetorius and Selle extended throughout the Baroque period. During Buxtehude's youth the new instrumental playing styles created by the North Italian composers such as Monteverdi, Rovetta, and Grandi enjoyed huge popularity on German soil. The Roman school of composition was less dependent upon the use of instruments, and it is striking that the German composers did not lessen their enthusiasm for instrumental participation in church music, even when the vocal style of their music was so heavily influenced by the Roman composers. Instrumental introductions to motets either led straight into the entry of the voices without a break, or took the form of an independent movement, which was often musically as well as structurally distinct from the motet proper. These independent movements, frequently entitled Sonata or Sinfonia, consisted of either a single section or a more elaborate structure. Although tripartite structures were not uncommon, the most favoured format was a bipartite structure, in which a slow section in homophonic style leads into a lively fugato section. Although the styles changed, this basic format remained in use throughout Buxtehude's lifetime, following the example of contemporary Italian church music. Sinfonias with the adagio–allegro structure by Italian composers can be found in both the Düben and Bokemeyer collections in works such as G. Cocci, *O pulcherrima inter mulieres*, and G. Alveri, *Arma, bella, proelia mortales*. Homophonic sections either maintained a continuous texture or were broken up by rests, whilst fugato sections were based on anything from the briefest up-beat figure to more extended themes.

Characteristic of the German tradition of string-playing was the fondness for full string textures with carefully composed middle parts. Rather than merely fleshing out the texture these were used to provide animated figuration in fast passages and expressive passing-note dissonances and suspensions in slower passages to a degree that was not usual in the Italian tradition. In works such as Ritter's *Vater unser*, the opening of which is shown in Ex. 8.14, it would be hard to imagine that the rich sonority of the opening string passage was not conceived as a whole, rather than as a trio texture which could be expanded at will. Another distinctive German characteristic was the prominence given to the viola da gamba. The standard trio texture of two violins and basso continuo was at times enriched by the composition of a viola da gamba or violono part that contained as much musical interest as the upper parts. It played an embellished continuo line alongside the regular continuo line played by the other bass instrument(s), as can be seen in the opening of Geist's *Domine qui das salutem* (see Ex. 7.1*b*).

But specific instances of Italian stylistic influence in North German instrumental writing are legion. During the early and mid-seventeenth century the contrasting idioms of the Italian canzona and toccata were both employed as brief instrumental introductions to motets by North German composers. The characteristic canzona

Ex. 8.14. Ritter, *Vater unser*

rhythm long–short–short can be seen, for example, at the opening of Förster's motet *Quanta fecisti Domine*, headed 'Canzona' in the manuscript. Moreover, the opening phrase of Bütner's setting of *Vom Himmel hoch* shows that the style was also taken over into chorale works. The toccata style is found in works scored for cornetts and/or trumpets. Monteverdi's Vespers of 1610 seems to have been a direct source of inspiration for the Danzig composer Christoph Werner. The opening of his Michaelmas motet *Es erhub sich ein Streit* betrays a notable motivic similarity to the start of Monteverdi's work, as shown in Ex. 8.15.[13]

One of the most popular Italian string idioms adopted by the North German composers was the *tremolo* style. Italian works in the Düben collection which contain the style include Peranda's *Vocibus resonent*, and Francesco Passerini's Psalm setting *Confitebor tibi Domine*. Not to be confused with the modern *tremolando*, the *tremolo* was similar to the organ tremulant, based on a fluctuation of intensity rather than pitch. The string-player performed repeated-note quavers in groups of two, or more usually four, within the same bow (the technique was fully described by Andreas Hammerschmidt, the most famous central German composer of the Buxtehude period, in the introduction to one of his many publications of church music).[14] Many examples survive in the North German repertoire where the bowing is clearly indicated by the use of slurs. The technique was

[13] The middle instrumental parts have been omitted in Ex. 8.15a.

[14] See S. Carter, 'The String Tremolo in the 17th Century', *Early Music*, 19/1 (1991), 44.

Ex. 8.15. (*a*) Monteverdi, Vespers of 1610; (*b*) Werner, *Es erhub sich ein Streit*

(*a*)

(*b*)

employed to create an intense and expressive mood for many devotional motets. One of the earliest examples of the style in the North German repertoire can be found in Tunder's Psalm setting *Dominus illuminatio mea*, in which just two violin parts are involved. Later generations of North German composers exploited the style more fully and composed extended passages in the style using four- and five-part textures, often containing chains of suspensions. A particularly innovative use of the style can be found in Weiland's motet *Nun dancket alle Gott*, where he combines the string *tremolo* with ascending scales in the voice parts, as shown in Ex. 8.16. At times a wavy line was used instead of the usual slur mark over groups of four repeated-note quavers. This may perhaps be suggesting the use of left-hand vibrato as well as the bowed *tremolo*, but the fact that both types of markings are used in the same passage in Meder's *Wie murren denn die Leute* suggests that both annotations were intended to

Ex. 8.16. Weiland, *Nun dancket alle Gott* (1661)

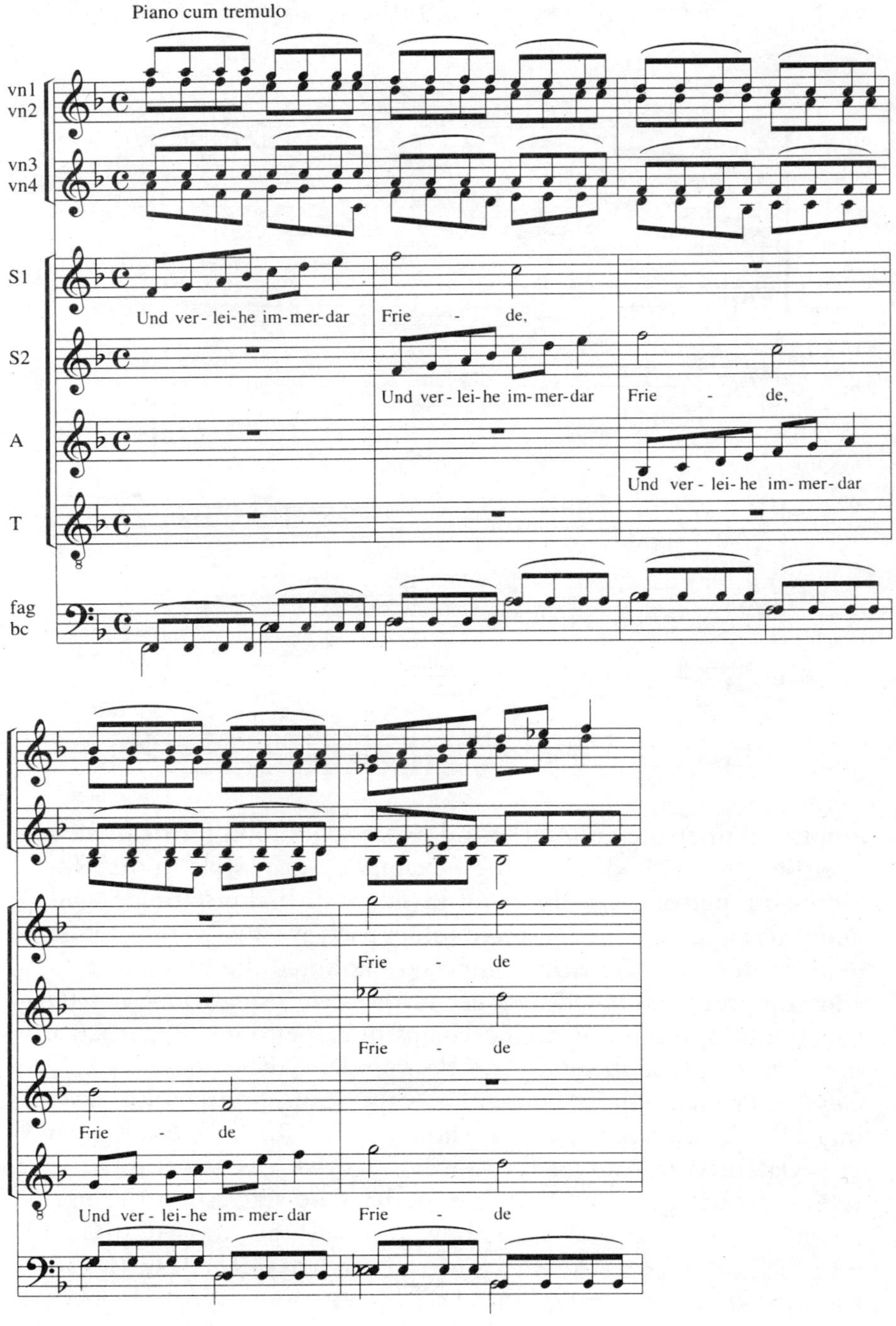

indicate the bowed *tremolo*. The same work by Meder opens with the indication 'tremulo' next to held chords rather than repeated-note quavers, a notation also found in some contemporary Italian works, such as P. Vertini, *Laudate Dominum*. Again, it would seem likely that the bowed technique is being implied here, which could be performed either by breaking up the minims and semibreves into repeated-note quavers, or by using a less strictly regulated rhythm.[15] The continued popularity of the *tremolo* style around the turn of the eighteenth century can be seen in the music of Österreich, von Bertuch, and others. Österreich employs the style as an accompaniment to a chorale melody in *Valet will ich dir geben*, and employs an unusual variation of the style in his motet *Weise mir Herr deinen Weg*, in which the indication 'tremulo doppelt' appears above groups of four repeated-note quavers following on from a passage of semiquavers, probably indicating the use of the bowed *tremolo* at double, i.e. semiquaver, speed. Less common than the *tremolo* style was the *spiccato* or *staccato* style found in a small number of Italian and North German works. In this style short notes are separated by rests, and the notes themselves are sometimes accompanied by vertical stroke marks in the manuscript. A section headed 'Spiccato' can be seen in Bassani's *Nisi Dominus*,[16] and North German examples can be found in Österreich's *Herr Jesu Christ*, where vertical strokes can be seen together with the instruction 'adagio e staccato', and Schieferdecker's *In te Domine speravi*.

The Italian school of virtuoso violin-playing was well known and imitated throughout Germany during the seventeenth century, and challenging parts for solo violin sometimes occurred in both Italian and North German church music. Advanced playing styles appear in the Italian sacred work *Peccai, è ver, fù grave il fallo mio*, attributed to both Bassani and Bononcini in the Bokemeyer collection, including three-note chords and rapid arpeggio passage-work. The most remarkable example of virtuoso string-writing in the North German repertoire is *Mein Herz ist bereit* by Bruhns, a virtuoso string-player himself as well as an organist, but several other composers occasionally adopted aspects of the style, notably Geist and Meder. The latter's *Jubilate Deo* contains a remarkable passage where the composer combines elements of the *tremolo*, *arpeggiando*, and *recitativo*

---

[15] The indication 'Tremolo con L'arco' is found against minims and semibreves in Biagio Marini's *Affetti musicali* (Venice, 1617); see Carter, 'The String Tremolo', 45–7.

[16] This is the setting listed as no. 54 in Kümmerling, *Katalog der Sammlung Bokemeyer*.

Ex. 8.17. Meder, *Jubilate Deo*

accompagnato styles, as shown in Ex. 8.17. In his motet *Sufficit nunc Domine* the opening Sinfonia, headed 'Lamento', is dominated by a quasi-improvisatory solo violin part which soars ecstatically above held chords marked 'tremolo' in the lower strings. However, Meder shows a characteristically German interest in the contribution made to the overall texture by the lower string parts, which take part in the octave runs towards the end of the Sinfonia, the whole of which is given in Ex. 8.18.

Meder's motet *Jubilate Deo* also contains a virtuosic solo trumpet part in addition to the solo violin part already mentioned, but in general trumpets (called either clarino or trombetta) were employed with timpani for toccata-style sections in large-scale compositions that were settings of joyful texts or themes associated with battle, in the tradition of Werner's *Es erhub sich ein Streit*. Geist's Michaelmas motet *Quis hostis in coelis*, the opening of which is shown in Ex. 8.19 (with the optional viola parts omitted), has two trumpet parts, though no timpani. He generates a high level of excitement by his use of a lively concertato style over a ground bass, and by the wide range of the trumpets. Later examples of the use of trumpets in the North German repertoire include Theile's *Herr unser Herrscher*, which opens with a seven-bar fanfare for trumpets, timpani, and continuo alone (see Ex. 6.3).

Towards the end of the seventeenth century the introduction of the oboe and bassoon added new colours to the palette of the North German composers. They were used either as solo instruments in the aria sections, or as a trio in combination with the standard string texture. Both uses can be seen in Österreich's motet *Weise mir Herr*

Ex. 8.18. Meder, *Sufficit nunc Domine*

Ex. 8.18. *cont.*

deinen Weg (dated 1695), the former in the aria section 'Ich dancke dir Herr', and the latter in the opening Sinfonia, where the oboes are heard as a contrast to the strings, as shown in Ex. 8.20. The oboes act here, as in other works, as a concertino within the full texture, betraying the influence of the contemporary Italian concerto grosso, and the patterned figuration employed from bar 5 over an harmonic sequence of a circle of fifths also demonstrates the importance of the contemporary Italian style.

Ex. 8.19. Geist, *Quis hostis in coelis*

Ex. 8.20. Österreich, *Weise mir Herr deinen Weg*

9

Performance Practice

◊

DETAILS concerning the size and nature of the musical forces employed in seventeenth-century North German church music survive either in the form of original documents or in nineteenth- and early twentieth-century musicological studies of sources that were lost in the Second World War. The archival studies by Lisette Krüger on Hamburg and by Hermann Rauschning on Danzig are particularly interesting as they contain transcriptions of several documents that provide information going far beyond a mere listing of numbers of musicians available.[1] Further information may be gleaned from the surviving music manuscripts and publications of the period. The Düben collection is of considerable interest in this respect since it contains parts as well as scores. Concerning manner of performance, the principal sources of information are the music treatises of the period, of which those by Daniel Friderici (*Musica Figuralis*, 1618), Michael Praetorius (*Syntagma musicum*, iii, 1619), Christoph Bernhard ('Von der Singe-Kunst oder Manier', c.1649), Johann Crüger (*Der Rechte Weg zur Singekunst*, 1660), and Martin Fuhrmann (*Musicalischer-Trichter*, 1706) are the most significant.

VOCAL AND INSTRUMENTAL FORCES

The vocal forces available to the typical North German *Kapellmeister* or cantor fell into three groups: trained boys, salaried men, and miscellaneous extras, either volunteer amateurs or visiting professionals. The number of trained boys available rarely reached double figures, and the number of salaried men rarely exceeded half a dozen. It was

[1] L. Krüger, *Die Hamburgische Musikorganisation im 17. Jahrhundert* (Strassburg, 1933), and Rauschning, *Geschichte der Musik und Musikpflege in Danzig*.

clearly a struggle for many musical directors to maintain even a minimum complement of able singers for church music. The sort of difficulties encountered can be readily appreciated from the letter sent
by Johann Meder to the town council at Danzig shortly after he
arrived at the Marienkirche there *c*.1685. He describes in detail the
abilities of the five salaried singers: a discantist who sings through his
nose and has an unpleasant and forced voice; an alto who, though
able, has almost lost his voice; a young weak tenor; a singer who is
too low to be a tenor and too high to be a bass; and a bass who is not
a regular singer since he has other church duties. Two extra singers
from the school were also available, but their ability was such that
they could only be used to sing in the 'Ripieno Choro' rather than
in 'Concertat-Music'.[2]

The distinction between concertato and ripieno is crucial for
understanding the nature of the vocal forces employed in church
music at this time. Concertato sacred music was written in essence
for solo voices, but extra voices could be added for the simpler music
found in tutti sections (see Ch. 6). Less able singers could thus be
drafted in to supplement the regular trained and salaried singers.
However, the surviving evidence concerning the size of such additional groups indicates that they were also small, usually either one
or two voices per part. This evidence comes from the parts marked
'Capella' or 'ripieno' in the Düben collection, and from comments
made by Fuhrmann. It is probably symptomatic of the optional
nature of the Capella that the survival of Capella parts in the Düben
collection seems so haphazard. In some cases mention is made of a
Capella on the title-page of a piece, but no such parts survive; in others, Capella parts were copied by Düben and others even though no
Capella is referred to on the title-page. In several sets of parts only
one or two Capella parts survive, and in some the additional parts are
indicated as being for either an extra voice or an extra instrument.
Nearly all the Capella parts which survive in the Düben collection
are single parts, suggesting that the Capella was only one voice per
part, or perhaps two if the part was shared between two people. Only
one set of parts survives in which more than one part per voice is
extant, Pfleger's *Laudate Dominum*, headed 'a 8, cum Capella'. The
work is scored for SSTB and four-part strings (making up the 'a 8' of

---

[2] Rauschning, *Geschichte der Musik und Musikpflege in Danzig*, 280.

the title), and two parts exist for each voice of the Capella, each marked 'ripieno'.

The use of two singers per part in a Capella is mentioned in Fuhrmann's *Musicalischer-Trichter* when describing the problems of more than one singer or instrumentalist performing the same part. When he refers to two singers taking the same part he adds '(welches man offt in *Capella* thun läst)' (which one often allows in a Capella).[3] However, although it is clear that the number of singers available was often small, even for a Capella, the overwhelming impression gained from the surviving comments in letters written by directors of music such as Thomas Selle in Hamburg (see p. 103) is that more was desirable, particularly in larger churches. Moreover, Fuhrmann eulogizes the famous choir of Orlando di Lasso, which had a regular complement of 16 boys, 13 altos, 15 tenors, 12 basses, and 6 castrati. A revealing comment in the score of Meister's chorale setting *Wie schön leuchtet der Morgenstern* concerning the performance of the second verse of the chorale, set in simple four-part harmony, reads as follows: 'Choral Tutti mit allerhand Instrumenten und vielen Vocal Stimmen' (Chorale full, with all kinds of instruments and many vocal parts). Other sources give open-ended instructions concerning numbers. Gerstenbüttel's *Dazu ist erschienen der Sohn Gottes* is headed 'a 10 l. 15 l. plur' (for 10, or 15, or more). Larger forces were desirable not only for use in Capella, but also for the singing of other non-soloistic music such as motets in the old style. Selle makes a clear distinction in his letter of 8 January 1642, between his normal minimum requirement of 2 basses, 2 tenors, 2 altos, and 4 discantists, and his requirements for motets. 'Zu Muteten', he says, 'müssen derer noch einmal so viel sein' (for motets there must be as many of them again), commenting that suitable extra forces can be found in the local orphanage as well the local schools.[4] A choir consisting of 8 discantists, 4 altos, 4 tenors, and 4 basses would thus have satisfied Selle for the performance of music in the *stile antico*, and this gives some guidance to the numbers that may actually or ideally have been involved in the performance of this type of music throughout the century, including the motets of the popular anthologies of Bodenschatz and Schadaeus, and more recent music composed in the *stile antico*, such as the *Missa brevis* settings by Buxtehude, Bernhard, Theile, and others. Theile's five-part *Missa* is headed 'a Capella', clearly indicating

---

[3] Fuhrmann, *Musicalischer-Trichter*, 77.
[4] Krüger, *Die Hamburgische Musikorganisation*, 68–9.

that at least two voices per part were envisaged by the composer. Moreover, some of his concertato works also carry this instruction, such as the *Benedicam Dominum* and *Laudate Dominum* found in the same Berlin manuscript as the *Missa*. Although these works have no particularly virtuosic pasages for individual voice parts, they nevertheless exhibit a lively concertato style, suggesting that within reasonable limits, works composed in the *stile moderno* were also at times performed by more than one voice to a part, when sufficient singers happened to be available.

Whilst it is self-evident that men sang the tenor and bass parts in concerted music, the question of who sang the alto and discantus parts is more problematic. Evidence from Furhmann and other sources suggests that these two parts were sung either by solo boys or by men singing in falsetto. In his discussion of the discantus part Furhmann refers principally to boys, though he notes that a good boy discantus is extremely rare, not even one in a thousand.[5] In his discussion of the alto part he also refers to boys, noting that a boy's voice normally changes from alto to tenor at the age of over 18.[6] Good solo boys in their early, mid, and even late teens could thus probably have been expected to hold their own as soloists alongside adult voices. However, Fuhrmann's comments about the rarity of such talent tie in with the fact that the discantus and alto parts were often sung by men rather than boys. When describing the falsetto voice, he gives the example of a tenor singing either the alto or the discantus part.[7] Many of the church and chapel records that indicate payments to a discantus singer make it clear that the discantus was a man, either by the size of salary given or by the length of duty. At the courts, the lack of a ready supply of schoolboys tended to favour the use of men for the top parts, of which the most highly prized form was the Italian castrato. Castrati are known to have been employed in the more wealthy and cosmopolitan courts in North Germany such as that at Hannover, but their high salaries put them beyond the reach of most of the smaller courts. Nevertheless, they are known to have given occasional performances away from the wealthy courts, and even to have sung in town churches, as recorded

[5] Fuhrmann, *Musicalischer-Trichter*, 81.

[6] Ibid. 36. At that time boys' voices broke often several years later than is normal today, so that they had the opportunity to develop their voices over a considerable number of years.

[7] Ibid. 80, under heading 9: *Voce contra fatta.*

at the Marienkirche in Lübeck and the Marienkirche in Danzig (see p. 50). But it would seem that at most North German churches and courts the discantus part was sung either by boys or by a man using falsetto, or possibly a combination of the two.

The surviving documents from the period indicate that the size of the instrumental forces available for church music was much the same as that of the vocal forces. One instrumentalist per part was the norm, with ripieno players added at times, according to availability. The instruments were usually owned by the church, and some of the musicians themselves were proficient both as singers and instrumentalists, thus giving greater scope to the director of music in his choice of music. The use of more than one instrument per part frequently corresponded to the use of the vocal Capella, as described in Chapter 5. As with the Capella parts in the Düben collection, only a few instrumental ripieno parts have survived, apparently almost at random, sometimes in conjunction with Capella parts, but sometimes on their own, as in the case of Erben's *Peccavi super numerum*. This is headed 'à 10 / 6 voci é 4 stromenti Concert: / Con li Riepieno [*sic*] Se piace'. Single parts survive for three independent violas and a 'violonne' which play throughout the work, together with single ripieno parts for three further violas (marked '2do choro') and a violono that play only in the tutti sections of the work. Ripieno parts for Förster's *Quanta fecisti Domine* are described as being either for an extra voice or an extra instrument, e.g. 'Viola sive Alto in Rip:'. In a small number of works the type of instrumental doubling indicated by the surviving parts or title-pages is not in the manner of a ripieno, but the more familiar modern practice of having more than one instrumentalist per part playing throughout an entire work. This occurs in a few works by Buxtehude[8] and a handful of other works, such as Johann Schröder's motet *Adesto virtutum chorus*, which survives in separate parts for SATB, basso continuo, SATB in ripieno, two cornetti in ripieno, and two copies each for Violin 1 and Violin 2 which play throughout the piece.

The use of more than one violin per part became a particular feature of some works which contain the instruction for violins to play 'In Unisono'. Kerala Snyder has noted that this was specified by Buxtehude in his now lost *Die Hochzeit des Lamms*, composed for an *Abendmusik* concert in 1678, which contained a passage for soprano

---

[8] Snyder, *Dieterich Buxtehude*, 383.

and eleven violins.[9] Multiple violin parts are also indicated in some of Buxtehude's last works dating from 1705, but these are extra-liturgical. However, the new Italian aria technique of employing many violins in unison over a basso continuo may be found in some of the church music in the Bokemeyer collection that dates from the early eighteenth century, such as Schürmann's *Es wird ein Stein* which contains a passage for violins marked 'Unissoni'.

BASSO CONTINUO

Considerable variety existed with regard to the instruments employed for the basso continuo. The most commonly used keyboard instrument was without doubt the organ, which was often a separate, small choir organ specifically for use with the singers, complete with its own organist. Fuhrmann gives some specific advice about the choice of organ stops, recommending the use of a soft 8-foot Gedackt for accompanying soloists, adding a 16-foot Sub-bass for larger forces.[10] No organ stops are specifically mentioned in the surviving musical sources, but a section in Meder's *Leben wir so leben wir* calls for the use of the organ's tremulant stop in conjunction with the related *tremolo* technique found in the string parts (see pp. 166–9). But besides the organ, other keyboard instruments such as the harpsichord and spinet were also employed for the basso continuo. Some of the continuo parts in the Düben collection suggest that the harpsichord was at times used as the sole keyboard instrument, as indicated in the title-page of Meder's *Ach Herr, straffe mich nicht* for 'Soprano con 3. Stroment[i] è Cembalo', but others suggest that it was also employed at times as a second keyboard in addition to the organ. This second keyboard part usually acted like a ripieno instrument, playing only at tutti sections. Its use in this capacity was thus, as with the other ripieno parts, optional. One ripieno bass part to Förster's motet *Ah peccatores*, for example, is marked 'spinetto overo Viol di gamba'. Further flexibility is suggested by the existence of several parts which although entitled 'violono' or 'viola' also contain figures. Harpsichords and spinets seem to have been used both in

[9] Snyder, *Dieterich Buxtehude*, 382.

[10] Fuhrmann, *Musicalischer-Trichter*, 80. A similar view is expressed by Friederich Niedt in ch. 11, para. 14 of *Die Musicalische Handleitung*, ii (Hamburg, 1706); see *Friederich Erhardt Niedt: The Music Guide*, transl. P. L. Poulin and I. C. Taylor (Oxford, 1989), 159.

court chapels and churches. The continuo part of Ritter's *Vater unser*, whose title-page contains a lengthy dedication to the German Church in Stockholm, is for cembalo rather than organ. More common as an additional continuo instrument than the harpsichord or spinet was the lute or theorbo. In a few cases the plucked instrument is the only surviving continuo part, but it is more generally found as an additional continuo instrument to the organ. Unlike the harpsichord or spinet, it was generally used throughout a whole work rather than as a ripieno instrument. Further evidence of the use of keyboard and plucked instruments as additional continuo instruments can be seen from the comment found in the violono part of Rubert's publication *Musicalische Seelen-Erquickung* (Stralsund, 1664), noting that the part can also be employed for a '*ClaviCymbal*, Harff, *Theorba* oder *Pandor*'.

The bass string instruments used to play along with the basso continuo part were either the violono (or violone), viola da gamba, or basso di viola. The instrument most frequently used was the violono. This played at 8-foot pitch, as is evident from the parts that survive in the Düben collection. Sometimes the violono is the only string bass part that is employed to play the bass line, and in works for which more than one string instrument playing the bass line survives, it is always the violono that plays throughout the work, whilst the gamba or viola is added for the tutti sections. The fagotto was also sometimes used as an additional ripieno instrument, and the difference between local variations in instrumentation is evident in the Düben collection from the way in which parts copied out for works by composers associated with the Dresden court nearly always contain such a ripieno fagotto part, whereas those copied for works by composers associated with the Stockholm court do not—a fact that matches with the well-documented lack of fagotto-players at the Stockholm court at this time. However, the scores of the Bokemeyer collection suggest that when the new French bassoon came into use along with the oboe, bassoonists often played throughout an entire work, rather than just as an additional tutti instrument.

Although the standard violono played at 8-foot pitch, there is some evidence from the period that a string instrument playing at 16-foot pitch was at times used for church music. The contemporary description of an instrument playing at the lower octave hinges on the use of a qualifying adjective such as 'gross' or 'contra'. The Hamburg cantor Thomas Selle wrote in the 1640s that 'Der grosse

Violon oder Contrabass-Geige' (the large violono or contrabass violin) should be available for use every Sunday. A similar point is made
by Fuhrmann in his *Musicalischer-Trichter* of 1706, in which he mentions specifically that the 'Violone Grosso' descends to 'das 16füßige
Contra-C' (the 16-foot Contra-C), and is suitable for use not only
for musical performances but also for use in playing chorales.[11]
Moreover, it is recorded that the Marienkirche in Lübeck purchased
a 'große Octav-geige' in 1672.[12] It may thus appear surprising that
no mention of the instrument appears in all the parts in the Düben
collection, but then there is no reference to such an instrument in
the records of the Royal court or German Church in Stockholm, for
which the collection was compiled. Moreover, the surviving lists of
instruments and instrumentalists at most other North German courts
and churches frequently lack the 16-foot instrument. Thus although
it was considered by some to be a desirable instrument for use in
church music, not all places seem to have had the resources to pur-
chase one. Given the struggle that most directors of music had to find
enough essential players and instruments, it is not surprising that the
non-essential 16-foot instrument was often not present. The earliest
North German reference to the use of a 16-foot stringed instrument
for a specific piece of music is found in the second part of Praetorius'
Syntagma Musicum: De Organographia (Wolfenbüttel, 1619). He suggests its use in his seventeen- and twenty-one-part *Lauda Hierusalem
Dominum*, shortly to be published in his *Polyhymnia* collection.[13] The
next such reference in the North German repertoire is found in the
Bokemeyer collection, dating from around the turn of the eighteenth century. The score of Österreich's *Actus funebris: Plötzlich
müßen die Leute sterben*, written for the funeral of Duke Friedrich IV,
who was killed in battle in 1702, lists the use of a 'Violono maggiore',
also described as a 'gross Violon'. The work also contains a rare mention of the use of a contra faggotto, probably the earliest surviving
specific use of the instrument. The score contains two instrumental
bass lines, one above the voice parts at the foot of the concertato
instrumental parts, and one below the voices. At the start of the score
the upper of these two parts is headed '2 bassoni, Cembalo und
Violoncello' and the lower 'NB Organo, Contra Fagott und Violono
maggiore'. Almost a century earlier, Praetorius had referred to a

---

[11] See pp. 39–40.   [12] See Snyder, *Dieterich Buxtehude*, 371.
[13] M. Praetorius, *Syntagma musicum, ii: De Organographia* (Wolfenbüttel, 1619; facs. repr.
ed. W. Gurlitt, Kassel, 1985), 46.

'Fagotcontra' playing at 16-foot pitch, but notes that the instrument existed only in theory and had not yet been built, although a builder in Berlin was shortly to make one. The earliest surviving instruments date from the early eighteenth century and are thus contemporary with Österreich's motet.[14]

SINGING STYLE AND EMBELLISHMENT

Concerning the manner of vocal performance, much useful information can be gleaned from the writings of Friderici, Praetorius, Bernhard, Crüger, and others. Friderici, whose singing treatise concerning boys' voices first appeared in Rostock in 1618 but was reprinted many times, provides the following recommendation:

Die Knaben sollen vom Anfang als bald gewehnet werden / die Stimmen fein natürlich / und wo möglich fein zitterend / schwebend oder bebend / *in gutture*, in dem Kehlen oder im Halse zu *formiren*.[15]

(The boys should right from the beginning be trained to form the voice in a pleasant and natural manner, and where possible nicely trembling, vibrating, or shaking, *in gutture*, in the larynx or in the throat.)

This type of singing would not seem to be far removed from the style of German boys' choirs today, particularly in its avoidance of a heady or straight tone.[16] This pleasant form of trembling is clearly quite different from the shaking that comes with old age, referred to by Bernhard, or the use of trembling to illustrate the text, as occurs at 'Ich zitte' in Schürmann's *Siehe, eine Jungfrau ist schwanger*, marked 'trem.'. Friderici also warns against various bad habits such as the addition of 'h' in dotted passages (as in Alle-he-he-luja) and the mispronunciation of vowels (as in 'Aumen' rather than 'Amen'). Bernhard's treatise 'Von der Singe-Kunst oder Manier' recommends the holding of a steady tone on all notes (not wavering like an old man), though with variations in volume, both within a note and on

---

[14] The important precedent set by Österreich for the use of 16-foot instruments in church music adds considerable weight to the possibility that the 'bassono grosso' referred to in the surviving parts for J. S. Bach's *Johannespassion* was indeed a 16-foot instrument. For details see L. Dreyfus, *Bach's Continuo Group: Players and Practices in his Vocal Works* (Cambridge, Mass. and London, 1987), 125–7.

[15] Friderici, *Musica Figuralis*, Caput VII, Regula 2. (The edition has no page numbers.)

[16] A similar reference to trembling from around the same time can be found in Praetorius, *Syntagma musicum*, iii, 229–30, reproduced and translated in Butt, *Music Education and the Art of Performance*, 73.

adjacent notes.[17] He urges careful observation of the text, both in terms of its pronunciation and meaning, and promotes strongly the use of an Italianate pronunciation of Latin, warning against obvious dangers for German singers such as the proper pronunciation of consonants such as 'd' and 't', and the use of clear, distinct vowel sounds.

Much of the space in the singing treatises of the period is given over to the art of improvised embellishment. Friderici refers to the use of improvised *Coloraturen*, pointing out that they should be employed only in the upper parts, and gives some examples of the simpler diminution patterns.[18] Regarding ornaments he states that they are in general too difficult for young boys and are the province of only the best singers. A fuller explanation, however, was provided in the following year by the greatest German champion of Italian music in the early decades of the seventeenth century, Michael Praetorius.[19] The standard Italian ornaments and diminutions described in the third part of his *Syntagma musicum* appear little changed in Crüger's treatise of 1660. Like Friderici, Crüger underlines that the more advanced Italian singing styles belong more to royal and princely chapels than to the activities of schoolboys, but this does not prevent him from giving explanations of several Italian ornaments, as well as examples of *passaggi*. Moreover, Crüger explicitly names the *accentus* and the easier forms of *passaggi* as being suitable for use by schoolboys.[20] Bernhard's treatise observes the same basic categorization as found in Praetorius and Crüger, consisting on the one hand of ornaments (a particular characteristic, he observes, of Roman singing) and on the other hand of diminutions (being characteristic of Lombardic singing).[21]

It is clear from the combined evidence of Friderici, Praetorius, Crüger, and Bernhard that the application of appropriate ornaments and *passaggi* was seen as fundamental to what Crüger calls 'Der Rechte Weg zur Singekunst' (The Correct Manner of Singing). As a guide to the nature of this style of improvised embellishment, Ex. 9.1 gives examples of the *accentus* and *passaggio* from Crüger's treatise of 1660.[22] His *accentus* concerns simple decorations of a single note and of intervals from a second to a fifth, both ascending and descending.

---

[17] See Hilse, 'The Treatises of Christoph Bernhard', 14–15.
[18] Reproduced in Butt, *Music Education and the Art of Performance*, 130–1.
[19] See ibid. 123–7. [20] Ibid. 128–9.
[21] Hilse, 'The Treatises of Christoph Bernhard', 13–25.
[22] Crüger, *Der rechte Weg zur Singekunst*, 21–31.

Ex. 9.1. Crüger, *Der rechte Weg zur Singekunst*

Ex. 9.1 contains all the single-note forms and most of the ascending versions of the interval forms; the *passaggi* are the first six out of a total of thirty-one examples given by Crüger. As the *accentus* and simpler forms of *passaggi* are described as being suitable even for schoolboys, they can perhaps now be taken as a guide for the modern performer seeking to aim at a miminum level of solo embellishment appropriate to German church music in the early and mid-Baroque period. But the modern performer should also take

note of the *Figuren* described by Bernhard as part of the standard
Roman style of ornamentation, particularly in relation to the performance of the large corpus of extant North German church music
composed under the influence of the mid-seventeenth-
century Roman school.[23] The most distinctive of these figures are
the *anticipatione della syllaba*, the *anticipatione della nota*, and *cercar della
nota*, that is, the anticipation of notes and syllables and the 'seeking
out' of notes. The three devices are closely related, as can be seen in
Ex. 9.2, which shows one of Bernhard's examples of each figure.
Similar written-out examples of the figures exist within the surviving repertoire itself.[24]

Ex. 9.2. Bernhard, 'Von der Singe-Kunst oder Manier'

anticipatione della syllaba

Can-ta - bo ti - bi   Can - ta - bo ti - bi

anticipatione della nota

Ex - ul - tet ter - ra   Ex - ul - tet ter - ra

cercar della nota

Deh   non la- sciar - mi,   deh   non la- sciar - mi,   deh   non la- sciar - mi

But if the modern performer can discover the nature of the improvised embellishment from the writings of Crüger, Bernhard, and others, the extent to which a performer should add such embellishment
to a particular composition is much harder to determine. Certainly the
fact that some authors warn against the use of too many embellishments suggests that some seventeenth-century performers may have
been inclined to over-use them, often at the expense of conveying the
text to the listener.[25] However, some help is given by Bernhard himself, who allies the application of embellishment to the nature of the

---

[23] Hilse, 'The Treatises of Christoph Bernhard', 17–19.

[24] See also the illustration of the use of Bernhard's figures in the *Rudimenta musices* of
W. M. Mylius (Mühlhausen, 1685), reproduced in Butt, *Music Education and the Art of
Performance*, 137.

[25] See e.g. Crüger, *Der rechte Weg zur Singekunst*, 19.

text, and thus more clearly to the concept of music as rhetoric, whereby the affections of the listener are moved by combined efforts of composer and performer (see pp. 23–6). For joy, anger, and similar emotions he recommends the use of a strong voice, a fast speed, and the comparatively sparing use of embellishments and *passaggi*, keeping to the notes given in the composition. By contrast, for sorrowful and gentle moods he advocates the use of a softer, more gentle voice, a slow tempo, even some sliding between the notes, and the comparatively liberal application of appropriate embellishments.[26] Crüger provides an even more specific connection between embellishment and the rhetorical nature of music under the title *exclamatio*.[27] He explains that the *exclamatio* is 'das rechte Mittel . . . die *affectus* zu *moviren*' (the correct method to move the affection), giving as his example a series of simple elaborations of the ascending *voces musicales*. The various patterns are labelled according to their particular moods— languid, affective, lively, and more lively, as shown in Ex. 9.3.[28]

Ex. 9.3. Crüger, *Der rechte Weg zur Singekunst*

[26] Hilse, 'The Treatises of Christoph Bernhard', 21.

[27] Crüger, *Der rechte Weg zur Singekunst*, 32.

[28] The final example, which is described more in terms of the vocal technique required ('Con Ribattuta di gola') has been omitted.

Although most of the ornaments, *passaggi*, and other *Figuren* propounded by Bernhard, Crüger, and others survived in the treatises of the early eighteenth century, their importance as improvised embellishments gradually declined during the period.[29] As far as church music was concerned, Bernhard's *Figuren* applied most importantly to the 'recitative-like' style (see pp. 146–8), an idiom that was eventually eclipsed by the increasing polarization between secco recitative and aria. In particular, the need for improvised *passaggi* waned as composers increasingly came to see virtuosic vocal writing as an important part of the compositional process. Written-out virtuoso passage-work thus becomes a common feature of church music dating from around the turn of the eighteenth century. Notable examples include the opening melisma of Luigi Mancia's *Ad arma volate*, and the concluding 'Alleluia' of the motet *Du Tochter Zion freue dich* by the military officer Georg von Bertuch, both of which require the performance of arpeggios in demisemiquavers. However, the use of ornaments remained crucial to vocal practice, as is evident from the continued appearance of signs for the *trillo* in the surviving compositions from this later period.

The *trillo*, indicated either by 'tr' or just 't', appears in compositions dating throughout Buxtehude's lifetime, but the meaning of the ornament changed during the period from a repeated-note to an adjacent-note form. Crüger's treatise of 1660 describes the *trillo* in the early seventeenth-century Italian sense as the rapid repetition of a single note, either in plain form or in two mildly decorated forms, shown in Ex. 9.4.[30] He does describe ornaments that are similar to the adjacent-note trill, but under the headings *gruppo* and *tremolo*; the *gruppo* is clearly intended as a vocal ornament, but the *tremolo* is described as being more suited to the keyboard than the voice. The manuscripts of the Düben collection contain a rare example of the

Ex. 9.4. Crüger, *Der rechte Weg zur Singekunst*

[29] See Butt, *Music Education and the Art of Performance*, 138–43.
[30] Crüger, *Der rechte Weg zur Singekunst*, 27. Crüger also gives an unusual wider explanation of the term involving a number of different cadential flourishes.

change in taste from the repeated-note to the adjacent-note trill. A setting of the Psalm 'Nisi Dominus' for three voices and continuo, ascribed to Rovetta, is in fact an altered version of Monteverdi's *Nisi Dominus* published in his *Messa a quattro voci, et Salmi* (Venice, 1650). The Gloria of Monteverdi's work opens with a long melisma for the tenor containing three brief written-out repeated-note trills, as shown in Ex. 9.5a. However, the arranger of the version in the Düben collection has replaced them with the more modern adjacent-note trill, as shown in Ex. 9.5b. Bruno Grusnick has suggested that the manuscript was acquired by Düben in 1665, fifteen years after the

Ex. 9.5. Monteverdi, *Nisi Dominus*: (a) *Messa a quattro voci, et Salmi* a 3 voci; (b) as found in the Düben collection

publication of the original composition.[31] Examples such as this illustrate the gradual eclipse of the repeated-note trill during the second half of the seventeenth century, a development that is confirmed by Fuhrmann's treatise of 1706 in which the *trillo* is clearly defined as the alternation of adjacent notes.[32]

TEMPO AND DYNAMICS

Concerning the fundamental interpretational problems of tempo and dynamics, one factor remained paramount: the text. The extreme care which the composers took over the clear presentation of the text speaks for itself, but there is also a considerable body of literary evidence concerning the matter, as well as evidence from the surviving scores. The theoretical distinction in tempo between C and ¢ time was closely allied to the style of music in question. As Crüger explains, ¢ is correctly employed for *Moteten* and C for *Concerten*, with a faster beat in the former and a slower beat in the latter, corresponding to the relative note-values used in the two styles.[33] However, much inconsistency can be found in the use of these two time signatures throughout the seventeenth century, as indeed one might expect from a time when the old proportional system was breathing its last, and when the use of Italian terms to indicate tempo was gaining ground. Praetorius noted this inconsistency in the third part of his *Syntagma musicum* of 1619,[34] and the extant church music of Buxtehude's lifetime provides plenty of examples of the confusion, with different copies of the same composition containing different time signatures, and pieces written in the *stile antico* employing the inappropriate C time signature. Concerning triple-time signatures, a similar hierarchy existed, in which the longer the note-values, the slower the speed. Thus both Friderici in 1619 and Fuhrmann in 1706 define 3/1, 'Tripla', as being a slow speed, and 3/2, 'Sesquialtera', a faster speed. However, as with the confusion between C and ¢, Friderici warns against being too strict about this

[31] Grusnick, 'Die Dübensammlung', 98.

[32] Fuhrmann, *Musicalischer-Trichter*, 64. The earliest German definition of the *trillo* as the alternation of adjacent notes is probably that found in the *Rudimenta musices* of Mylius (1685). See Butt, *Music Education and the Art of Performance*, 135.

[33] Crüger, *Der rechte Weg zur Singekunst*, 16.

[34] Praetorius, *Syntagma musicum*, iii. 51, reproduced and transl. in Butt, *Music Education and the Art of Performance*, 96.

difference since many composers did not make a careful distinction between the two. He continues:

Ists derwegen an der *discretion* eines *Directoris* gelegen / daß er / nach dem die Worte des *Textus* es mit bringen / den *Tact* so wol in Triplâ / als in Sesquialterâ, langsam oder geschwinde schlagt.[35]

(For this reason it lies in the discretion of a conductor, that he beats slowly or quickly according to what is suggested by the words of the text, whether in tripla or sesquialtera.)

Friderici also advances the idea that the tempo of a composition should even change within a single section in one time signature, according to the nature of the text, and this view is supported by evidence provided by surviving scores.[36] Although indications of slow tempi for serious and penitential texts and fast tempi for joyous texts are ubiquitous, either applying to an entire piece or to whole sections of a piece, markings such as 'adagio' and 'allegro' also appear within a single section. A passage composed in aria style in Geist's *Laudet Deum*, for example, contains the annotations 'adagio' and 'presto' at a place where a performer might well have sung through at the same speed had the tempo indications not been there. The brief change of speed is employed to illustrate the text 'indignissimus ego' (I am most unworthy), as shown in Ex. 9.6.

As with tempo, the approach to dynamics was similarly bound up with textual considerations. 'Forte' and 'piano' are used in the main for whole sections, with the former often linked to joyous passages and the latter to more sober reflections, as suggested by Bernhard. However, one interesting case survives in which the markings are used to indicate changes of volume within a single phrase to bring out the expression of the text. The passage occurs at the opening of Förster's motet *O bone Jesu*, shown in Ex. 9.7. This type of detailed volume control is also suggested by Bernhard in his singing treatise, though he does not link it specifically to textual expression.[37]

Further evidence concerning the importance of conveying the text in performance can be seen in comments by Weckmann contained in a Lüneburg manuscript dating from 1663.[38] All four pieces in the manuscript are highly expressive works, but at the start of the

---

[35] Friderici, *Musica Figuralis*, Caput VI: 'Von den *Proportionibus* oder *Triplen*'.

[36] The relevant passage is reproduced in Butt, *Music Education and the Art of Performance*, 98.

[37] Hilse, 'The Treatises of Christoph Bernhard', 15.

[38] Lüneburg, Ratsbücherei, Mus. ant. pract. K. N. 207/6. See Weckmann, *Four Sacred Concertos*, ed. Silbiger.

Ex. 9.6. Geist, *Laudet Deum*

second work, *Zion spricht: Der Herr hat mich verlassen*, Weckmann has written 'NB: Diß Stück muß durchaus langsam und affettuos gemachet werden' (NB. This piece must be performed slowly and affectively throughout), whilst at the start of the final piece, *Wie liegt die Stadt so wüste*, Weckmann recommends a spatial separation between

Ex. 9.7. Förster, *O bone Jesu*

the two performers to enhance the dialogue nature of the piece: 'NB der Discantist muß in diesem Stück nicht stracks neben den Bassisten, sondern etwas von Ihm ab gestellet werden' (NB. the discantist in this piece must not be positioned right next to the bass, but at some distance from him).

Echo effects are frequently indicated in the surviving scores of the period, and were a particularly important part of the musical language of the composers active around the middle of the seventeenth century, such as Förster and Geist. Following Italian models, the North German composers employed echo effects both for textual reasons and for their purely decorative musical value. A number of scores show the use of echos either for the repeat of whole phrases or for brief groups of semiquavers within *passaggi*. The performance of such passages with echo effects thus seems to have been a well-established practice. Modern performers can thus with justification apply echos to appropriate passages where echo markings are absent, and also apply them to improvised *passaggi*. Ex. 9.8 illustrates the use of echos within semiquaver passage-work; Ex. 9.8*a*, taken from Geist's *Pastores dicite*, illustrates a simple alternation between forte and piano, whilst Ex. 9.8*b* reveals the use of several different levels of echo within a melisma, ranging from 'f.' down to 'p.p.p.', as found in Meder's motet *Sufficit nunc Domine*.

Ex. 9.8. (*a*) Geist, *Pastores dicite*; (*b*) Meder, *Sufficit nunc Domine*

Conclusion

◊

THE widely held perception of North German church music in the age of Buxtehude is of a repertoire that was increasingly free from Italian influence. Modern scholars have tended to contrast the state of German church music in the first half of the seventeenth century with that of the second half of the century, suggesting that whereas the influence of Italian church music was paramount in the earlier period its importance declined substantially in the later period, so that the German composers 'now took and held the lead' in the composition of church music.[1] In this book, however, I have sought to highlight the continued supremacy of Italian church music during Buxtehude's lifetime, and to examine in detail the channels through which this influence was transmitted. A substantial quantity of Italian church music is known to have been in circulation throughout the North German region in the second half of the seventeenth century, and several influential North German composers followed the example of Schütz by studying in Italy. Those that did not visit Italy themselves nevertheless had the opportunity to encounter Italian musicians working in the North German region. But the most compelling evidence of the continued importance of Italian church music can be found from a detailed study of the North German repertoire itself, as is demonstrated in Chapters 5 to 8.

The chief sources of Italian influence on the North German repertoire changed with the general progress of Italian church music during the seventeenth century. Thus, Monteverdi and the Venetian school were of greatest importance during Buxtehude's youth, then the Roman school of Carissimi and his successors came to the fore,

---

[1] Kirwan-Mott, *The Small-Scale Sacred Concertato*, 373. For a similar view see Roche, *North Italian Church Music*, 150–1, where the author refers to 'Italy's loss of supremacy in sacred music'.

and finally individuals mostly from North Italy came to dominate, notably G. B. Bassani at Bologna and Ferrara. A study of Italian influence in the North German repertoire not only reveals countless direct examples of Italian influence but also exposes the way in which Italian compositional techniques were sometimes adapted by the North German composers to suit their own ends, as with the accompaniment of chorale verses by concertato string-writing or the composition of idiosyncratic ostinato bass lines. Moreover, it also helps to clarify what, in addition to the chorale, is distinctively North German in the repertoire, such as the greater preoccupation with the instrumental writing, seen in features such as the imaginative exploitation of the middle parts of a string ensemble, the wider use of wind instruments, and, in the earlier part of the repertoire, the importance of the viola da gamba.

The principal textual development in the church music of Buxtehude's lifetime was the gradual increase in the use of German rather than Latin texts. Latin texts based on mystical themes were particularly popular during the 1650s, 1660s, and 1670s, but subsequently the use of Latin came to be connected with strictly liturgical items such as Vespers Psalms. By contrast, the use of composite texts in German became increasingly popular during the 1680s and 1690s. The chorale, despite its importance in the early seventeenth-century repertoire of Michael Praetorius and others, received comparatively little attention from North German composers during Buxtehude's lifetime, particularly those who worked at courts rather than in towns. One of the principal reasons for this was the growth in popularity of the strophic aria, which, with its Italian-influenced style and contemporary Pietist texts, came to be used increasingly as a substitute for the traditional chorale. But although some composers made use of either the aria or chorale, or even both within the same composition, others preferred to concentrate on more strictly liturgical music such as Psalm settings, or on motets with exclusively biblical texts.

One of the most revealing results of surveying the repertoire as a whole comes from exploring the correlation between what is known of the background and careers of different composers and the nature of their extant compositions. In general, court composers took advantage of the presence of virtuoso, operatic singers by writing more ambitious vocal lines than their town counterparts, whilst town composers, serving a local congregation rather than a princely ruler, made greater use of the chorale than the court composers. The most Italianate music composed by the North Germans was written by those known to have had close connections with Italian music, such as Kaspar Förster, whilst the more old-fashioned music belongs to composers whose careers brought them into less contact with Italian music and musicians, as was the case with Johann Rubert.

A study of the overall corpus of North German church music of the second half of the seventeenth century also provides a fuller context for understanding Buxtehude's surviving church music. It has been suggested that his church music is both higher in quality and more modern in style than the church music of his contemporaries.[2] But although his organ music can certainly be hailed as the finest achievement amongst the organ music of his contemporaries, his church music does not stand out in the same way. Moreover, the style of his church music shows both modern and conservative traits. This is not to denigrate Buxtehude's achievement, but rather to arrive at a more accurate picture of the nature of his output, and at the same time to give due appreciation to the music of his contemporaries. Most of Buxtehude's surviving church music dates from the 1670s and 1680s, and so can most appropriately be compared with outputs of composers such as Christian Geist and Johann Valentin Meder. Mattheson reported that both Geist and Meder were acknowledged in their day as leading exponents of the Italian style, and their surviving music bears this out. Their music is arguably more thoroughly Italianate in style than Buxtehude's, and contains many works whose expressive quality and technical accomplishment rival the best of Buxtehude's output.

Buxtehude's church music has often been viewed as representing the state of North German church music during the formative years of J. S. Bach. Unfortunately, we have little evidence of how Buxtehude's style developed during the 1690s, but it is clear that by this time the baton had been taken up by the next generation of composers, including Georg Österreich, Johann Theile, and Georg Schürmann. It is to this generation of composers, writing under the influence of Italians such as Giovanni Bassani, Ruggiero Fedeli, and Antonio Giannettini, that one should turn for a fuller understanding

---

[2] 'None of his contemporaries could rival the penetration of Buxtehude's expressiveness or the richness of his methods of text interpretation or his romantic lyricism. At the same time, he was the most advanced musician in respect to style.' F. Blume, in F. Blume *et al.*, *Protestant Church Music: A History* (London, 1974), 275.

of the state of North German church music during Bach's youth. Bach certainly spent time in Lübeck in order to learn from Buxtehude, but, as Christoph Wolff has explained, this concerned many aspects of the composer's art in general, rather than the assimilation of a specific compositional style.[3]

A large proportion of the musical examples in this book are taken from unpublished sources. Much work is still needed to produce modern published editions of the under-explored repertoire of composers throughout the period spanned by Buxtehude's life, ranging from Cratone Bütner and Kaspar Förster to Christian Ritter, Martin Köler, and Balthasar Erben, and finally to Johann Theile, Georg Österreich, and Georg Schürmann. If this general survey of the repertoire has served its purpose, it will have played some part in making the names of these and other North German composers more familiar, and in encouraging the editing and performing of their works.

[3] See the article 'Buxtehude, Bach, and Seventeenth-Century Music in Retrospect', in id., *Bach: Essays on His Life and Music* (Cambridge, Mass., 1991), 41–55.

APPENDIX I

Summary List of Extant Church Music by North German Composers

◊

The following list indicates the number of extant sacred works in manuscript (MS) and print (PR) by each composer.[1] Concordances between the principal manuscript sources are shown by the formula 'x-y', where x is the number of works in the source also present in source y. Further concordances are indicated in the footnotes. Settings of the Passion narrative, and publications of sacred songs or single works for weddings or funerals are not included. The list also indicates the nature, location, and date of commencement of the chief musical appointments held by each composer.

BECKER, DIETRICH (1623–79)
Violinist, Celle court (1658) and Hamburg (1662); Director of Music, Hamburg (1674)
MS Düben collection   2[2]
    Bokemeyer collection   2
    Wolfenbüttel, Herzog August Bibliothek, 294
      (Vogel catalogue)[3]   1

---

[1] Information on the Düben collection has been taken from the typed catalogue by Folke Lindberg and the more recent card catalogue by O. Rudén in the Carolina Rediviva in Uppsala. Details of the Bokemeyer collection have been taken from Kümmerling, *Katalog der Sammlung Bokemeyer*. Information concerning other sources comes principally from Krummacher, *Die Überlieferung der Choralbearbeitungen in der frühen evangelischen Kantate*, and D. P. Walker and P. Walker, *German Sacred Polyphonic Vocal Music between Schütz and Bach: Sources and Critical Editions* (Warren, Mich., 1992) (concerning compositions for three or more voices only). For further details of the Düben and Bokemeyer collections, see pp. 3–6

[2] One of these works (*Laeta nobis*) is attributed in the Düben collection both to Becker (3:5) and to Francesco Foggia (43:1, 77:67).

[3] Vogel, *Die Handschriften der Herzoglichen Bibliothek zu Wolfenbüttel*, 61. Only the vocal parts and the basso continuo are extant; the obbligato instrumental parts are lost.

BERNHARD, CHRISTOPH (1628–1692)
Cantor, Hamburg (1663)

MS Düben collection	24[4]
Bokemeyer collection	6[5]
Berlin, Staatsbibliothek (Unter den Linden), Mus. ms. 30167	1[6]
Berlin, Staatsbibliothek (Unter den Linden), Mus. ms. 1190	4[7]
Berlin, Staatsbibliothek (Potsdamer Straße), Mus. ms. 1620	2
PR *Geistlicher Harmonien, erster Theil* (Dresden, 1665)	20

BERTUCH, GEORGE VON (1668–1743)
Various military appointments

MS Bokemeyer collection	3

BOHLEN, ADRIAN
Cantor, Aurich court (1700)

MS Bokemeyer collection	1

BÖHM, GEORG (1661–1733)[8]
Organist, Lüneburg (1698)

MS Bokemeyer collection	7[9]
Frankfurt am Main, Stadt- und Universitätsbibliothek, MS Ff. Mus. 163	1

BRONNER, GEORG (1667–1720)
Organist, Hamburg (1689)

MS Bokemeyer collection	3[10]
PR *Geistliche Concerten* (Hamburg, 1696)	6

---

[4] Of these, seven are copies of works from the printed collection *Geistlicher Harmonien, erster Theil*, two are copies of published funeral pieces, and one is a misattribution: *Weine nicht* is by M. Weckmann; see Weckmann, *Four Sacred Concertos*, ed. Silbiger, p. xi.

[5] Of these, one is a copy of a published funeral piece, and one is taken from the printed collection *Geistlicher Harmonien, erster Theil*.

[6] This composition (a five-part *Missa brevis*) also survives in Berlin, Staatsbibliothek (Potsdamer Straße), Mus. ms. 1610.

[7] One of these compositions is a copy of a published funeral piece, and three of the compositions can also be found in a manuscript in Dresden: Sächsiches Landesbibliothek, Mus. Part. A 571.

[8] Böhm's motets in the central German style (see p. 81) have been omitted.

[9] One of the works is also attributed to 'Bruhns'. Some anonymous works in the Bokemeyer collection have also been attributed to Böhm. See the *Vorwort* to G. Böhm, *Sämtliche Werke: Vokalwerke*, ed. J. Wolgast, rev. H. Kümmerling (Wiesbaden, 1963).

[10] One of these works, *Es wol uns Gott*, is also extant under the name of N. A. Strungk in Luckau (see below under N. A. Strungk).

BRUHNS, FRIEDRICH (1637–1718)
Director of Music, Hamburg (1682)
MS Bokemeyer collection   2[11]

BRUHNS, NICOLAUS (1665–1697)
Organist, Husum (1689)
MS Bokemeyer collection   11
   Lund, Universitetsbiblioteket, Wenster M 60   1

BRUNCKHORST, ARNOLD MATTHIAS (1670–1725)
Organist, Celle (1697)
MS Bokemeyer collection   2

BÜTNER, CRATO (1616–1679)
Organist, Danzig (c.1652)
MS Düben collection   12[12]
   Dresden, Sächsische Landesbibliothek, Mus.
      Löb. 53 (Löbau collection)   2 (1-Gdańsk)
   Dresden, Sächsische Landesbibliothek, Mus.
      U 515/T (Grimma, St. Jacobi collection)   1
   Berlin, Staatsbibliothek (Potsdamer Straße),
      Mus. ms. 2627 (Erfurt collection)   1
   Berlin, Staatsbibliothek (Unter den Linden),
      Mus. ms. 131 (Breslau collection)   1
   Gdańsk (Danzig), Biblioteka Polskiej Akademii Nauk,
      Ms. Joh. 406 (St. Johannis collection)   2
PR *Geistliche Concerte* (Hamburg, 1651)   1
   Musicalische Concerto (Danzig, 1652)   1
   Musicalische Hertzens-Frewde (Danzig, 1653)   1
   Aria Sunamithica (Danzig, 1654)   1
   Anima Christi (Danzig, 1661)   1
   Lobet den Herrn (Danzig, 1661)   1
   Wo der Herr nicht bei uns wäre (Danzig, 1661)   1
   Te Deum (Danzig, 1662)   1

BUXTEHUDE, DIETERICH (c.1637–1707)
Organist, Lübeck (1668)
MS Düben collection   95[13]
   Bokemeyer collection   9 (5-Düben)[14]

---

[11] One of these is also attributed to Böhm (see n. 9). If it is by either N. or F. Bruhns then it is probably by Friedrich on account of its later style. See Böhm, *Sämtliche Werke: Vokalwerke*, p. vi.
[12] Of these, three are copies of extant printed works.
[13] Of these, two are copies from published funeral works.
[14] One of these is a copy of a published funeral work.

Brussels, Bibliothèque du Conservatoire Royal de Musique, Mus. mss. 758–9	2 (1-Bok.)
Lübeck, Bibliothek der Hansestadt, Mus. A373, now in Berlin, Staatsbibliothek	21 (10-Düben)
Lund, Universitetsbiblioteket, Wenster A 29	1
Lund, Universitetsbiblioteket, Engelhardt 712	1

COBERG, JOHANN ANTON (1665–1708)
Organist, Hannover court (1670s), Berlin court (1680s)

PR *Einer in Gott gelassen* (Hamburg, 1683)	10

DÜBEN, GUSTAV (c.1628–1690)
Kapellmeister, Stockholm court (1663)

MS Düben collection	4[15]

EBELING, JOHANN (1637–1676)
Cantor, Berlin (1662)

MS Bokemeyer collection	1
Göttingen, Niedersächsische Staats- und Universitätsbibliothek, Cod. Ms. philos. 84e Ebeling 1	1

ERBEN, BALTHASAR (1626–1686)
Kapellmeister, Danzig (1658)

MS Düben collection	19
Bokemeyer collection	5 (2-Düben)
PR *Halt Auff! grosses Himmelslicht* (Königsberg, 1668)	1

FLOR, CHRISTIAN (1626–1697)
Organist, Lüneburg (1654)

MS Düben collection	2
Bokemeyer collection	1

FÖRSTER, KASPAR (1616–1673)
Kapellmeister, Danish court (1652, 1661), Danzig (1655)

MS Düben collection	35[16]
Bokemeyer collection	5 (5-Düben)
Strasbourg, Bibliothèque du Séminaire Protestant / Collegium Wilhelmitanum (St. Thomas collection)	1
PR *Ecce ancilla Domini* (canon), included in M. Scacchi, *Cribrum musicum* (Venice, 1643)	1

[15] The Düben collection also contains nineteen simple strophic sacred works by Düben for solo voice and instruments.

[16] One of these compositions (*O bone Jesu*) can also be found in a manuscript in Dresden: Sächsische Landesbibliothek, Mus. ms. 1715-E-500 (Grimma, St. Jacobi collection).

FÖRTSCH, JOHANN PHILIPP (1652–1732)
Kapellmeister, *Gottorf court (1680)*
MS Bokemeyer collection   82

FRANCK, JOHANN WOLFGANG (1644–*c.*1710)
Director of Music, Hamburg (1682)
MS Bokemeyer collection   5
    Wolfenbüttel, Herzog August Bibliothek, 294
    (Vogel catalogue)   6[17] (1-Bok.)

FUNCKE, FRIEDRICH (1642–1699)
Cantor, Lüneburg (1664)
MS Lüneburg, Ratsbücherei, Mus. ant. pract. K. N. 201   1
PR *Danck- und Denck-Mahl* (Hamburg, 1666)   1
    Der ewig-feste (1652)   1

GEIST, CHRISTIAN (*c.*1640–1711)
Organist, Stockholm court (1670), Copenhagen (1685)
MS Düben collection   57[18]
    Bokemeyer collection   2 (1-Düben)

GERSTENBÜTTEL, JOACHIM (*c.*1650–1721)
Cantor, Hamburg (1675)
MS Bokemeyer collection   31

HAHN, MICHAEL
Cantor, Narva
MS Düben collection   3

HANFF, JOHANN NICOLAUS (1665–1711/12)
Organist, Eutin court (c.1696)
MS Bokemeyer collection   3

HASSE, NICOLAUS (*c.*1617–1672)
Organist, Rostock (1642)
MS Lund, Universitetsbiblioteket, Wenster M 39   1

JACOBI, MICHAEL (1618–1663)
Cantor, Lüneburg (1651)
MS Kaliningrad (Königsberg), Oblastnaya Biblioteka[19]   1

---

[17] These works are all ascribed to 'J. W. F.', but it seems likely that this refers to Franck, as suggested by Krummacher in *Die Überlieferung der Choralbearbeitungen*, 184. He states that there are seven works by 'J. W. F.', but one is headed 'Secunda pars' and belongs to the previous piece.

[18] One of these compositions (*Jesu delitium vultus*) can also be found in a manuscript in Frankfurt am Main: Stadt- und Universitätsbibliothek, MS Ff. Mus. 204.

[19] According to the entry on Jacobi in *The New Grove*.

PR   *Timor Domini* (Lüneburg, 1663)[20]   1

KAPLER, H. CONRAD
Kapellmeister, *Husum (1660)*
MS Düben collection   1

KLINGENBERG, FRIEDRICH GOTTLIEB (*d.* 1720)
Organist, Stettin (1699)
MS Lund, Universitetsbiblioteket, Wenster collection   7

KÖLER, MARTIN (*c.*1620–1703/4)
Kapellmeister, *Wolfenbüttel court (1663), Gottorf court (1675)*
MS Düben collection   1
    Bokemeyer collection   14
    Dresden, Sächsische Landesbibliothek (Grimma,
        St. Jacobi collection)   2
    Wolfenbüttel, Herzog August Bibliothek, 44
        (Vogel catalogue)   1[21]

LÖWE, JOHANN JACOB (1629–1703)
Kapellmeister, *Wolfenbüttel (1655); organist, Lüneburg (1683)*
MS Düben collection   1[22]
PR *Neue geistliche Concerten* (Wolfenbüttel, 1660)   12

LÜBECK, VINCENT (1654–1740)
Organist, Stade (1675), Hamburg (1702)
MS Bokemeyer collection   3

MEDER, JOHANN VALENTIN (1649–1719)
Cantor, Reval (1674); Kapellmeister, Danzig (1687); cantor, Riga (1700)
MS Düben collection   12
    Bokemeyer collection   1
    Wolfenbüttel, Herzog August Bibliothek, 294
        (Vogel catalogue)   2 (1-Bok.)
    Luckau, Nikolaikirche Ms. 221A   1
    Gdańsk (Danzig), Biblioteka Polskiej Akademii Nauk,
        Mus. Joh. 191–4 (St. Johannis collection)   4

MEISTER, JOHANN FRIEDRICH (1638–1697)
Organist, Flensburg (1683)
MS Bokemeyer collection   14

---

[20] The entry on Jacobi in *The New Grove* suggests that this publication is a collection of several works, whereas it is in fact a single piece.

[21] According to the entry on Köler in *The New Grove*, this work is found in the Murhardsche Bibliothek der Stadt und Landesbibliothek, Kassel.

[22] This piece is taken from Löwe's *Neue geistliche Concerten.*

ÖSTERREICH, GEORG (1664–1725)
Kapellmeister, *Gottorf court (1689); singer, Wolfenbüttel court (1702)*
MS Bokemeyer collection   33[23]

ÖSTERREICH, MICHAEL
MS Bokemeyer collection   13[24]

PFLEGER, AUGUSTIN (c.1635–1686)
Kapellmeister, *Gottorf court (1665)*
MS Düben collection   98[25]
   Bokemeyer collection   3 (3-Düben)
PR *Psalmi, dialoghi et motettae* (Hamburg, 1661)   18

RADECK, JOHANN MARTIN (1623?–1684)
Organist, Copenhagen (1660)
MS Düben collection   1

REINCKEN, JOHANN ADAM (1623–1722)
Organist, Hamburg (1663)
MS Berlin, Staatsbibliothek (Potsdamer Straße),
   Mus. ms. 18254   1

RITTER, CHRISTIAN (1645/50–AFTER 1717)
Organist, Vice-Kapellmeister, Stockholm court (1681)
MS Düben collection   16
   Bokemeyer collection   4
   Lüneburg, Ratsbücherei, Mus. ant. pract. K. N.
   207/13   1

RUBERT, JOHANN MARTIN (1614–1680)
Organist, Stralsund (1646)
PR *Musicalische Seelen-Erquickung* (Stralsund, 1664)   12

SCHÜRMANN, GEORG CASPAR (1672/3–1751)
Wolfenbüttel court (1697)
MS Bokemeyer collection   10

SCHWENCKENBECKER, GÜNTER (1682–1714)
Cantor, Königsberg
MS Bokemeyer collection   1

---

[23] See n. 24.
[24] It seems possible that the thirteen works attributed to the otherwise unknown Michael Österreich, bound together as 'Mus. ms. autogr. Michael Österreich', may in fact be by Georg Österreich. Certainly one of them, the arrangement of a motet by Della Porta, is attributed to G. Österreich (see Kümmerling, *Katalog der Sammlung Bokemeyer*, 122).
[25] One of these works (*Missus est angelus*) is also found in Pfleger's 1661 publication.

SEBASTIANI, JOHANN (1622–1683)
Cantor, Königsberg (1661)
MS Düben collection   4[26]
  Bokemeyer collection   2

SLÖPKE, MAURITZ
Organist, Stade
MS Düben collection   2

STRUNGK, DELPHIN (1600/1–1694)[27]
Organist, Braunschweig (1637)
MS Wolfenbüttel, Herzog August Bibliothek, [252]
  (Vogel catalogue)   1

STRUNGK, NICOLAUS ADAM (1640–1700)
Hannover court (1665, 1682); Director of Music, Hamburg (1678)
MS Bokemeyer collection   5
  Luckau, Nikolaikirche, Ms. 302   1[28]
  London, British Library, Mus. R.M. 24.a.3 (7) 1

STRUTZ, THOMAS (*c.*1621–1678)
Organist, Danzig (1642)
MS Düben collection   4
  Bokemeyer collection   1
  Dresden, Sächsische Landesbibliothek, Mus. ms.
   1914-E-500 (Grimma, St. Jacobi collection) 1
PR *Psalmus C* (Danzig, 1658)   1

STÜBENDORF, GEORG
Organist, Stockholm (1663)
MS Düben collection   1

THEILE, JOHANN (1646–1724)
Kapellmeister, Gottorf court (1673), Wolfenbüttel court (1685)
MS Düben collection   5
  Bokemeyer collection   21 (2-Düben)
  Berlin, Staatsbibliothek (Potsdamer Straße),
   Mus. ms. 21825 ('Andächtige Kirchen-Music') 8[29]
  Berlin, Staatsbibliothek (Unter den Linden),
   Mus. ms. theor. 913   2

---

[26] Two of these are copies of published funeral works.

[27] *The New Grove* also states that there are five works by Delphin Strungk in Berlin, but these works are by his son Nicolaus Adam Strungk.

[28] This work is also extant under the name of Georg Bronner in the Bokemeyer collection.

[29] One composition in this manuscript (*Wirf dein Angliegen*) can also be found in a manuscript in the Berlin Staatsbibliothek (Under den Linden): Mus. ms. 30177.

Berlin, Staatsbibliothek (Unter den Linden),
    Mus. ms. 30172   1
PR *Pars prima missarum* (Wismar, 1673)   6

TUNDER, FRANZ (1614–1667)
Organist, Lübeck (1641)
MS Düben collection   17

VIERDANCK, JOHANN (*c.*1605–1646)
Organist, Stralsund (1635)
MS Düben collection   1
PR *Geistliche Concerten . . . Erster Th.* (Greifswald,
    1641)   21
    Geistliche Concerten . . . Ander Th. (Greifswald,
    1643)   20
    Profe anthology RISM B/I/1: 1641[3]   1

WECKMANN, JAKOB (1643–1680)
MS Düben collection   1
    Bokemeyer collection   2 (1-Düben)

WECKMANN, MATTHIAS (*c.*1619–1674)
Organist, Hamburg (1655)
MS Düben collection   5
    Bokemeyer collection   3
    Lüneburg, Ratsbücherei, Mus. ant. pract.
    K. N. 207/6   4 (1-Düben)

WEILAND, JULIUS JOHANN (d. 1663)
Wolfenbüttel court (1655)
MS Düben collection   3[30]
    Bokemeyer collection   1
PR *Erstlinge musicalische Andachten* (Bremen, 1654)   22
    Deuterotokos (Bremen, 1656)   15
    Nun dancket alle Gott (Wolfenbüttel, 1661)   1
    Ich will singen (Wolfenbüttel, 1661)   1
    Uns ist ein Kind geboren (Wolfenbüttel, 1663)   1

WERNER, CHRISTOPH (1617/18–1650)
Cantor, Danzig (1646)
MS Lüneburg, Ratsbücherei, Mus. ant. pract.
    K. N. 206   8[31]
PR *Praemessa musicalia* (Königsberg, 1646)   15

---

[30] All three are copies of printed works from Weiland's 1656 collection.
[31] Seven of these eight works are copies of pieces in Werner's printed collection of 1646.

APPENDIX II

List of Compositions Cited, with Details of Sources and Modern Editions

◊

This list gives the original sources of all the North German and Italian compositions mentioned in the text, together with details of principal modern editions, where they exist. In the case of the Italian works, only North German and Scandinavian sources are listed. The scoring details do not include instruments that double the basso continuo line.

ABBREVIATIONS

BuxWV	Buxtehude-Werke-Verzeichnis: G. Karstädt, *Thematisch-systematisches Verzeichnis der musikalischen Werke von Dietrich Buxtehude* (Wiesbaden, 1974; 2nd edn., 1985)
D-B (PS)	Germany, Berlin, Staatsbibliothek (Potsdamer Straße)
D-B (UdL)	Germany, Berlin, Staatsbibliothek (Unter den Linden)
DBW	*Dietrich Buxtehudes Werke*, ed. W. Gurlitt and others (8 vols., Klecken and Hamburg, 1925–58; repr. New York, 1977)
DdT 3	F. Tunder, *Kantaten und Chorwerke*, ed. M. Seiffert (Denkmäler deutscher Tonkunst, 3; 1990)
DdT 6	M. Weckmann und C. Bernhard, *Solokantaten und Chorwerke mit Instrumentalbegleitung*, ed. M. Seiffert (Denkmäler deutscher Tonkunst, 6; 1901, repr. 1957)
EdM 2/1	N. Bruhns, *Gesamt Ausgabe der Werke*, ed. F. Stein (Das Erbe deutscher Musik, Zweite Reihe: Schleswig-Holstein und Hansestädte, 1; 1937)
EdM 48	C. Geist, *15 Ausgewählte Kirchenkonzerte*, ed. B. Lundgren (Das Erbe deutscher Musik, 48; 1960)
EdM 64	A. Pfleger, *Geistliche Konzerte Nr. 12–23, aus dem Evangelien-Jahrgang*, ed. F. Stein (Das Erbe deutscher Musik, 64; 1964)

EdM 65   C. Bernhard, *Geistliche Harmonien*, ed. M. Geck (Das Erbe
              deutscher Musik, 65; 1972)
EdM 90   Christoph Bernhard, *Geistliche Konzerte und andere Werke*,
              ed. O. Drechsler (Das Erbe deutscher Musik, 90; 1982)
GBSW   G. Böhm, *Sämtliche Werke: Vokalwerke*, ed. J. Wolgast, rev.
              H. Kümmerling (Wiesbaden, 1963)
HK   H. Kümmerling, *Katalog der Sammlung Bokemeyer* (Kassel,
              1970)
RRMBE 46   Matthias Weckmann, *Four Sacred Concertos*, ed. A. Silbiger
              (Recent Researches in the Music of the Baroque Era, 46;
              1984)
S-Uu   Sweden, Uppsala, Universitetsbiblioteket (Vokalmusik i
              handskrift)

NORTH GERMAN CHURCH MUSIC

BECKER, D.
Schaf in mir Gott, A, 2vn, 2va, bc
   Düben collection: S-Uu 3:6, 86:68

BERNHARD, C.
Ach Herr, strafe mich nicht, SB, bc
   Geistlicher Harmonien erster Theil (Dresden, 1665)
   modern edn., EdM 65, no. 3
Anima sterilis, SB, 2vn, bc
   Düben collection: S-Uu 3:10, 81:62
   modern edn., EdM 90, no. 9
Aus der Tiefe ruf' ich Herr, zu dir, S, 2vn, bc
   Geistlicher Harmonien erster Theil (Dresden, 1665)
   modern edn., EdM 65, no. 6
Currite pastores, S, 2vn, bc
   Düben collection: S-Uu 80:93
   modern edn., EdM 90, no. 6
Das ist ein köstlich Ding, TT, bc
   Geistlicher Harmonien erster Theil (Dresden, 1665)
   modern edn., EdM 65, no. 5
Euch ist's gegeben, SB, 2vn, bc
   Geistlicher Harmonien erster Theil (Dresden, 1665)
   modern edn., EdM 65, no. 20
Fürchtet euch nicht (Fruchten Ehr ey), S, 2vn, bc
   Düben collection: S-Uu 41:12, 67:20, 79:33
   modern edn., B. Grusnick (Kassel, 1975)

Heute ist Christus von den Toten auferstanden, B, 2vn, bc
  Geistlicher Harmonien erster Theil (Dresden, 1665)
  modern edn., EdM 65, no. 9
Ich sahe an alles Thun, SATB, 2vn, 2va, bc
  Bokemeyer collection: D-B (UdL), Mus. ms. 30096 (HK 144)
  Düben collection: S-Uu 4:3, 86:22
  Letzter Ehren-Nachklang (Hamburg, 1669)
  modern edn., DdT 6, no. 3
Jubilate Deo, STB, bc
  Düben collection: S-Uu 42:19, 80:109
  modern edn., EdM 90, no. 8
Missa Christ unser Herr zum Jordan kam, SSATB
  D-B (PS), Mus. ms. 162
  modern edn., R. Gerber, Das Chorwerk, 16 (1932, repr. *c.*1955)
Missa Durch Adams Fall, SATTB
  D-B (PS), Mus. ms. 1620
  modern edn., O. Drechsler, Das Chorwerk, 107 (1969)
Prudentia prudentiana, SATB
  Prudentia prudentiana (Hamburg, 1669)
  modern edn., EdM 90, no. 14
Salve mi Jesu, A, bc
  Düben collection: S-Uu 86:59
  modern edn., EdM 90, no. 11

BERTUCH, G. VON
Gott der Herr, der mächtige redet, SATB, 3vn, 3va, bc
  Bokemeyer collection: D-B (UdL), Mus. ms. 30096 (HK 149)
Du Tochter Zion freue dich, B, 2vn, 2va, bc
  Bokemeyer collection: D-B (UdL), Mus. ms. 30096 (HK 151)

BÖHM, G.
Das Himmelreich ist gleich einem Könige, SSATB, 2vn, 2va, bc
  Bokemeyer collection: D-B (UdL), Mus. ms. 30099 (HK 158)
  modern edn., GBSW, no. 1
Nun komm der Heyden Heylandt, SSATB, 2vn, 2tbn, bc
  Bokemeyer collection: D-B (UdL), Mus. ms. 30099 (HK 159)
  modern edn., GBSW, no. 5
Wie lieblich sind deine Wohnungen, SATB, 2cl, 2vn, 2va, bc
  Frankfurt am Main, Stadt- und Universitätsbibliothek, Ms. Mus. 163
  modern edn., GBSW, no. 4

BRONNER, G.
Gott hilff mir, S, 2vn, bc
  Geistliche Concerten (Hamburg, 1696)

BRONNER, G. (*cont.*):
Gott sey mir gnädig, S, 2vn, bc
  Geistliche Concerten (Hamburg, 1696)
Lobet den Herren alle Heyden, S, 2ob, bc
  Geistliche Concerten (Hamburg, 1696)

BRUHNS, N.
Die Zeit meines Abschieds ist vorhanden, SATB, 2vn, 2va, bc
  Bokemeyer collection: D-B (UdL), Mus. ms. 30101 (HK 176)
  modern edn., EdM 2/1, no. 1
Hemmt eure Thränenflut, SATB, 2vn, 2va, bc
  Bokemeyer collection: D-B (UdL), Mus. ms. 30101 (HK 171)
  modern edn., EdM 2/1, no. 11
Mein Herz ist bereit, B, vn, bc
  Lund, Universitetsbiblioteket, Wenster Litt. M 60
  modern edn., EdM 2/1, no. 5

BÜTNER, C.
Du heilige Brunst süsser Trost, SATB, 2fl, 2vn, 2va, bc
  Düben collection: S-Uu 5:8
Ei du frommer und getreuer Knecht, SSAATTBB, 2vn, 3va/tbn, bc
  Düben collection: S-Uu 5:16
Frohlocket mit Händen, SSAB, ATTB, 2ct, 2vn, 3tbn, bc
  Düben collection: S-Uu 5:10
Te Deum, SSAB, SATB, ATTB, 2vn, va, 2 ct, 2cl, timp, 4tbn, bc
  Te Deum (Danzig, 1662)
Vom Himmel hoch, SATB, SATB, 3vn, 2tbn, bc
  Düben collection: S-Uu 5:19
Wirff dein Anliegen auf den Herrn, TT, 2vn, vdg, bc
  Geistliche Concerte (Hamburg, 1651)
  modern edn., F. Kessler, *Danziger Kirchen-Musik: Vokalwerke des 16. bis
    18. Jahrhunderts* (Stuttgart, 1973), no. 15

BUXTEHUDE, D.
Benedicam Dominum (BuxWV 113), SSATB, SATB, 2vn, vno, 4cl, posauna,
    tbn grossa, 2ct, fag, 3tbn
  Düben collection: S-Uu 50:6
  modern edn., *DBW* iv. 23
Canite Jesu nostro (BuxWV 11), SSB, 2vn, bc
  Düben collection: S-Uu 82:43
  modern edn., *DBW* v. 21
Dixit Dominus (BuxWV 17), S, 2vn, 2va, bc
  Bokemeyer collection: D-B (PS), Mus. ms. 2680 (HK 192)
  Düben collection: S-Uu 50:8
  modern edn., *DBW* ii. 27

Ecce super montes (*Membra Jesu nostri*, BuxWV 75), SSATB, 2vn, bc
    Düben collection: S–Uu 6:2, 50:12
    modern edn., B. Grusnick (Kassel, 1963)
Gott hilf mir (BuxWV 34), SSATBB, 2vn, 2va, bc
    Düben collection: S–Uu 50:19
    modern edn., D. Buxtehude, *Abendmusiken und Kirchenkantaten*, ed. M.
      Seiffert (DdT, 14; 1903; 2nd edn., H. Moser, 1957), no. 4
Ich habe Lust abzuscheiden (BuxWV 46), SSB, 2vn, bc
    Düben collection: S–Uu 51:4, 82:42 (earlier version)
    Lübeck, Bibliothek der Hansestadt, Mus. A373, now in D–B (UdL)
      (later version)
    modern edn., *DBW* v. 56, 62
Ich suchte des Nachts (BuxWV 50), TB, 2ob, 2vn, bc
    Brussels, Bibliothèque du Conservatoire Royal de Musique, Mus. ms. 759
    modern edn., *DBW* iii. 41
Jesu dulcis memoria (BuxWV 57), ATB, 2vn, bc
    Düben collection: S–Uu 51:8
    modern edn., *DBW* vii. 72
Jesu, komm, mein Trost und Lachen (BuxWV 58), ATB, 2vn, va, bc
    Düben collection: S–Uu 6:12
    modern edn., *DBW* vii. 81
Jesulein, du Tausendschön (BuxWV 63), ATB, 2vn, bc
    Düben collection: S–Uu 51:9
    modern edn., *DBW* vii. 89
Jubilate Domino (BuxWV 64), A, vdg, bc
    Düben collection: S–Uu 51:12
    modern edn., *DBW* ii. 19
Lauda Sion salvatorem (BuxWV 68), SSB, 2vn, bc
    Düben collection: S–Uu 51:14, 82:42
    Lübeck, Bibliothek der Hansestadt, Mus. A373, now in D–B (UdL)
    modern edn., *DBW* vi. 24
Laudate pueri (BuxWV 69), SS, 5vdg, bc
    Düben collection: S–Uu 6:17, 84:29
    modern edn., *DBW* iii. 59
Membra Jesu nostri (cycle of motets, BuxWV 75), SSATB, 2vn, 5vdg, bc
    Düben collection: S–Uu 6:1, 2, 3, 6:18, 46:25, 51:10, 50:12
    modern edn., B. Grusnick (Kassel, 1963)
Missa brevis (BuxWV 114), SSATB, bc
    Düben collection: S–Uu 6:16
    modern edn., *DBW* iv. 12
Mit Fried und Freud ich fahr dahin (BuxWV 76), SB, 4 instrumental parts
    Fried- und Freudenreiche Hinfahrt (Lübeck, 1674)
    modern edn., *DBW* ii. 86

BUXTEHUDE, D. (*cont.*):

Nimm von uns, Herr, du treuer Gott (BuxWV 78), SATB, 2vn, 2va, bc
  Düben collection: S–Uu 82:38
  modern edn., D. Buxtehude, *Collected Works*, ix, ed. K. Snyder (New
    York, 1987), 109
Nun laßt uns Gott (BuxWV 81), SATB, 2vn, bc
  Düben collection: S–Uu 51:17, 85:1–18
  modern edn., *DBW* viii. 9
Singet dem Herrn (BuxWV 98), S, vn, bc
  Düben collection: S–Uu 51:27, 82:43
  modern edn., *DBW* i. 108
Surge anima mea (*Membra Jesu nostri*, BuxWV 75), SSATB, 2vn, bc
  Düben collection: S–Uu 6:1, 50:12
  modern edn., B. Grusnick (Kassel, 1963)
O clemens, o mitis (BuxWV 82), S, vn, 2va, bc
  Düben collection: S–Uu 51:18, 84:29–42
  modern edn., *DBW* i. 65
O Gottes Stadt (BuxWV 87), S, 2vn, va, bc
  Düben collection: S–Uu 51:19, 85:1–18
  modern edn., *DBW* i. 84
O wie selig (BuxWV 90), TB, 2vn, bc
  Düben collection: S–Uu 51:21
  modern edn., *DBW* iii. 83
Wie schmeckt es so lieblich (BuxWV 108), SAB, 2vn, bc
  Düben collection: S–Uu 82:43
  modern edn., *DBW* vii. 39

DÜBEN, G.
Fadher wår, ATTB, 2vn, 2va, bc
  Düben collection: S–Uu 19:5

ERBEN, B.
Ach dass ich doch in meinen Augen, S, 2vn, va, 2vdg, bc
  Düben collection: S–Uu 20:1/1a, 85:86
Ante oculos tuos, S, 2vn, va, bc
  Düben collection: S–Uu 20:2, 83:39
Dixit Dominus, SSATTB, 2vn, 3va, bc
  Düben collection: S–Uu 20:4
Erbarm dich mein o herre Gott, SATTB, 4va, bc
  Bokemeyer collection: D–B (UdL), Mus. ms. 30294 (HK 292)
Herr Christ der einige Gottes Sohn, SSATB, 2vn, 2va, bc
  Düben collection: S–Uu 20:7
    modern edn., F. Kessler, *Danziger Kirchen-Musik: Vokalwerke des 16. bis
      18. Jahrhunderts* (Stuttgart, 1973), no. 21

O Domine Jesu Christe, SATB, bc
  Düben collection: S-Uu 20:8a
Peccavi super numerum, SSATTB, 3va, bc
  Bokemeyer collection: D-B (UdL), Mus. ms. 30294 (HK 294)
  Düben collection: S-Uu 20:9, 80:26
Salve suavissime Jesu, SS(TT), 2vn, 2va, bc
  Düben collection: S-Uu 20:11

FÖRSTER, K.
Ad arma fideles, SSB, 2–5va, bc
  Bokemeyer collection: D-B(UdL), Mus. ms. 30298 (HK 330)
  Düben collection: S-Uu 21:7, 78:14, 84:5
  ed. S. Sørensen (Copenhagen, 1967)
Ah peccatores, SSATTB, 2fl, 2vn, 2va, bc
  Düben collection: S-Uu 21:8
Beatus vir, SAB, 2vn, bc
  Düben collection: S-Uu 21:9
Confitebor tibi Domine, SSATTB, 2vn, 2va, bc
  Düben collection: S-Uu 21:12
Confitebor tibi Domine, SATB, 2vn, bc
  Düben collection: S-Uu 21:13
Congregantes Philistei, SATB, 2vn, va, bc
  Bokemeyer collection: D-B (UdL), Mus. ms. 30298 (HK 327; HK 329,
    with additional instrumental parts by G. Österreich)
  Düben collection: S-Uu 54:7, 78:54
Et cum ingressus, ATB, bc
 Düben collection: S-Uu 83:18
Gentes redemptae, ATB, 2vn, bc
  Düben collection: S-Uu 22:3, 85:58
In tribulationibus, SATB (2vn, va), bc
  Düben collection: S-Uu 22:5 (version without instruments)
  Düben collection: S-Uu 22:5a, 85:18 (version with instruments)
  modern edn., M. Wöldike (Copenhagen, c.1982)
Intenderunt arcum, SAB, bc
  Düben collection: S-Uu 22:4, 86:9
Lauda Jerusalem, SSATB, 2vn, 2va, bc
  Düben collection: S-Uu 22:6
O bone Jesu, SAB, 2vn, bc
  Düben collection: S-Uu 22:9, 84:7
Quanta fecisti Domine, SATB, 2vn, bc
  Düben collection: S-Uu 54:13, 86:46
Repleta est malis, ATB, 2vn, bc
  Düben collection: S-Uu 22:2, 78:89

FÖRSTER, K. (*cont.*):
Vanitas vanitatum, STB, 2vn, 2va, bc
  Düben collection: S-Uu 22:19, 81:77
Viri Israelite, SATB, 2vn, va, bc
  Düben collection: S-Uu 54:11, 78:34

FÖRTSCH, J.P.
Christ der du bist der helle Tag
  D-B (PS), Mus. ms. 6473
Ich vergeße was dahinten ist, SSATB, 2vn, 2va, bc
  Bokemeyer collection: D-B (PS), Mus. ms. 6470 (HK 349)

F[RANCK], J.W.
Herr Jesu Christ du höchstes Gut, S (2vn, missing), bc
  Wolfenbüttel, Herzog August Bibliothek, Mus. ms. Slg 294, no. 9

FUNCKE, F.
Danck- und Denck-Mahl (Gelobet sei der Herr aus Zion), SSAATTBB, 2vn,
  2va, bc
  Danck- und Denck-Mahl (Hamburg, 1666)

GEIST, C.
Alleluia. Virgo Deum, SSB, 2vn, vdg, bc
  Düben collection: S-Uu 25:3, 84:53
Dixit Dominus, SATB, 2vn, bc
  Düben collection: S-Uu 25:8
  modern edn., EdM 48, no. 11
Domine qui das salutem, SSATB, 2vn, va (optional), vdg, bc
  Düben collection: S-Uu 54:18, 84:19
Jesu delitium vultus, SATB, 2vn, bc
  Düben collection: S-Uu 25:15, 84:20
  Frankfurt am Main, Stadt- und Universitätsbibliothek, MS Ff. Mus. 204
Laudet Deum, SSB, 2vn, vdg (optional), bc
  Düben collection: S-Uu 26:2, 84:41
  modern edn., B. Lundgren (Stockholm, 1953)
Media vita in morte sumus, SSB, 3va, bc
  Düben collection: S-Uu 54:19, 26:3
O caeli sapientia, SSB, bc
  Düben collection: S-Uu 26:4
O Jesu amantissime, SST, 2vn, bc
  Düben collection: S-Uu 84:36
O Jesu dulcis, SST, 2vn, bc
  Düben collection: S-Uu 26:5
Pastores dicite, STTB, 2vn, bc
  Düben collection: S-Uu 26:9, 84:54
  modern edn., EdM 48, no. 13

Quis hostis in coelis, SSATB, 2cl, 2vn, 2va (optional), vno, bc
  Düben collection: S-Uu 54:20, 84:18
Resurrexi et adhuc tecum sum, S, 2vn, vdg, bc
  Düben collection: S-Uu 26:13, 84:45
Seelig, ja seelig, SSTB, 2vn, bc
  Düben collection: S-Uu 26:15
Veni sancte spiritus et emitte, SS, 2vn, vdg, bc
  Düben collection: S-Uu 26:20, 82:2:1
Veni sancte spiritus reple tuorum, SSB, 2vn, bc
  Düben collection: S-Uu 26:21, 85:34a
Verbum caro, SS, 2vn, vdg (optional), bc
  Düben collection: S-Uu 26:22, 84:52

GERSTENBÜTTEL, J.
Dazu ist erschienen der Sohn Gottes, SSATB, 2vn, 2va, bc
  Bokemeyer collection: D-B (PS), Mus. ms. 7310 (HK 440)
In dich hab ich gehoffet, SSATB, 2vn, 2va, bc
  Bokemeyer collection: D-B (PS), Mus. ms. 7310 (HK 427)
Lobet den Herrn ihr seine Engel, SATB, 2cl/ob, 2ob/va, bc
  Bokemeyer collection: D-B (PS), Mus. ms. 7310 (HK 446)
Wohl dem der in Gottes Furcht steht, SSATB, 2vn, 2va, bc
  Bokemeyer collection: D-B (PS), Mus. ms. 7310 (HK 430)

JACOBI, M.
Timor Domini, SSATB, 2vn, 2va, bc
  Timor Domini (Lüneburg, 1663)

MEDER, J.V.
Ach Herr mich armen Sünder, SATB, vn, 2va, bc
  Gdańsk (Danzig), Biblioteka Polskiej Akademii Nauk, Ms. Joh. 191
Ach Herr, straffe mich nicht, S, 2vn, bc
  Düben collection: S-Uu 28:5
Gott! mein Hertz ist bereit, SSB, 2vn(ob), 2va, bc
  Düben collection: S-Uu 28:7
In tribulatione, S, 4vn, bc
  Bokemeyer collelction: D-B (UdL), Mus. ms. 30236 (HK 633)
  Wolfenbüttel, Herzog August Bibliothek, 294 (Vogel catalogue), no. 21
Jubilate Deo, B, cl, vn, bc
  Düben collection: S-Uu 28:8
Leben wir so leben wir, SATB, vn, 2vdg, bc
  Düben collection: S-Uu 61:6
Sufficit nunc Domine, S, vn, 4vdg, bc
  Düben collection: S-Uu 61:8
Wie murren denn die Leute, AB, 2vn, 2va, bc
  Düben collection: S-Uu 28:9

MEISTER, J. F.

Unser Wandel ist im Himmel, SSB, 2vn, bc
  Bokemeyer collection: D-B (UdL), Mus. ms. 30236 (HK 630)
Wie schön leuchtet der Morgenstern, SATBB, 2vn, bc
  Bokemeyer collection: D-B (UdL), Mus. ms. 30236 (HK 626-7)

ÖSTERREICH, G.

Ach Herr wie sind meine Feinde, T, cl, 2vn, va, bc
  Bokemeyer collection: D-B (UdL), Mus. ms. autogr. Georg Österreich
    1 (HK 651)
Alle Menschen müßen sterben, SATBB, 3ob, 2vn, 2va, 2bn, bc
  Bokemeyer collection: D-B (UdL), Mus. ms. autogr. Georg Österreich
    2 (HK 675)
Aller Augen warten auf dich, SATB, 2vn, 2va, bc
  Bokemeyer collection: D-B (UdL), Mus. ms. autogr. Georg Österreich
    2 (HK 674)
Du Tochter Zion freue dich, SATB, 2vn, 2va, bc
  Bokemeyer collection: D-B (UdL), Mus. ms. autogr. Georg Österreich
    2 (HK 676)
Herr Jesu Christ, SATB, 2vn, 2va, bc
  Bokemeyer collection: D-B (UdL), Mus. ms. autogr. Georg Österreich
    2 (HK 679)
Herr Jesu Christ meins Lebens Licht, SATB, 2vn, 2va, bc
  Bokemeyer collection: D-B (UdL), Mus. ms. autogr. Georg Österreich
    2 (HK 680)
Ich bin die Auferstehung, SATBB, 2ob, 2vn, 2va, bc
  Bokemeyer collection: D-B (UdL), Mus. ms. autogr. Georg Österreich
    1 (HK 652)
Plötzlich müßen die Leute sterben ('Actus funebris'), SATBB, 2ob, 2vn, 2va,
    bc
  Bokemeyer collection: D-B (UdL), Mus. ms. autogr. Georg Österreich
    3 (HK 692)
Ubi eras, o bone Jesu (arrangement of motet by F. Della Porta), SA, 3va, bc
  Bokemeyer collection: D-B (PS), Mus. ms. autogr. Michael Österreich
    (HK 708)
Und Jesus ging aus, SSATB, 2vn, 2va, bc
  Bokemeyer collection: D-B (UdL), Mus. ms. autogr. Georg Österreich
    1 (HK 656)
Valet will ich dir geben, SATB, 3va, bc
  Bokemeyer collection: D-B (UdL), Mus. ms. autogr. Georg Österreich
    1 (HK 660)
Weise mir Herr deinen Weg, SATB, 2ob, 2vn, 2va, bc
  Bokemeyer collection: D-B (UdL), Mus. ms. autogr. Georg Österreich
    1 (HK 659)

Wie eilstu edler Geist, SSATB, 2vn, 2va, bc
  Bokemeyer collection: D-B (UdL), Mus. ms. autogr. Georg Österreich
  3 (HK 682)

ÖSTERREICH, M.
Sursum corda, SATB (possibly by Georg Österreich)
  Bokemeyer collection: D-B (UdL), Mus. ms. autogr. Michael Öster-
  reich, located with a setting of the *Sanctus* (HK 710)

PFLEGER, A.
Laudate Dominum, SATB, 2vn, 2va, bc
  Düben collection: S-Uu 31:14, 85:38
O pulcherrima mulier, SSATB, bc
  Psalmi, Dialogi et Motettae (Hamburg, 1661)
So spricht der Herr, SSTB, 3va, bc
  Düben collection: S-Uu 72:18
  modern edn., EdM 64, no. 21
Und es war eine Hochzeit zu Kana, SSATB, 2vn, 2va, bc
  Düben collection: S-Uu 72:13
  modern edn., EdM 64, no. 13
Und Jesus ward verkläret, SSATBB, 2vn, 2va, bc
  Düben collection: S-Uu 72:17
  modern edn., EdM 64, no. 17

RITTER, C.
Gelobet sey der Name des Herren, SATB, 4cl, timp, 2vn, 2va, 2ct, 3tbn, bc
  Bokemeyer collection: D-B (PS), Mus. ms. 30260 (HK 767)
Herr wer wird wohnen, ATB, bc
  Düben collection: S-Uu 32:19
Miserere Christe mei, SATB, 3va, bc
  Düben collection: S-Uu 63:17, 86:44
O amantissime Sponse Jesu, S, 2vn, 2va, bc
  Bokemeyer collection: D-B (PS), Mus. ms. 30260 (HK 769)
  modern edn., D. Krüger (Copenhagen, 1976)
Vater unser, S, 2vn, 2va, bc
  Düben collection: S-Uu 63:20, 85:77
Wie lieblich sind deine Wohnungen, SSATB, 2cl, 2vn, 2va, bc
  Düben collection: S-Uu 63:21, 84:102
  modern edn., E. Selén (Kassel, 1967)

RUBERT, J. M.
Ich weis mein Gott, SS, B (optional), 2vn, 2va (optional), bc
  Musicalische Seelen-Erquickung (Stralsund, 1664)

SCHIEFERDECKER, J. C.
In te Domine speravi, T, vn, bc
  Bokemeyer collection: D-B (UdL), Mus. ms. 30095 (HK 1081)

SCHRÖDER, J.
Adesto virtutum chorus, SATB, 2vn, bc
  Düben collection: S-Uu 34:19

SCHÜRMANN, G.
Es wird ein Stern aus Jacob auffgehen, SATB, 2vn, 2va, bc
  Bokemeyer collection: D-B (UdL), Mus. ms. 30272 (HK 945)
Siehe, eine Jungfrau ist schwanger, SATB, 2vn, 2va, bc
  Bokemeyer collection: D-B (UdL), Mus. ms. 30272 (HK 948)

SEBASTIANI, J.
Ad sacram mensam, SSATB, 2vn, 2va, 3tbn, bc
  Düben collection: S-Uu 35:3, 84:11
Jesu, Jesu du mein Licht, SS, 2vn, bc
  Düben collection: S-Uu 42:8
  Parnaß Blumen (Königsberg, 1672)

STRUNGK, N. A.
Laudate pueri Dominum, T, 2vn, bc
  Bokemeyer collection: D-B (UdL), Mus. ms. 30272 (HK 940)

STÜBENDORF, G.
O Jesu dulcissime, S, 2vn, bc
  Düben collection: S-Uu 35:12

THEILE, J.
Beatus vir, SATB, 2vn, 2va, bc
  Bokemeyer collection: D-B (PS), Mus. ms. 21822 (HK 1002)
Benedicam Dominum, SATB, 3vn, 2va, bc
  Bokemeyer collection: D-B (PS), Mus. ms. 21822 (HK 1004)
Cum invocarem, SATB, 2vn, 2va, bc
  Bokemeyer collection: D-B (PS), Mus. ms. 21822 (HK 1003)
Herr unser Herrscher, SSATB, 2cl, timp, 2ct, 3tbn, 2vn, 2va, bc
  Bokemeyer collection: D-B (PS), Mus. ms. 21823 (HK 1010)
Laudate Dominum, SATB, 2vn, 3va, bc
  Bokemeyer collection: D-B (PS), Mus. ms. 21822 (HK 1006)
Missa, SSATB, bc
  Bokemeyer collection: D-B (PS), Mus. ms. 21822 (HK 1005)
  D-B (PS), Mus. ms. 21820 (no. 1)
  modern edn., R. Gerber, Das Chorwerk, 16 (1932, repr. *c.*1955)
Warum toben die Heyden, SSATB, 2cl, timp, 2vn, 2va, bc
  Bokemeyer collection: D-B (PS), Mus. ms. 21823 (HK 1019)

TUNDER, F.
An Wasserflüssen Babylons, S, 2vn, 2va, bc
  Düben collection: S-Uu 36:13, 81:45
  modern edn., DdT 3, no. 13

Dominus illuminatio mea, SSATB, 2vn, bc
   Düben collection: S-Uu 36:1, 86:17
   modern edn., DdT 3, no. 7
Nisi Dominus (SSATB, 2vn, 2va, bc)
   Düben collection: S-Uu 36:8, 81:69, 86:56
   modern edn., DdT 3, no. 8
Salve coelestis Pater, B, vn, bc
   Düben collection: S-Uu 36:10
   modern edn., DdT 3, no. 1
Wend' ab deinen Zorn, lieber Herr, mit Gnaden, SSATTB, 5va, bc
   Düben collection: S-Uu 36:15
   modern edn., DdT 3, no. 16

WECKMANN, M.
Gegrüsset seist du, ST, 2fl, 2vn, bc
   Düben collection: S-Uu 79:80
   modern edn., DdT 6, no. 4
Kommet her zu mir alle, B, 2vn, 3vdg, bc
   Düben collection: S-Uu 79:72
   modern edn., DdT 6, no. 2
Weine nicht, ATB, 3vn, 3vdg, bc
   Düben collection: S-Uu 79:109
   Lüneburg, Ratsbücherei, Mus. ant. pract. K. N. 207/6
   modern edns., DdT 6, no. 6, and RRMBE 46, no. 1
Wie liegt die Stadt so wüste, SB, 2vn, 3vdg, bc
   Lüneburg, Ratsbücherei, Mus. ant. pract. K. N. 207/6
   modern edn., RRMBE 46, no. 4
Zion spricht: Der Herr hat mich verlassen, ATB, 2vn, 3vdg, bc
   Lüneburg, Ratsbücherei, Mus. ant. pract. K. N. 207/6
   modern edn., RRMBE 46, no. 2

WEILAND, J. J.
Jesu dulcis memoria, T, 2vn, bc
   Deuterotokos (Bremen, 1656)
Jesu dulcis memoria, B, 2vn, bc
   Deuterotokos (Bremen, 1656)
Jesu dulcis memoria, STB, 2vn, bc
   Deuterotokos (Bremen, 1656)
Nun dancket alle Gott, SSAT, 4vn, bc
   Nun dancket alle Gott (Wolfenbüttel, 1661)
Salve o Jesu, ATB, 2vn, bc
   Düben collection: S-Uu 45:13
   Deuterotokos (Bremen, 1656)

WERNER, C.
Es erhub sich ein Streit, SATB, SATB, SATB, 2cl, tbn, 2ct, vno, bc
Lüneburg, Ratsbücherei, Mus. ant. pract. K. N. 206

ITALIAN CHURCH MUSIC

ALBRICI, V.
Cogita o homo, SATB, 2vn, bc
Bokemeyer collection: D–B (PS), Mus. ms. 501 (HK 16)
Düben collection: S–Uu 1:5, 77:89, 79:6
Fader wår, SSATB, 2vn, bc
Düben collection: S–Uu 1:6
In convertendo Dominus, SSATB, SATB, 2vn, bc
Düben collection: S–Uu 1:10
Jesu dulcis memoria, SAB, 2va, bc
Düben collection: S–Uu 1:9, 82:4
O quam terribilis (also attributed to Carissimi), SS, bc
Düben collection: S–Uu 29:8a
Quo tendimus mortales, SSB, bc
Düben collection: S–Uu 1:19, 78:11
Sive vivimus, SAB, 3vn, bc
Düben collection: S–Uu 2:2/2a, 78:68

ALDROVANDINI, G.
Volate nubila, B, 2vn, bc
Bokemeyer collection: D–B (UdL), Mus. ms. 30094 (HK 24)

ALVERI, G.
Arma, bella, proelia mortales, B, 2vn, va, bc
Bokemeyer collection: D–B (UdL), Mus. ms. 30094 (HK 29)

ANTONELLI, A.
Amor Jesu dulcissime, SATB, bc
Düben collection: S–Uu 2:8

BASSANI, G. B.
Alma Redemptoris Mater (Alme Rex Coelorum), B, 2vn, bc
Bokemeyer collection: D–B (PS), Mus. ms. 1162 (HK 108)
Nisi Dominus, SAB, 2vn, bc
Bokemeyer collection: D–B (PS), Mus. ms. 1161 (HK 54)
Peccai, è ver, fù grave il fallo mio (also attributed to Bononcini), A, vn, bc
Bokemeyer collection: D–B (PS), Mus. ms. 1162 (HK 104)
Quid arma quid bella, S, 2vn, bc
Bokemeyer collection: D–B (PS), Mus. ms. 1162 (HK 74)

Wolfenbüttel, Herzog August Bibliothek, 294 (Vogel catalogue), no. 33
Salve Regina (*Salve Rex Christe*), A, 2vn, bc
  Bokemeyer collection: D-B (PS), Mus. ms. 1162 (HK 101)

BERNARDI, S.
Non habemus vinum, SATBBB, bc
  Düben collection: S-Uu 4:10
  A. Profe, *Vierdter und letzter Theil geistlicher Concerten . . . aus den berühmbsten italiänischen und andern Autoribus* (Leipzig, 1646)

BICILLI, G.
Gloriosum diem colimus, ATB, bc
  Düben collection: S-Uu 4:13
Perge curre sequere, SS, bc
  Düben collection: S-Uu 4:14

BONONCINI, [G.?]
Peccai, è ver, fù grave il fallo mio (also attributed to Bassani), A, vn, bc
  Bokemeyer collection: D-B (PS), Mus. ms. 1162 (HK 104)

CARISIO, G.
Benedicam Dominum, SS, bc
  Düben collection: S-Uu 10:18, 81:138
Jesu dulcis memoria, SS, bc
  Düben collection: S-Uu 10:19, 81:154

CARISSIMI, G.
Ecce nos reliquimus omnia, TTB, bc
  Düben collection: S-Uu 53:10:25
Jubilemus omnes, SSB, bc
  Düben collection: S-Uu 11:14
O quam terribilis (also attributed to Albrici), SS, bc
  Düben collection: S-Uu 11:16
O vos populi, ATB, 2vn, va (optional), bc
  Düben collection: S-Uu 11:17, 11:17a
Salve Regina (*Salve Rex Christe*), SSB, bc
  Düben collection: S-Uu 11:20, 80:117
  For an edition of the original version of this motet, see Jones, *The Motets of Carissimi*, ii. 455
Surrexit Pastor, SSS, bc
  Düben collection: S-Uu 12:4, 53:10:2, 80:115
Vanitas vanitatum, SSATB, 2vn, bc
  Düben collection: S-Uu 83:68, 70:16

CASATI, G.
Descende dilecti mi, S, bc
  Düben collection: S-Uu 12:7

CASATI, G. (*cont.*):
Laudate pueri, ATB, 2vn, bc
  Düben collection: S-Uu 81:32
Quid vidistis, o Magi, SAATB, bc
  A. Profe, *Cunis solennibus* (Leipzig, 1646)

CAZZATI, M.
Carissime frater, S(T), bc
  Düben collection: S-Uu 12:8

CECCHELLI, C.
Per rigidos montes, SSB, 2vn, bc
  Düben collection: S-Uu 12:11, 80:21

COCCI, G.
O pulcherrima inter mulieres, SSSATB, 2vn, 2va, bc
  Bokemeyer collection: D-B (PS), Mus. ms. 30305 (HK 204)
  Düben collection: S-Uu 44:22, 45:5 (anonymous)
Salve Regina (*Salve mi Jesu*), SS, 2vdg, bc
  J. Havemann, *Erster Theil geistlicher Concerten . . . aus den berühmtesten, itali-
    iänischen und andern Autoribus* (Jena and Berlin, 1659)

COLONNA, G.
Ecce jubar, S, 2vn, bc
  Bokemeyer collection: D-B (UdL), Mus. ms. 30095 (HK 277)

COSSONI, C.
Morior misera, SSB, bc
  Düben collection: S-Uu 83:11

DALLA TAVOLA, A.
Laudate pueri Dominum, SATB, 2ct, 2vn, bc
  Bokemeyer collection: D-B (PS), Mus. ms. 730 (HK 982)

DELLA PORTA, F.
O amantissime Jesu, ATB, bc
  Düben collection: S-Uu 83:15a
O dulcissime Jesu, ATB, bc
  Düben collection: S-Uu 32:12, 83:16a
Ubi eras, o bone Jesu (arranged by G. Österreich), SA, (3va), bc
  Bokemeyer collection: D-B (PS), Mus. ms. autogr. Michael Österreich
    (HK 708)

FOGGIA, F.
Excelsi luminis, SSB, 2vn, bc
  Düben collection: S-Uu 23:6, 77:63
Laetantes canite, SSB, 2vn, 2va (added by Düben), bc
  Düben collection: S-Uu 23:10, 77:61

GIANETTINI, A.
Dixit Dominus, SSATB, 2vn, 2va, bc
Bokemeyer collection: D-B (UdL), Mus. ms. 30211 (HK 459)

MANCIA, L.
Ad arma volate, T, 2vn, bass instrument, bc
Bokemeyer collection: D-B (UdL), Mus. ms. 30095 (HK 1077)

MELANI, A.
Exultent concinant, S, 2vn, bc
Düben collection: S-Uu 28:10

MONTEVERDI, C.
Beatus vir, SSATTB, 2vn, 3va/tbn, bc
Düben collection: S-Uu 29:21
Lüneburg, Ratsbücherei, Mus. ant. pract. K. N. 206
For an edition taken from the original Italian publication, see C.
Monteverdi, *Tutte le opere*, ed. G. F. Malipiero, xv/2 (Asolo, 1940),
368
Nisi Dominus, STB, 2vn, bc
Düben collection: S-Uu 35:9b (version without instruments, attributed
to G. Rovetta)
For an edition of the original form of this composition, taken from the
original Italian publication, see Monteverdi, *Tutti le opere*, xvi. 229

PASSERINI, F.
Confitebor tibi Domine, ATB, 2vn, bc
Düben collection: S-Uu 61:13

PERANDA, M. G.
Dedit abyssus, SSBB, bc
Düben collection: S-Uu 30:4, 78:51
Per rigidos montes, A, 2vn, bc
Düben collection: S-Uu 30:8
Te solum aestuat, SSB, 2vn, bc
Bokemeyer collection: D-B (PS), Mus. ms. 17081 (HK 735)
Düben collection: S-Uu 30:12, 78:73
Vocibus resonent, SAB, 2vn, vdg, bc
Düben collection: S-Uu 30:13, 78:43

PHILETARI, D.
Salve Regina (*Salve Rex Christe*), S, 3va, bc
Düben collection: S-Uu 32:1, 79:36

RIGATTI, A.
Ave Regina coelorum (*Ave regnator coelorum*), S, 4va, bc
Düben collection: S-Uu 32:15, 77:111

RIGATTI, A. (*cont.*):

A. Profe, *Vierdter und letzter Theil geistlicher Concerten* . . . *aus den berühmb-sten italiänischen und andern Autoribus* (Leipzig, 1646)

ROVETTA, G.

Laudate Dominum, SSATB, 2vn(ct), 2 tbn, bc
Düben collection: S-Uu 33:14

Salve Regina (*Salve mi Jesu, Jesu mein Heyland*), SATTB, bc
Düben collection: S-Uu 33:15

A. Profe, *Corollarium geistlicher collectaneorum, berühmter authorum* (Leipzig, 1649)

Salve Regina (*Salve Rex Christe*) TB, bc

J. Havemann, *Erster Theil geistlicher Concerten* . . . *aus den berühmtesten, ital-iänischen und andern Autoribus* (Jena and Berlin, 1659)

Salve Regina (*Salve mi Jesu*), A, 2vn, 2va, bc
Düben collection: S-Uu 36:11, attributed to F. Tunder

VERTINI, P.

Laudate Dominum, A, 2vn, 3va, bc
Düben collection: S-Uu 37:10, 79:39

BIBLIOGRAPHY

◊

PRIMARY SOURCES

Hymn-books and liturgical books

Braunschweig-Lüneburg: *Kirchen-Ordnung des Durchleuchtigen . . . Herrn Friederichen, Hertzogen zu Braunschweig und Lüneburg* (Lüneburg, 1643).

Dresden: *Kirchen- und Hauß-Buch* (Dresden, 1694).

Hamburg: *Melodeyen Gesangbuch* (Hamburg, 1604).

Hannover: *Hannoverisch Voll-Ständiges Gesangbuch* (Lüneburg, 1657).

Mecklenburg: *Revidirte Kirchenordnung . . . Im Hertzogthumb Mecklenburg* (Lüneburg, 1650).

MÜLLER, H., *Geistliche Seelen-Musik* (Rostock, 1659; 2nd edn., 1668).

NICOLAI, P., *Freuden-Spiegel des ewigen Lebens* (Frankfurt am Main, 1599; facs. rep. 1963).

OPITZ, M., *Die Psalmen Davids* (Lüneburg, 1641).

Literature

ALBERT, H., Introduction to *Arien*, vi (Königsberg, 1645), ed. in Denkmäler deutscher Tonkunst, 13 (1904).

BERNHARD, C., 'Von der Singe-Kunst oder Manier', 'Tractatus compositionis augmentatus', 'Ausführlicher Bericht vom Gebrauche der Con- und Dissonantien', ed. J. M. Müller-Blattau in *Die Kompositionslehre Heinrich Schützens in der Fassung seines Schülers Christoph Bernhard* (Kassel, 1926; repr. 1963); transl. in W. Hilse, 'The Treatises of Christoph Bernhard', *Music Forum*, 3 (1973), 1–196.

BURMEISTER, J., *Musica Poetica* (Rostock, 1606; facs. repr. ed. M. Ruhnke, Kassel, 1955); transl. B. V. Rivera, *Musical Poetics* (New Haven, 1993).

CRÜGER, J., *Der rechte Weg zur Singekunst* (Berlin, 1660).

FRICK, C., *Music-Büchlein* (Lüneburg, 1631; facs. repr., Leipzig, 1976).

FRIDERICI, D., *Musica Figuralis* (Rostock, 1618; repr. 1649).

FUHRMANN, M., *Musicalischer-Trichter* (Frankfurt an der Spree, 1706).

GERBER, C., *Unerkandte Sünden der Welt* (Dresden, 1690).

GIBELIUS, O., *Seminarium Modulatoriae vocalis* (Celle, 1645).

GIBELIUS, O., *Kurtzer, jedoch gründlicher Bericht von den Vocibus musicalibus* (Bremen, 1659).

GROßGEBAUER, T., *Wächterstimme aus dem verwüsteten Zion* (Rostock, 1661), repr. in *Drey Geistreiche Schrifften* (Rostock, 1667).

KIRCHER, A., *Musurgia Universalis* (2 vols., Rome, 1650; repr. 1969).

MATTHAEI, C., *Bericht von den Modis Musicis* (Königsberg, 1652).

MATTHESON, J., *Der vollkommene Capellmeister* (Hamburg, 1739; facs repr. 1987); transl. E. C. Harris (Ann Arbor, 1981).

—— *Grundlage einer Ehren-Pforte* (Hamburg, 1740), ed. M. Schneider (Berlin, 1910, repr. 1969).

METZELIUS, H., *Compendium Musices tam Choralis quam Figuralis* (Hamburg, 1660).

MITHOBIUS, H., *Psalmodia Christiana* (Jena, 1665).

MOTZ, G., *Die vertheidigte Kirchen-Music* (n.p., 1703).

MUSCOVIUS, J., *Bestraffter Mißbrauch der Kirchen-Music* (Lauban, 1694).

NIEDT, F. E., *Die Musicalische Handleitung*, ii (Hamburg, 1706); *Friederich Erhardt Niedt: The Musical Guide*, transl. P. L. Poulin and I. C. Taylor (Oxford, 1989), 56–232.

NUCIUS, J., *Musices poeticae* (Neisse, 1613).

PRAETORIUS, M., *Syntagma musicum*, ii: *De Organographia* (Wolfenbüttel, 1619; facs. repr. ed. W. Gurlitt, Kassel, 1985).

—— *Syntagma musicum*, iii (Wolfenbüttel, 1619; facs. repr., Kassel, 1954).

QUANTZ, J. J., *Versuch einer Anweisung die Flöte traversiere zu spielen* (Berlin, 1752), transl. as *On Playing the Flute*, ed. E. R. Reilly (London, 1966).

SCHACHT, M. H., 'Musicus Danicus aller Danske sangmester (1687)', ed. G. Skjerne (Copenhagen, 1928).

SCHÜTZ, H., Introduction to *Symphoniarum sacrarum secunda pars* (Dresden, 1647), ed. in H. Schütz, *Neue Ausgabe sämtliche Werke*, xv, ed. W. Bittinger (Kassel, 1964), p. xxv.

SELLE, T., Introduction to 'Opera omnia' (Liber primus tabulatura), Hamburg, Staats- und Universitätsbibliothek, Musiksammlung.

SPENER, J., *Pia Desideria* (Frankfurt am Main, 1675), transl. and ed. T. G. Tappert (Philadelphia, 1964).

THEILE, J., *Opus Musicalis Compositionis* (Merseburg, 1708).

WALTHER, J., *Praecepta der musicalischen Composition*, ed. P. Benary (Leipzig, 1955).

SECONDARY LITERATURE

ADRIO, A., 'Ambrosius Profe (1589–1661) als Herausgeber italienischer Musik seiner Zeit', in *Festschrift Karl Gustav Fellerer* (Regensburg, 1962), 20–7.

BEREND, F., *Nicolaus Adam Strunck, 1640–1700: Sein Leben und seine Werke. Mit Beiträgen zur Geschichte der Musik und des Theaters in Celle, Hannover und Leipzig* (Freiburg, 1915).

BLANCKENBURG, W., 'Der mehrstimmige Gesang und die konzertierende Musik im evangelischen Gottesdienst', *Leiturgia*, 4/5 (1961), 661–719.

BLUME, F., et al., *Protestant Church Music: A History* (London, 1974), originally published as *Geschichte der evangelischen Kirchenmusik* (Kassel, 1964).

BOHN, E., *Bibliographie der Musik-Druckwerke bis 1700, welche in der Stadtbibliothek, der Bibliothek des Academischen Instituts für Kirchenmusik und der Königlichen und Universitäts-Bibliothek zu Breslau aufbewahrt werden* (Berlin, 1883; repr. 1969).

BROCKPÄHLER, R., *Handbuch zur Geschichte der Barockoper in Deutschland* (Emsdetten, 1964).

BUELOW, G., 'National Predilections in Seventeenth-Century Music Theory, a Symposium: Germany', *Journal of Music Theory*, 16 (1972), 36–49.

BUNNERS, C., *Kirchenmusik und Seelenmusik: Studien zu Frömmigkeit und Musik im Luthertum des 17. Jahrhunderts* (Berlin and Göttingen, 1966).

BUTT, J., *Music Education and the Art of Performance in the German Baroque* (Cambridge, 1994).

CARSTENN, T., 'Katalog der St. Marienbibliothek zu Elbing', *Kirchenmusikalisches Jahrbuch*, 11 (1896), 40–9.

CARTER, S., 'The String Tremolo in the 17th Century', *Early Music*, 19/1 (1991), 43–59.

CONRADY, K. O., *Lateinische Dichtungstradition und deutsche Lyrik des 17. Jahrhunderts* (Bonn, 1962).

CULLEY, T. D., *Jesuits and Music, i: A Study of the Musicians connected with the German College in Rome during the 17th Century and of their Activities in Northern Europe* (Rome, 1970).

DREYFUS, L., *Bach's Continuo Group: Players and Practices in his Vocal Works* (Cambridge, Mass., and London, 1987).

FISCHER-KRÜCKEBERG, E., 'Johann Crüger als Musiktheoretiker', *Zeitschrift für Musikwissenschaft*, 12 (1929), 609–29.

FÜRSTENAU, M., *Zur Geschichte der Musik und Theaters am Hofe zu Dresden* (Dresden, 1861; repr. 1971).

GECK, M., *Die Vokalmusik Dietrich Buxtehudes und der frühe Pietismus* (Kieler Schriften zur Musikwissenschaft, 15; Kassel, 1965).

GÖBEL, M., *Die Bearbeitungen des Hohen Liedes im 17. Jahrhundert* (Halle, 1914).

GRIBBLE, F., *The Court of Christina of Sweden, and the Later Adventures of the Queen in Exile* (London, 1913).

GRUSNICK, B., 'Die Dübensammlung: Ein Versuch ihrer chronologischen Ordnung', *Svensk tidskrift för musikforskning*, 46 (1964), 27–82, and 48 (1966), 63–186.

GÜNTHER, O., *Die musikalischen Kirchenbibliothek von St. Katharinen und St. Johannis in Danzig* (Katalog der Handschriften der Danziger Bibliothek, 4; Danzig, 1911).

HAMMERICH, A., *Dansk Musikhistorie indtil ca. 1700* (Copenhagen, 1921).

HILSE, W., 'The Treatises of Christoph Bernhard', *Music Forum*, 3 (1973), 1–196.

HOFFMEISTER, G. (ed.), *German Baroque Literature: The European Perspective* (New York, 1983).

JAACKS, G. (ed.), *300 Jahre Oper in Hamburg* (Hamburg, 1977).

JONES, A. V., *The Motets of Carissimi*, 2 vols. (Ann Arbor, 1982).

JUNGHANS, W., 'J. S. Bach als Schüler der Partikularschule zu St. Michaelis in Lüneburg, oder Lüneburg einer Pflegestätte kirchlicher Musik', *Programm des Johanneums zu Lüneburg, Ostern 1870* (Lüneburg, 1870), 3–42.

KARSTÄDT, G., *Thematisch-systematisches Verzeichnis der musikalischen Werke von Dietrich Buxtehude* (Wiesbaden, 1974; 2nd edn., 1985).

KESSLER, F., Introduction to *Danziger Instrumentalmusik des 17. und 18. Jahrhunderts* (Stuttgart, 1979).

KIRBY, D., *Northern Europe in the Early Modern Period: The Baltic World 1492–1772* (London and New York, 1990).

KIRWAN-MOTT, A., *The Small-Scale Sacred Concertato in the Early Seventeenth Century*, 2 vols. (Ann Arbor, 1981).

KJELLBERG, E., 'Kungliga musiker i Sverige under stormaktstiden. Studier kring deras organisation, verksamheter och status ca 1620–ca 1720' (Ph.D. thesis, Uppsala, 1979).

KRÜGER, L., *Die Hamburgische Musikorganisation im 17. Jahrhunderts* (Strassburg, 1933).

KRUMMACHER, F., *Die Choralbearbeitung in der protestantischen Figuralmusik zwischen Praetorius und Bach* (Kassel, 1977).

—— *Die Überlieferung der Choralbearbeitungen in der frühen evangelischen Kantate* (Berlin, 1965).

—— 'Das geistliche Aria in Norddeutschland und Skandinavien. Ein gattungsgeschichtlicher Versuch', in D. Lohmeier (ed.), *Weltliches und geistliches Lied des Barock: Studien zur Liedkultur in Deutschland und Skandinavien* (Stockholm and Amsterdam, 1979), 229–64.

KÜMMERLING, H., *Katalog der Sammlung Bolemeyer* (Kassel, 1970).

LILIENCRON, R. VON, *Liturgisch-musikalische Geschichte der evangelischen Gottesdienste von 1523 bis 1700* (Schleswig, 1893).

MEYER, C., *Geschichte der Mecklenburg-Schweriner Hofkapelle* (Schwerin, 1913).

MOBERG, C.-A., 'Vincenzo Albrici und das Kirchenkonzert', in *Natalicia musicologica Knud Jeppesen* (Copenhagen, 1962), 199–216.

MÜLLER, J., *Die musikalischen Schätze der Königlichen und Universitäts-Bibliothek zu Königsberg in Preußen aus dem Nachlasse F. A. Gottholds* (Bonn, 1870).

MÜLLER-BLATTAU, J. M., *Die Kompositionslehre Heinrich Schützens in der Fassung seines Schülers Christoph Bernhard* (Kassel, 1926; repr. 1963).

MUNCK, T., *Seventeenth Century Europe: State, Conflict and the Social Order in Europe 1598–1700* (London, 1990).

NAUSCH, A., *Augustin Pfleger: Leben und Werke* (Kassel, 1954).

NOACK, F., *Das Deutschtum in Rom* (Berlin and Leipzig, 1927).

NORLIND, T., 'Vor 1700 gedruckte Musikalien in den schwedischen Bibliotheken', *Sammelbände der Internationalen Musik-Gesellschaft*, 9 (1908), 196–231.

NOSKE, F., *Saints and Sinners: The Latin Musical Dialogue in the Seventeenth Century* (Oxford, 1992).

PALISCA, C. V., 'Marco Scacchi's Defence of Modern Music (1649)', in *Words and Music: The Scholars's View . . . in Honor of A. Tillman Merritt* (Cambridge, Mass., 1972), 189–235; repr. in id., *Studies in the History of Italian Music and Music Theory* (Oxford, 1994), 88–145.

RAUSCHNING, H., *Geschichte der Musik und Musikpflege in Danzig* (Danzig, 1931).

Répertoire international des sources musicales, B/I/1: Recueils imprimés, XVIᵉ–XVIIᵉ siècles (Munich, 1960) (RISM).

RIEDEL, F. W., 'Strenger und freier Stil in der nord- und süddeutschen Musik für Tasteninstrumente des 17. Jahrhunderts', in *Norddeutsche und nordeuropäische Musik* (Kieler Schriften zur Musikwissenschaft, 16; Kassel, 1965), 63–70.

ROCHE, J., *North Italian Church Music in the Age of Monteverdi* (Oxford, 1984).

—— 'Rovetta and Tunder: An Interesting Example of Plagiarism', *Early Music*, 3 (1975), 58–60.

RUHNKE, M., *Joachim Burmeister* (Schriften des Landesinstituts für Musikforschung Kiel, 5; Kassel, 1955).

SACHS, C., *Musik und Oper am kurbrandenburgischen Hof* (Berlin, 1910; repr. Hildesheim, 1977).

SADIE, S. (ed.), *The New Grove Dictionary of Music and Musicians*, 20 vols. (London, 1980).

SCHARLAU, U., *Athanasius Kircher (1601–1680) als Musikschriftsteller* (Marburg, 1969).

SCHILLING, H., *T. Eniccelius, Fr. Meister, N. Hanff: Ein Beitrag zur Geschichte der evangelischen Frühkantate in Schleswig-Holstein* (Kiel, 1935).

SCHMIDT, E., *Der Gottesdienst am kurfürstlichen Hofe zu Dresden* (Göttingen, 1961).

SCHMIEDER, W., and HARTWIEG, G., *Kataloge der Herzog-August-Bibliothek Wolfenbüttel*, xii (Frankfurt am Main, 1967).

SEHLING, E., *Die evangelischen Kirchenordnungen des XVI. Jahrhunderts*, iv (Leipzig, 1911).

SEIFFERT, M., 'Die Chorbibliothek der St. Michaelis-Schule in Lüneburg', *Sammelbände der Internationalen Musik-Gesellschaft*, 9 (1908), 593–621.

—— 'Matthias Weckmann und das Collegium Musicum in Hamburg', *Sammelbände der Internationalen Musik-Gesellschaft*, 2 (1901), 76–132.

SMALLMAN, B., *The Background of Passion Music: J. S. Bach and his Predecessors* (2nd edn., New York, 1970).

SNYDER, K., *Dieterich Buxtehude: Organist in Lübeck* (New York, 1987).

SØRENSEN, S., *Diderich Buxtehudes vokale kirkemusik* (Copenhagen, 1958).

—— 'Monteverdi–Förster–Buxtehude: Entwurf zu einer entwicklungsgeschichtlichen Untersuchung', *Dansk Aarbog for Musikforskning*, 3 (1963), 87–100.

STAHL, W., *Franz Tunder und Dietrich Buxtehude* (Leipzig, 1926).

—— *Die Musikabteilung der Lübecker Stadtbibliothek in ihren älteren Beständen* (Lübeck, 1931).

STOEFFLER, F. E., *The Rise of Evangelical Pietism* (Studies in the History of Religions, 9; Leiden, 1965).

SZWEYKOWSKI, Z. M., 'Stile imbastardito i stile rappresentativo w systemie teoretycznym Marka Scacchiego', *Muzyka*, 19/1 (1974), 11–34.

VICKERS, B., 'Figures of Rhetoric / Figures of Music?', *Rhetorica*, 2/1 (1984), 1–41.

VIERHAUS, R., *Deutschland im Zeitalter des Absolutismus (1648–1763)* (Göttingen, 1978), transl. as *Germany in the Age of Absolutism* (Cambridge, 1988).

VOGEL, E., *Die Handschriften der Herzoglichen Bibliothek zu Wolfenbüttel, 8: Die Handschriften nebst älteren Druckwerken der Musik-Abtheilung* (Wolfenbüttel, 1890).

WALKER, D. P., and WALKER, P., *German Sacred Polyphonic Vocal Music between Schütz and Bach: Sources and Critical Editions* (Detroit Studies in Music Bibliography, 67; Warren, 1992).

WALTER, H., *Musikgeschichte der Stadt Lüneburg: Vom Ende des 16. bis zum Anfang des 18. Jahrhunderts* (Tutzing, 1967).

WEBBER, G., 'A Study of the Italian Influence on North German Church and Organ Music in the Second Half of the Seventeenth Century, with Special Reference to the Collection of Gustav Düben" (D.Phil. thesis, Oxford, 1988).

—— 'Italian Music at the Court of Queen Christina: Christ Church, Oxford, Mus. MS 377 and the Visit of Vincenzo Albrici's Italian ensemble, 1652–54', *Svensk tidskrift för musikforskning*, 75/2 (1993), 47–53.

WELTER, F., *Katalog der Musikalien der Ratsbücherei Lüneburg* (Lippstadt, 1950).

WOLFF, C., 'Buxtehude, Bach, and Seventeenth-Century Music in Retrospect', in id., *Bach: Essays on His Life and Music* (Cambridge, Mass., 1991), 41–55.

INDEX

◇